New Testament
Life and Literature

New Testament Life and Literature

BY DONALD W. RIDDLE
FORMERLY UNIVERSITY OF CHICAGO
AND HAROLD H. HUTSON
BIRMINGHAM-SOUTHERN COLLEGE

THE UNIVERSITY OF CHICAGO PRESS
CHICAGO · ILLINOIS

The University of Chicago Press · Chicago 37
Agent: Cambridge University Press · London

Copyright 1946 by The University of Chicago. All rights reserved
Published 1946. Composed and printed by the University
of Chicago Press, Chicago, Illinois, U.S.A.

Preface

THIS book is the result of several years of experimentation in the teaching of New Testament history and literature to college students. Its aim is simple: to present the results of scholarship to the student who is seriously interested in the New Testament as a book of literature, of history, and of religion. It will not prove exhaustive enough for scholars, since it is intended rather as a "first reader" for the student. If it succeeds in picturing with some degree of clarity the conditions under which the New Testament came to be written and in stimulating the reader to further study, it will have accomplished its purpose. The Select Bibliography should serve as a guide to continued reading.

The graduate and the undergraduate fields have joined efforts in the production of the volume. Mr. Riddle prepared the first draft for his sections of the volume while he was Associate Professor of New Testament and Early Christian Literature at the University of Chicago. Entry into the United States Army Air Corps interrupted his work on this project, so that the main responsibility for revision and re-writing has been Mr. Hutson's. The end of World War II has permitted Mr. Riddle's participation in the final stages of manuscript preparation and publication. The following was the original division according to chapters: i–iii, x–xiii, xvi–xx (Riddle); iv–ix, xiv–xv, Appendix (Hutson).

<table>
<tr><td>DONALD W. RIDDLE</td><td>HAROLD H. HUTSON</td></tr>
<tr><td>CAMBRIDGE, MASS.</td><td>BIRMINGHAM-SOUTHERN COLLEGE</td></tr>
<tr><td>January 14, 1946</td><td>January 14, 1946</td></tr>
</table>

Table of Contents

I

BEFORE ALEXANDER AND AFTER

TO UNDERSTAND the history and literature of early Christianity, it is necessary to understand the world in which Christianity appeared—the world which in part brought it into being. To appreciate the world in which early Christianity appeared, it is necessary to begin with the Hellenistic age, for this was one of those fruitful transition periods which welded its past and its present into an eventful future.

Before Alexander, the East had been more important in the development of culture and of civilization than the West; after Alexander, the East and the West flowed together to form Western civilization. Before Alexander the large and powerful empires of the Orient had overshadowed the small political units of the Greek city-states. Not yet had the power of Rome become the major factor in Western politics, nor had it even registered upon the great world of the East.

The far-flung oriental empires prior to Alexander were simply miscellaneous congeries of peoples and cultures. Religion was the most evident thread in the slight pattern of relationships. After Alexander there were more observable relationships throughout the world at large; and there were certain aspects of a general, working unity—for example, a single language which, besides the many local tongues and dialects, made possible some communication throughout the ancient world.

Before Alexander commercial intercourse and communication (although in certain cases extensive) was largely localized; after Alexander the Mediterranean Sea became the center of commercial activity, which soon thrust its way to Britain, to western Africa, and beyond the Near East.

1

This development witnessed rapid and continuous change. The change involved not only political and military shifts but also social attitudes as well. Before Alexander the given local political organization necessarily determined the particular culture of a people; after Alexander's work had been done, the former political lines were obliterated, and new loyalties, values, and social attitudes were demanded by the changed world. In one way or another, directly or indirectly, all people were affected.

The military and political exploits of Alexander mark the high-water line of Macedonian encroachment upon the Greek city-states. The early stages of this influence can be seen in the Philippics of Demosthenes, who warned the Athenians against the barbarian Philip. Alexander utilized and improved the innovations in military technique which his father had devised, but he was not content to stop with the subjection of the Greek city-states. He challenged the mighty power of Persia. At the Granicus River, near the location of legendary Troy, Alexander in 334 B.C. led his army to the first victory over Persia. The following year he won a crushing victory at the Battle of Issus. The offer of extensive territories from the defeated king did not deter Alexander from his further conquests. Damascus, Tyre, and Gaza capitulated, and the way was open to Egypt. This ancient land surrendered without a fight. It was during his brief stay in Egypt that Alexander's deification occurred, a significant event for later religious attitudes. When he returned to Persia, the Battle of Arbela in 331 resulted in his complete victory, and the entire "world" to the south and east of his much smaller "Greek" territory was at his feet. Alexander's penetration as far east as the Ganges and his sending of expeditions to the region of the Caspian Sea indicate not only his crushing military force but also his insatiable interest in things new and foreign.

Alexander's remarkable intellectual grasp of the significance of his military conquests is suggested by the details of his plan for world rule. Not less interesting than his commercial and political schemes is the scientific interest which led him to collect and send to his teacher, Aristotle, specimens from the places visited.

The significance of the commercial implications is not to be minimized. Although Alexandria in Egypt, developed as an outpost of commercial communication, became the greatest in importance of all, there were many other "Alexandrias," which were founded for the same purpose.

Likewise, it is clear that the shrewd conqueror was actuated by intelligence of the highest order when he had himself deified at the Egyptian oasis of Siwa. It is obvious that he realized the magnitude of the political entity which he was molding. He saw clearly that so expansive a territory, peopled by subjects of infinitely diverse cultures, must have an effective symbol of unity. He found that symbol in himself as elevated to divine status. Alexander was not the last to see the value of displaying the emperor as a human flag. However questionable may have been the wisdom of his choice—for his Western friends and associates frowned upon his requirement that they prostrate themselves in his presence—it is evident that he had a purpose and that he was aware of the potentialities of religion as a unifying force.

Of tremendous importance for the unity of Alexander's world was the spread of Greek as the common language. Regions retained in many instances their own dialects for local use, but international commerce and government soon made Greek the universal tongue. But the Greek which spread over the Mediterranean world was not the speech of "classical" Athens; it was a modified or developed form of the language which came to be described as *koine* ("common"). For language, like all cultural tools, is changed by generations of use, particularly where whole areas come within a short period of time to adopt it.

It was the common Greek of the Hellenistic world in which the New Testament was written. Scholars who once referred to New Testament Greek as "biblical" or "degenerate" discovered that it shared the characteristics of the common language which followed Alexander's conquests. The rude awakening of these scholars occurred in the last decades of the nineteenth century, when the Egyptian papyri were discovered. The commonplace correspondence on these discarded sheets made from the papyrus plant showed the same linguistic character as the Greek New

Testament. The "puzzle" was solved; the language universalized by Alexander had been the ready instrument for the first Christian documents.

The major purpose of Alexander collapsed, of course, with his death. Instead of the one-world empire, there appeared three recognizable entities. The Persian power was succeeded by the Seleucid kingdom, whose "capital" was significantly located in Antioch rather than in the Mesopotamian region. This clearly indicates that in the mixture of Eastern and Western elements the West was dominant. Egypt came under the dominance of the Ptolemies. The "Greek" areas were ruled by "the successors"; their devious history, since it is unimportant for the particular subject of this book, may be disregarded. When the localities and peoples of this area reappear in early Christian history and literature, they are organized as provinces of the Roman Empire.

But although Alexander's primary purpose perished with his death, other features of his grandiose plan were continued, and certain outgrowths were of basic importance in the ensuing developments. The common dialect Greek remained the vehicle of communication and of culture, and the fused elements of East and West brought into being a culture which was distinctive. The outcome was Hellenism—a development of Greek culture whose characteristics were as distinctive as had been those of Athens and the classical Hellenic civilization.

The Hellenistic period has been called the "silver age," a phrase meant to stand in obvious and negative contrast to the "golden age"—as classical Hellenic civilization is commonly described. The value-judgment may be disregarded. However, it is inescapably true that the literature of the Hellenistic period is not so "good" as that of classical Greece. In the Hellenistic age there were no philosophers comparable to Plato and Aristotle. But in Hellenistic days the writings of the earlier Greeks were collected into libraries, and something like library science was developed; philosophy left the cloistered academy and lyceum and, democratized, was brought to the common man. Such a Hellenistic philosopher as Epictetus was no "scholar," in the basic meaning of the word; but the literary form by which the

Cynic-Stoic philosophy was propagated was one of the typical products of Hellenism. In literature and in thought Alexander's work formed a watershed between cultures. It is a fact that in quality these products of culture were inferior to those of the Hellenic age; what is significant is that the dissemination and popularization of literature and philosophy were characteristic of the Hellenistic period, while excellence had been the glory of the classical age.

Perhaps no development was of greater importance than the world view of the Hellenistic age. Before Alexander localism was dominant; after him there came a cosmopolitanism and an individualism which were vitally complementary even though they seemed contradictory. Both grew out of the political and cultural changes which were effected by Alexander's conquests. As the former political lines were obliterated and the conception of world-state emerged, inevitably the old localisms were deeply affected. It was no longer possible for the Athenian or the Ephesian to consider his homeland as the world, for his homeland no longer existed as a state. Thus the awareness of the larger world brought into being the cosmopolitanism which had been perceived by philosophers but which awaited an exceptional political leader to give it vitality.

But, by the same token, thoroughgoing individualism arose as the only practical social attitude. Ultimately it sprang from the judgment of value. "The world" is a large place, however limited may be one's apprehension of it. The small and homogeneous state no longer existed; gone were the old sanctions, the old means of protection and satisfaction of needs. Thus the individual was thrown back upon himself; he, at least, had value and existed. Side by side, each supplementing and giving meaning to the other, were cosmopolitanism and individualism.

There was one important exception to this, as to many of the developments of Hellenistic culture. Between the territories of the West—the "Greek" and the Anatolian localities of the Aegean Peninsula and Asia Minor—and the broadly sweeping kingdoms of the South and the East—now the Ptolemaic and the Seleucid kingdoms—was Palestine, the land of Israel. Although by no means all Jews were domiciled there, it was, in a certain sense, accurately described as the "land of Israel." Alexander had covered it in the movement of his armies; he had viewed the sacrifices in the "Temple." But he had not subjected Palestine to the same control he had insisted upon elsewhere. It is a strange but important fact that (with such exception as shall be noted presently) the Jewish people—especially those resident in Palestine—were the sole significant exception to the otherwise complete domination of Hellenistic culture.

True, Jews were influenced and affected. Many influential Jews participated in the universal development of the culture which emerged with and after Alexander. It is significant, however, that this participation was engendered and directed chiefly outside Palestine, particularly in Antioch and Alexandria. While it is true that many intellectual Jews took over and furthered Hellenistic science and thought, the Jews, generally speaking, maintained their traditional religious conceptions and customs. Where Hellenistic culture impinged upon Palestine, it was resisted. The ultimate effect, as we shall show, was to strengthen the particular characteristics which were a development of the Judaism of the old days.

The entry of Rome upon the stage of the great powers materially altered this picture. This book will not consider the expansion of Rome in the early days but is concerned rather with the period when the inexorable trend of Roman power was felt in the eastern half of the Mediterranean basin, when Rome met Hellenistic culture and, in conquering, was conquered.

Earlier Rome had been deeply influenced by Hellenic culture; this is plainly evident in literature and religion. But later Rome—and particularly imperial Rome—was profoundly affected by Hellenistic ways. It was at this time, indeed, that the confluence of East and West reached maximum volume. The West controlled in politics and in military might; the East subtly infused itself and transformed the controlling power. So effective was this phenomenon that historians note as the distinguishing characteristic in Roman life the degree to which oriental elements are to be observed in the West.

Thus in the Roman Empire, roughly coincident with the rise and growth of Christianity, the forces which came into being with and after Alexander were in the ascendance. Roman Stoicism was the further development of a philosophy which had assumed particular character in the Hellenistic age. The Roman religion was an eclectic mixture of indigenous elements and of values which had become current in the new age of transition. Elements which had been born in the East were to be found in the life of the city of Rome itself. The commercial development which was no less important than the political control was the direct outgrowth of Hellenistic civilization. Art, in Rome as elsewhere, was not local but Hellenistic. The common Greek of the Hellenistic world was used in Rome besides the local, native language.

It was therefore of the greatest significance that Christianity had its beginning after, rather than before, Alexander. Although Judaism, its mother-religion, had resisted and successfully avoided most of the elements of Hellenism, it was a developed Judaism which bore and nurtured Jesus. And when Christianity emerged, it came into being in a world which was, as it were, set for the developments which took place. As shall be pointed out, Christianity was a missionary religion; it is of the utmost significance that the cosmopolitanism of the world after Alexander gave the readiest impulse to the extension of religion. As had not been true before, there was a single language in which its messages could be expressed and be heard and understood everywhere. And this was the language, not of a race, or a nation, or of a people, but of all peoples, all races, all nations. Hellenistic commerce had made highways on land and charted paths on the seas; travel and transportation had for decades followed these paths. The breakdown of the former political divisions had caused a mixture of peoples, so that a man could find some of his own people wherever he went. And the widespread social attitude of individualism, with consequent effect upon all current religions, made it possible for older religions to propagate themselves throughout the Mediterranean world and, by the same token, made it possible for a new one to be extended from the place of its beginning to the limits of East and West.

As shall be seen, every aspect of Hellenistic culture was of importance in the development of Christianity. Although Jesus was, in the direct sense, the flower of Judaism—the only significant exception to the otherwise complete extension of Hellenistic culture—and the religion which he lived and taught were within the framework of Judaism, Christianity was so intimately connected with and related to Hellenistic culture that the religion and literature cannot be understood without comprehension of the Hellenistic age. To this background we must now turn.

II

THE HELLENISTIC AGE OF TRANSITION

AFTER Alexander the political world fell into three parts. The "Greek" territories and cities of Macedonia, the Greek Peninsula, and Asia Minor formed the westernmost part of the older Hellenistic world. The Seleucid kingdom, with Antioch as the most important western city, included much of the vast expanse to the east which Alexander had conquered. Egypt under the Ptolemies continued as part of the old Egypt but was infused with the genuinely new life of the Hellenistic age of transition.

As it had for centuries past, Palestine played the role of a small buffer state. Lying between the Seleucid kingdom and Egypt, it was nominally under the political control of the Ptolemies. But in culture and in influence it was far more effectively in the orbit of the northern power.

In spite of political differentiation, there was a remarkable unity of the Hellenistic world. It is the purpose of this chapter to suggest the general character of the Hellenistic age and to show how this so permeated the world that rising Christianity and its literary expressions could not fail to be affected by it.

The geographic unity of the Hellenistic world was the basis of economic, cultural, and religious development. Alexander had brought under at least nominal control the vast expanse to the east as far as India; but the only articulate unity of the Hellenistic age, until the rise of Carthage and of Rome to power, was the eastern end of the Mediterranean. The old Greek cities gradually adopted the quality of the new age; and to these were added several new cities, of which Alexandria in Egypt and Antioch in Syria serve as examples. It is significant that these cities were

9

now of great commercial importance. A Hellenistic historian, Polybius,[1] illustrates the solidarity of the Hellenistic world in his account of the earthquake which destroyed large portions of the city of Rhodes in 224 B.C. Commercial credit was extended to the Rhodians by rival cities, for all seemed to realize that Mediterranean trade would be disrupted by the destruction of this important city. The fact that Rhodes would thus be restored as a military power did not deter the extension of credit for commercial ends.

The Hellenistic world had commercial unity. Ships plied between Spain and the Indian Ocean. Trade included spices from the Orient, British tin, Chinese silk, and Indian cotton. Coins struck off by Alexander in India were in use two hundred years later. Merchants from all lands migrated and settled in foreign lands.

For this commercial development on a world-wide scale, basic advance in science was necessary. The advancement of knowledge in this period is strikingly similar to the contributions, centuries later, of Copernicus and Galileo, with practical application by Columbus. In the Hellenistic age of transition the name of Eratosthenes stands high. His achievements were numerous: he abandoned the idea that the world was the center of the universe, he assumed that the earth was spherical, and he calculated (with not too erroneous result) the earth's circumference. Although these findings are more striking to the modern student, his application of his knowledge to practical geography was more important to the people of his day and after. It is not a serious discount of his achievement to discover that he maintained the orthodox belief that the inhabited world was an island; what is remarkable is that his "maps" exhibit the generally correct shape of known countries, with fairly accurate relative distances. His use of lines, corresponding to latitude and longitude, give his charts a modern quality.

The practical use of this increased knowledge in commercial navigation necessarily involved corresponding advance in mathematics and astronomy. It is necessary to mention only Archi-

[1] Polybius *The Histories* v. 88–90.

medes and Euclid to indicate the remarkable development of mathematics. But the mystical, semicult studies of the Neo-Pythagoreans also call attention to the semireligious aspects of Hellenism. However, the geometry of Euclid and the perception of higher mathematics by Archimedes—which had to be rediscovered centuries later in the beginning of the "modern" age—also illustrate the religious element in Hellenism.

Astronomy, too, is basic to navigation. There was an "observatory" in Alexandria (of course, without a telescope), where some nine hundred fixed stars were catalogued. The great name in Hellenistic astronomy was that of Aristarchus of Samos. His view, that the sun is the center of our solar system and that the earth revolves around it, was too advanced for his time; it was opposed even by philosophers. Aristarchus also attempted to compute the distance between planets, but with considerable error. The practical application of astronomy included studies in chronometry; public clocks, either of the shadow or water type, were common. Under the Ptolemies solar calculation resulted in the correction of the calendar by the addition of the three hundred and sixty-sixth day to each fourth year. This, like the heliocentric view of Aristarchus, was too radical and was not generally used.

A well-known monument, which symbolizes the convergence of these scientific findings and their practical application to navigation, was the lighthouse in the harbor of Alexandria. Equaling the height of a thirty-seven-story modern building, its beacon shone less bright than the scientific discoveries which it assumed.

There was a Hellenistic counterpart of Columbus. This was Pytheas of Marseille, a contemporary of Alexander. He sailed along the coast of Europe as far as the Elbe, and later he crossed to Britain. Doubtless it was the information which he published in his book, *A Treatise on the Ocean*, which enabled Eratosthenes to enter Britain and Ireland on his maps with roughly correct outline. Pytheas, observing the noon location of the sun at the various places in his voyages, typifies the Hellenistic application of mathematics and astronomy to practical science.

But it must not be thought that the Hellenistic age was merely a matter of the practical application of science to commerce. The Hellenistic period had its characteristic culture, and it was a culture of a high order. Its chief products were not in creative literature; the Hellenistic aptitude was more on the systematizing side. To be sure, there was some Hellenistic literature. But few of its examples attain high excellence. The "Hymn to Zeus" of Cleanthes is perhaps the best known of the religious poetry of Hellenistic days. Epic and idyllic poetry was produced, with Apollonius of Alexandria (called "the Rhodian") and Callimachus as the most noted exponent of each, respectively. Both tragic and comic drama were written; Menander stands as the great name in the latter. The epigram was particularly a form of Hellenistic literature—the same Callimachus was its leading exponent. Theocritus of Syracuse was another notable idyllic poet, especially since he directly influenced Latin writers.

It is interesting that the close association between literary activity and science is to be seen in Hellenistic writing; Apollonius the Rhodian was one of the librarians in the great institution in Alexandria, with which Callimachus was also associated. Here something of library science had its beginning: philology was generalized as a discipline; textual criticism (e.g., of Homer) was begun and practiced; the division and arrangement of "books" by types of literature was made; and the mechanical division into the "books" was devised, with suitable classification and "filing" systems and a catalogue.

In content, as well as in organization, the relation of science and literature was close. For example, Aratus of Soli wrote *Phenomena*, which put into hexameter verse an earlier astronomical work. This is another Hellenistic product which had direct influence upon Latin literature. Nicander of Colophon worked a curious subject matter into verse: scientific data on poisons and their antidotes.

But it was in history that Hellenistic literature reached its highest point. The great name was that of Polybius, but there were many lesser historians. One of these worthy writers was Hieronymus of Cardia. In a later period, but none the less genu-

ine products of this culture, were Josephus the Jewish historian
and Strabo the Roman. Since his "biographies" were based upon
the work of historians, Plutarch may also be counted.

If there was obvious inferiority in Hellenistic (as compared
with classical Hellenic) literature, the same judgment cannot be
accorded Hellenistic art. One has but to mention the well-known
examples which have survived to appreciate this extraordinary
aspect of Hellenistic culture: the Victory of Samothrace
("Winged Victory"); the great frieze from the Altar of Pergamum, more than 400 feet long, depicting the battle of the gods
and the Titans; the Aphrodite of Melos ("Venus of Milo"); the
Apollo Belvedere; the Dying Gaul; the Laocoön. What is distinctive in these sculptures is that, abandoning the restraint of
the classical sculpture (such as that of Phidias), these depict human expression most movingly. Painting also flourished, although, naturally, much less of it has survived.

The genius of Hellenistic culture—that adaptation of science,
philosophy, and art to popular and practical use—is to be seen
in the architecture of the period. Not only was it beautiful; it
was practical. There was an obvious distinction between Hellenistic and earlier cities. City-planning was practiced; it must be
remembered that many new cities were founded during the period, and earlier cities were modernized. The market place—a much
older feature of the Greek city—was now beautified with extensive high colonnades; the Corinthian column and capital were
widely used. Many cities had their public auditorium, basilicas
with high clerestory windows, gymnasia, baths, and theaters.
The great theater of Ephesus seated twenty-five thousand people.
This beautification of cities was another aspect of Hellenistic culture which the Romans took up with enthusiasm. There can be
no doubt that in this respect the world was much more beautiful
during this era of transition than at any previous period.

While philosophy and religion are to be discussed later, it is
necessary in the present connection to mention the characteristic
adaptations in these realms. The essential feature to be noted in
philosophy is that, while individual thinkers of the period are
hardly to be compared with the philosophers of the classical

Greek periods, the Hellenistic age developed, applied, and democratized philosophy. Plato's Academy and Aristotle's Lyceum were succeeded by the Porch of the Stoics and the Garden of Epicurus. The traditional conception of the philosopher as a scholar—which meant, literally, a man of leisure; a man of sufficient wealth that he could be and was a man of leisure—gave way to the function of the philosopher as a popular teacher who took his thoughts to the people wherever they were to be found. The difference can be observed in the content of the Stoic philosophy of the later Hellenistic period compared with that of Zeno, the founder. Earlier Stoicism was much more concerned with metaphysical speculation, while later Stoicism, as can be observed in the teaching of Epictetus and Seneca, was much more concerned with ethics. The difference can be seen also in the popular form by which the Hellenistic teaching was expressed. The characteristic vehicle was the diatribe, which was in dialogue form, shaped in crisp, brief sections, obviously intended to catch the interest. Indeed, the diatribe is curiously like the technique of the soap-box orator. Very properly, a historian of the period entitles one of his chapters "The Cynic-Stoic Missionary." For the wandering philosophers, wearing characteristic garb, were to be found everywhere, haranguing people as they traveled. It is indicative of the vast difference between classical and Hellenistic philosophy that Epictetus, one of the foremost representatives of later Stoicism, had been a slave.

Similarly in religion the Hellenistic age had its own characteristic development. Here the effect of the new world is plainly to be seen. The obliteration of the old national boundaries and the mixture of peoples had two immediate effects. Both have been mentioned. First, the breakdown of the old nationalities denationalized the religions which had been indigenous. For example, before Alexander the cult of Isis and Osiris had been thoroughly Egyptian. Obviously, it was Egyptian in its origin; it was a religion which had grown out of the life-giving fact of the recurrent fertility in the annual inundation of the Nile. Naturally, its priesthood and its devotees were Egyptian. Until the Hellenistic era it was peculiarly Egyptian. But after Alexander, in the dissemination of the common culture throughout the world, the Isis-Osiris cult was a religion of individual salvation, widespread and functional for the benefit of peoples wherever it was to be found. Similarly, religions of the farther East had been transferred to the West; what was in effect the old Ishtar-Tammuz cult of early Accadia was current in one form or another throughout the Mediterranean world. One of its forms, the Attis-Cybele cult, with the particular characteristics of the Phrygian locality of Asia Minor, was introduced into Rome by official act during the Punic Wars. The Mithra cult, originally Persian, in later Hellenistic days had a thorough distribution throughout the Roman Empire.

Together with denationalization, the Hellenistic age of transition brought about another equally important effect upon religions: they were thoroughly individualized in application and function. The significant point is that they now existed and functioned for the sole purpose of bringing the sense of salvation to the individual as an individual. This, obviously, was an outgrowth of the breakdown of nationalism. As has been mentioned, cosmopolitanism and individualism were complementary social attitudes of the period. In the days of the old city-states, for example, it was the business of Athena to protect and to give complete religious satisfaction to the Athenians as Athenians; of Artemis, to do the same for the Ephesians; while Isis and Osiris served as exclusive deities for Egyptians. When the city-states and the empires fell before Alexander, this did not obliterate local and indigenous religions. Instead, they were transformed. Since their state or national functions had been ended, they functioned with reference to the individual. With the mixture of peoples in the new world the religions accompanied the worshipers, functioning wherever they were taken, now not solely for the benefit of Egyptians, or Persians, or Phrygians but for the benefit of anybody and everybody who was attracted to the particular cult.

Thus, the Isis cult was to be found throughout the Mediterranean world. There is a very effective story,[2] for example, of an

----

[2] Apuleius *Metamorphoses*.

adventurous young man who attempted, without sufficient information, to practice magic. He found himself transformed into an ass and was restored to his human state after he had a vision of Isis and found his way to a procession of her cult at a point near Corinth. The author of the story was a "Roman" from northern Africa, the "hero" was a Greek, but the "Egyptian" religion was embraced and utilized far from its river-valley home. Obviously, the "foreign" devotee did not have to become an Egyptian when he did so. He embraced the religion because of a felt need; he was welcome to join, whoever he was and wherever he was, and anyone who joined it was given the assurance of salvation and welfare. This was individualism—as characteristic of religion in the Hellenistic age of transition as it was basic in Christian Protestantism or in the revivals on the American frontier.

It will be remembered, however, that Judaism was an exception to both these features. Since (save for a brief period, as will be sketched later) the Jewish people did not constitute a nation, it is improper to speak of nationalization or of denationalization in referring to Judaism. But Judaism, then as now, was the religion of a people; and in Hellenistic days it remained so. Further, there was no counterpart in Judaism of the thoroughgoing individualism which has been pointed out and emphasized. As shall be shown, Jews and Judaism were importantly affected by Hellenistic culture, but this was one of its features which was successfully resisted. In this period, as before, to practice Judaism required that one be a Jew. Normally and in most cases, he would be born a Jew; if he were a Gentile and wished to practice Judaism, he must become a Jew. For Judaism was not a religion of individual salvation. To be sure, Judaism possessed and applied the concept of salvation, and ultimately it was the individual person who was "saved." But the concept was different from that of the gentile religions of the Hellenistic age in that the good life came through identification with the people and obedience to their code of behavior. One could never be saved as an individual, apart from the group.

There was much greater influence of Hellenistic culture upon

Judaism in certain localities outside Palestine. Alexandrian Judaism was deeply affected, and Jews in Antioch felt the impact to a lesser degree. Evidence has been presented recently which indicates that Judaism in certain areas of the Dispersion became a "mystery religion," with Moses functioning as Orpheus and Hermes-Tut imparting the mystic way of salvation.[3] Archeological remains in extra-Palestinian and in Palestinian synagogues also indicate that art was used to a degree and in ways not conforming to the strict interpretation of the First Commandment— a certain evidence of the influence of Hellenistic culture. Jewish thinkers reinterpreted traditional Judaism in the light and terms of Greek philosophy.

This type of Judaism must be taken into account in depicting the spread of Hellenistic ways, and especially in studying certain aspects of the rise of Christianity: Dispersion Judaism became a sort of bridge between Jesus and gentile Christianity.

Yet in the main, as has been insisted, Judaism formed an exception to the otherwise complete extension of Hellenistic values in culture and religion. Judaism, in the Dispersion as in Palestine, remained the religion of a people. This accounts for the characteristics mentioned above.

The reader must bear in mind that after the Punic Wars (264–146 B.C.) the balance of political power in the Mediterranean world shifted to the West—for the remainder of the period Rome was dominant. Roman legions asserted their power over northern Africa, Egypt, the Iberian Peninsula, "Gaul," and Britain. All this was accomplished before the death of Julius Caesar. Imperial Rome pushed her sway into the East; and by the time that Christianity emerged, the Roman armies were keeping the Roman peace throughout another vast world empire. There was uncertainty at the eastern border and the territory along the Danube, but within these limits the power of Rome was supreme.

But in conquering by military and political force, the Roman power itself was transformed by the more insidious values of

[3] Erwin R. Goodenough, *By Light, Light: The Mystic Gospel of Hellenistic Judaism* (New Haven: Yale University Press, 1935).

Hellenistic civilization and culture. The Hellenistic age of transition did not come to its end with the crushing might of Roman power. Rather, the development of Hellenistic values went on, albeit with modifications and new directions. Indeed, the transforming power of Greek culture is to be seen in the significant fact that, as late as the early fourth century after Christ, the eastern part of the Roman Empire was more important than the western. When Constantine relocated his capital, it was in the eastern city, which he chose to call Constantinople. What began with Alexander had its culmination under the Caesars and their successors.

III

JUDAISM

THE determining date line for Judaism is earlier than the rise of Hellenistic culture. In Judaism it was the so-called "Exile," and the developments in and after it, which marked the most significant dividing-point. The story of Ezra, in the Old Testament, gives an idealized account of the adoption of, and subsequent commitment to, legalism. This was the dominant characteristic of subsequent Judaism, so that "late Judaism" is distinguished from other phases of the religion and history of the people of Israel.

In this development the "law of Moses" was consciously and deliberately adopted as the pattern of the life of the Jewish people, by which they tenaciously and successfully maintained their particular values and cultural characteristics. The Jewish leaders and teachers knew fully that this ancient pattern (of course, less ancient than its ascription to Moses implied) had to be interpreted for its provisions to be applicable to the current life. They therefore developed a class of professional interpreters, the scribes, whose business it was to make the old code apply to modern situations. With practical unanimity the people at large followed this leadership. Thus the consciousness that they were a peculiar people, to whom God had revealed himself as he had not revealed himself to any other people, was the foundation of a religious culture which held a widely dispersed people together.

In this period, subsequent to Ezra, the Jews developed their characteristic ways of life and their particular religious institutions. The adoption of "the Torah" (the written "law of Moses" and its traditional interpretations) was fundamental.

The synagogue, which probably appeared first in the Persian period, was an efficient means for the dissemination of the Torah, both in its legalistic and its more generally didactic elements. A Temple, the particular concern of the hereditary priesthood, functioned in Jerusalem. Of these two institutions, however, the synagogue was by far the more influential, effective, and important. Teachers were honored; a high intellectualism was native in ancient Judaism. The importance of the synagogue and the universal necessity for "legal" interpretation gave the lay officials, such as the scribes, far more practical influence than the priests.

In Palestine the economy was chiefly agricultural, with a certain amount of trade in the cities, particularly Jerusalem. Outside Palestine—and the reader must remember that only a fraction of the Jews lived in Palestine—there was great variety in the economic status of the Jewish people. But wherever there were Jews, their particular way of life, now crystallized into customs which had the sanction of law, was readily and cheerfully observed.

Jews were widely distributed. Only a small proportion of the large Babylonian colony had returned to Palestine when Cyrus the Persian became for the Jews the God-sent deliverer (called "my Anointed"—i.e., my Messiah, my Christ—in Isa. 45:1). During the Hellenistic period there were many Jews in Egypt, and the "people of the Law" were to be found throughout the Western part of the world as well.

Inevitably Judaism felt the impact of the conquest of Alexander. Josephus tells[1] that Alexander visited Jerusalem and was impressed by the priests. However this may have been, at least the conqueror crossed Palestinian territory; and in his reorganization of political administration he assigned the land of Israel to Syria. In the struggles for power after Alexander's death, however, Palestine came under the nominal control of Egypt in 320 B.C.; and for several years afterward she suffered frequently the fate of the buffer state. During this time, however, the effective cultural relationship was with Syria. Finally, in 198 the political

---

[1] *Antiquities* xi; *Against Apion* ii.

control was again seized by Syria, and remained so until the advent of the power of Rome.

During the Hellenistic period Judaism was, then, under the effective influence of Syria, in which Antioch was the central force as well as the chief city. There can be no doubt that Palestinian Judaism was affected by Hellenism to a considerable degree. The story of the corrupt high priests outbidding one another to the Seleucid king is an indication of their willingness to accept and to further the culture of Hellenistic Syria. That the priests followed their trend was natural. It resulted that there was a considerable acceptance and spread of Hellenistic customs. The building of a gymnasium in Jerusalem is a practical symbol; some people—doubtless a considerable portion—took up various Greek ways. They wore items of Greek dress. These are the points that are emphasized in the historical accounts; what is to be borne in mind is that these particular matters were only conspicuous symbols of the insidious spread of Hellenistic culture. It is possible to conclude that in Jerusalem the priests, at least, became more Greek then Jewish.

But this tendency was resisted, particularly by the scribes and their followers. The Jews furnished the one significant exception to the otherwise complete subjection of the world to Alexander's control and to the effects of Greek culture. As was stated, they did not adopt the thoroughgoing individualism which was everywhere else universal. For the Jews felt themselves God's people in a peculiar way; God had revealed himself to them as he had not to any other people, and it was part of their accepted tradition to keep themselves separate from others. Their practice of circumcision symbolized the covenant relation into which God had entered with Abraham for the benefit of Abraham's descendants. It was the greatest value to be born a Jew, thus to become one of the people who were God's, to whom God had revealed himself in the perfect law. The encroachment of any foreign culture, it was plainly perceived by their most influential religious leaders, would result in the breakdown of this relationship and the loss of this possession.

Probably, if the current of affairs had been allowed to take its natural development, the influence of Hellenistic culture upon Judaism would have effected as profound a synthesis as had occurred in the earlier history of the Hebrew groups.

But this did not occur, except in certain localities outside Palestine (see above, p. 17). Antiochus IV (Epiphanes) undertook to hasten the process by forcing the Hellenization of his Palestinian subjects. This precipitated the revolt under the leadership of Mattathias, a priest who had never accepted Hellenistic culture. Mattathias began the revolution by striking down a Jew who was about to submit to the king's decree and offer a pig as sacrifice. Summoning all who were loyal to their ancestral religion, he was joined by a band of "pious ones" (*Chasidim*). After his death his sons, Judas, Jonathan, and Simon, proved to be able leaders who successfully achieved the political, religious, and cultural independence of the Palestinian Jews. No small part of the victory was due to the foreign wars, which prevented the Seleucid kings from exerting their full force against the Jews.

Political independence of the Palestinian Jews lasted for about a century—from the recapture of Jerusalem in 165 B.C. to the completion of Roman sway in 63, when Pompey captured the city of Jerusalem—"city of peace" which had seen so much of war!

During this period the character of late Judaism was formed. This character was the further development of that which had begun in the "restored" community when the people adopted the "law of Moses" as the basis of their culture. Many of the institutions which existed in the days of Jesus and Paul go back to this earlier time; some came into being between the time of Ezra and the Maccabean period (e.g., the synagogue). The conservative reaction leading to the Maccabean revolt intensified already present tendencies. Even so, Hellenistic influence, although checked and lessened by the Maccabean revolution, was effective to some degree. But the Judaism of Jesus' day developed through these earlier, formative periods.

For example, the basic divisions of the Jewish people were formulated at that time. The priests, of course, had existed as a class long before, and their place and function continued. The "party" of the Sadducees was a growth of the priestly class. Its

counterpart, the Pharisees, seems to have emerged in the reign of
John Hyrcanus, successor of Simon the Maccabee (135–105 B.C.).
These people were laymen, as distinct from the priestly Sadducees. As the institution of the Sadducees was the Temple, the
institution of the Pharisees was the synagogue. Both "parties"
were in agreement in acceptance of the "law of Moses," but the
Pharisees became its chief interpreters. Scribes came from both
groups but predominantly from the Pharisees. The Pharisees em-
bodied the fierce loyalty and devotion to the "law of Moses"
which had been so heroically evidenced by the very life-blood of
"the pious ones" (the *Chasidim* of the Maccabean revolt). Their
whole aim was to live according to the law and to bring others
to do the same. Consequently, it was the Pharisees who brought
into being the intricate system of custom which existed in Jesus'
day.

A third group, which was considerable in number even
though the nature of their way of life made them less influential
than either the Sadducees or the Pharisees, was the Essenes.
These were communities of Jews who, also stemming from "the
pious ones," acted upon the judgment that only complete with-
drawal from the world enabled people to live their religious lives
completely. Therefore they formed closed communities, within
which they practiced a much more ascetic and rigorous discipline
than was characteristic of Jews generally. So rigid was their interpretation of the law that they refused to perform their bodily
functions on the Sabbath, regarding this as "work." Their life
was monastic; they practiced strict celibacy, rejected animal
sacrifice, and completely eschewed politics. They wore a distinctive white garb and had their own religious and civil government.

As to politics, the Sadducees were entirely willing to cultivate
relations with civil government; and when Palestine was under
foreign sway, they were equally ready to deal with their overlords. The reason for this was simple: the Sadducees were the
people who maintained the Temple cultus and, enjoying the
considerable income from tithes enjoined by the Mosaic law,
they were a wealthy class. Indeed, they were the great landed

class of the Palestinian Jews. People of wealth naturally desire the maintenance of the political status quo; hence the Sadducees were ready to deal with political administrators of their own or of foreign people.

The Pharisees maintained a position midway between the rejection of politics (the ideal of the Essenes) and the cultivation of civil power (the practice of the Sadducees). The Pharisees acted upon the practical position that the primary value in life was religion, and they made it their sincere effort to make religion cover all aspects of life. But they sensibly recognized that the state inevitably impinges upon the common life. The ideal was to avoid politics, as far as this was possible; but where it was not possible, to accept the obligation of dealing with civil law and political administration. There is no difference between their ideal and the saying of Jesus: "Pay Caesar what is owing him, and pay God what is owing him."

The attitudes of the Pharisees and the Sadducees are to be seen in their contrasting reactions to the developing ideas of the resurrection and of angels. Contacts with Eastern religions, notably Persian Zoroastrianism and its outgrowths, had confronted the Jews with these two doctrines. The Pharisees readily adapted these concepts to their own purposes; the Sadducees consistently rejected both angels and the resurrection.

The different attitudes of various Jewish groups emerge in their views of the Messiah. All Jews had some expectation of the Messiah, for this was a religious conception found in their Scripture, with particular ideas of it developed from the interpretation of Scripture. The messianic expectation of the Sadducees, however, was not at all ardent—also an aspect of their preference for the maintenance of the status quo. It is not clear what the Essenes taught about the Messiah. The flowering of the messianic hope occurred within Pharisaism. What must be borne in mind is that there was almost infinite variety in the messianic expectation of various Jews. Some, like the Sadducees, accepted the idea but had no ardor in their expectation. Of those who did eagerly hope for the appearance of the Messiah, some expected him soon, some in the indefinite future, some in the remote future. Some conceived the expected Messiah as king, some thought of him as a warrior leader, some pictured a heavenly being who would come on the clouds in the end of the age.

There was similar variation in the closely related thought concerning the Kingdom of God. The Sadducees were more concerned with this world than with such an abstraction. Some Pharisees pictured God's rulership in terms of something like the glorious reign of David. Others had a view which connected the idea with their expectation of a catastrophic end of the age— they thought of an apocalyptic Kingdom with an apocalyptic Messiah introducing it.

Indeed, perhaps during the days of Jesus, and certainly not long after his death, these related religious values brought into being a definite group, the Zealots. Although they agreed with many of the religious concepts of the Pharisees, the Zealots differed strongly at the significant point of political action. Whereas the Pharisees avoided politics as much as possible, leaving it to God to bring about changes in political conditions, the Zealots conceived it to be their purpose to bring in the apocalyptic Kingdom of God by resistance to the Roman administrative and military forces. They believed that the Messiah would bring the Kingdom by destroying the Roman power and that it was their duty to initiate the divine purpose by assassinating as many Romans as they could. They became known to the Romans as *sicarii* ("dagger-carriers").

It is not in the realm of ideas, however, that the essential nature of late Judaism is to be observed. This essential nature has been mentioned; now it must be detailed. Late Judaism was legalistic. The willing adoption of the "law of Moses" meant for the Jewish people generally the application to their lives of the customs which had developed as a result of the attempt to make an older law contemporary. These customs were numerous and detailed. However, for practical purpose they grouped around two poles: diet and Sabbath observance. Not only must the faithful Jew refrain from eating pork, rabbits, and oysters; his food must be prepared in a certain way, meat slaughtered according to strict rules, different foods cooked in certain vessels, and some foods must not be mixed with others. No work could be done on the Sabbath—and many legal minds wrestled with the problem of defining what constituted "work." It must not be thought, however, that the Jewish Sabbath was a somber day (like the New England Sunday of Colonial days). On the contrary, it was a joyous day of entertainment and feasting.

Specific interpretations of the written law brought differences of opinion among the great scribes and teachers (rabbis) of Judaism, just as ethical judgments vary among free minds in the twentieth century. Not only were there debates on matters of diet and "work" on the Sabbath, but the question of divorce saw scribal differences. In Jesus' day there were two prevailing interpretations of the Deuteronomic law which permitted a man to divorce his wife for any "indecency" or "unseemly conduct."[2] The followers of the conservative teacher, Shammai, declared that adultery alone constituted "the unseemly thing." The students of the great liberal scribe, Hillel, declared (with characteristic oriental overemphasis) that burning the bread would give adequate cause under the law.

But, as a matter of fact, Jewish legalism was regarded by the Jews as positive in its nature and effect, not negative. There were indeed many "laws"; but the Jewish people accepted them gladly and found, not only satisfaction, but joy, in their observance. There is no basis for the view that multitudes of Jews groaned under the intolerable weight of a legal system which had been forced upon them. Rather, they enjoyed the religion whose obligations they voluntarily accepted, legalistic though it was.

It must be remembered by the reader that the volume of Jewish law was accounted for by its inclusion of what modern Western nations separate as "civil" and "criminal" law. It is a simple fact that the ancient Jew lived under fewer laws and felt them to be no more a burden than the citizen of any city of the United States.

Judaism during the Hellenistic period focused its activities about two institutions: the Temple and the synagogue. The

[2] Deut. 24:1.

Temple was the center of the sacrificial cultus and the symbol of
Jewish unity under the Covenant. Its hereditary priesthood,
drawn from the Sadducees, was retrogressive in matters religious.
But far more influential in Jewish life was the synagogue, an institution of worship and of learning. It may have had its faint
beginnings during the Exile; certainly it grew to power as the
center of developing Judaism after Ezra. Here the scribe and the
Pharisee interpreted the law; here the Jew came on the Sabbath
to worship and to learn the meaning of Torah; here the youth
came for proper instruction. There were many synagogues, for
one could be formed wherever there were ten male Jews over
thirteen years of age; there was only one "legitimate" Temple.
Yet it was not simply a matter of numbers which preserved the
synagogue after the fall of the Temple and the Jewish nation in
the rebellion of 132 A.D. The synagogue had become the heart of
Judaism; the Temple and its cultus had degenerated into an almost useless appendix.

As the period of the life of Jesus was reached, the development
of Jewish legalism had resulted in the production of a voluminous
code of interpretation of the Scripture upon which Judaism was
based. The professional interpreters, the so-called "scribes,"
especially after the rise and growth of Pharisaism, were a numerous class in Judaism, highly respected by the people. They regarded the Scripture as sacred and used it as a guide to their activities
and attitudes. They recognized its three divisions: the Law (i.e.,
the Pentateuch), the prophets (former and latter prophets; this
division included what we call the "historical books": Joshua,
Judges, I and II Samuel, I and II Kings, as well as those which
we classify as "prophets"), and "the writings" (i.e., the remainder when the first two groups are identified; e.g., Ruth,
Esther, Psalms, Chronicles, Daniel). Deriving more from "the
Law" than from the other divisions, they drew from the whole
the interpretations which made the Scripture apply to daily life.

Their interpretations were later incorporated into the Talmud. But in the days of Jesus the corpus of interpretation
was carried in memory—the so-called "tradition of the elders."

Scripture and the traditional interpretation were known as "the Torah" ("the Teaching"). Torah had absolute authority; for practical purposes there was little distinction between the attitudes toward Scripture and Torah. What must be remembered is that the Jewish people accepted it voluntarily and enjoyed its observance.

After all, the daily life of the common people did not involve the burdensome discharge of numerous obligations. It was a matter of custom, and there is slight difference between custom and law. A Jew lived according to the code which was customary in his group. There were local and group differences, too. Some Jews lived according to highly detailed laws; these *Chaberim* ("associates") applied to themselves as laymen all the laws, even those applicable to priests when on service. Others had much less detailed codes. Some particularists attempted to make their codes normative for others, even endeavoring to force them upon fellow-Jews who offered resistance. After all, a number of points were debatable and were vigorously discussed by those whose logic drove them to different interpretations of the law.

Anyone who learns and understands Judaism must see that it was a vigorous, living religion, noble in its spiritual values, high in its achievement of personal and group righteousness. That Pharisaic Judaism was capable of ruthless cruelty to opponents and foreign enemies can scarcely be doubted in the light of II Macc. 15:28 ff.; but, in the main, the moral and religious teachings of Judaism were humanitarian and enlightened.

By the time of the life of Jesus the Jewish people were under the political control of Rome, as was all the Hellenistic world. Jesus was born during the days of Herod the Great, an autonomous king whose Idumean forebears had been forced by John Hyrcanus to accept circumcision and thus become Jews. After his death the land was ruled by his sons, Archelaus having Judea and Samaria, Antipas having Galilee and the region known as "the Ten Cities," Philip having certain territories to the northeast. Archelaus proved to be unsuitable to Rome; consequently he was replaced by a procurator who was directly responsible to the emperor.

The rule of Rome was firm, often severe. Palestine was not far from the eastern frontier, always a danger point to the empire. Like all provincial areas, it was exploited for the benefit of Rome. But as the Romans were capable colonial administrators, they exercised the control necessary to keep the country at peace.

The traditions record that it was in Bethlehem of Judea, where his parents had gone for enrolment for census or tax purposes, that Jesus was born—born a Jew into the late Judaism which now flourished in the Hellenistic world.

IV

GENTILE RELIGIOUS LIFE

PARTICULARLY misleading is the oft-cherished belief that the first-century Greco-Roman world was devoid of vital religious life and was impatiently awaiting the coming of a new and dominant religious type. This misimpression has caused casual students of the beginnings of Christianity to suppose that the gentile world welcomed the new movement with open arms, having laid aside every vestige of previous decadent religions. This view ignores the historical fact that the Christian movement found itself, from the beginning, in the center of the mad scramble for religious loyalty which was being waged by competing cults of the first century. The battle scars which the new movement acquired in the first three centuries of this era are irrefutable witnesses of the power which the competing religions could muster. Certainly the early Church Fathers were as convinced of their vigor as they were of their error.

Variety marked the first-century religious scene. Under the tolerant spirit of Roman administration a great many types of religious activity flourished. Nor were the numerous cults always mutually exclusive. An ardent devotee of the cult of Magna Mater might hold in high regard several of the deities of the Capitoline system, invoke the medical aid of the hero-god Asclepius, and perform his patriotic and religious duties in connection with emperor-worship. While philosophy brought the critical spirit to bear upon all religious practices, it was never regarded as an exclusive cult. Judaism, indeed, was almost exclusive; but it was regarded as a highly peculiar faith.

Supernatural beings were not strangers in the Mediterranean world of the first century. They often interfered with the daily

30

activities of human beings—sometimes to help, at other times to injure. Since men could not know all the desires which motivated the behavior of spirits, the exact course of events was indeed difficult to predict. The degree of uncertainty varied according to a person's background and training. The whimsicality of the spirits determined the course of events, in the thinking of many. To others, nature seemed orderly and her path was well marked: one had but to observe natural history to conclude that a stern Necessity or Fate determined the destiny of man. Thus the prosperous and happy man had reason to believe that his actions had been in accordance with the ways of nature; otherwise poverty and distress would have been his lot. To the masses of people whose fortunes were at a low ebb, however, the controlling forces of the universe seemed capricious and lacking in justice. Chance and whim seemed the main factors in a confusing life.

In a world of chance, superstition played an important role. When cause-effect relationships are illogical, life under the spirits becomes a hazardous affair. Efforts to insure favors and avert calamities ranged from the humorous to the pitiful. Thunderstorms drove Augustus to the cellar and Caligula under the bed, while Domitian regarded as highly ominous the seeming preference of the lightning for his imperial palace and other public buildings. Outstanding men of letters, such as Dio Cassius, Suetonius, Petronius, and Apuleius, bear witness to the prevalence of superstition in high and low places. So intertwined did religion and superstition seem to Lucretius that he proposed that both should be removed from the thought of intelligent men. In place of capricious gods, Lucretius advised his age to substitute a rational concept of nature. To the writer Plutarch, it appeared that religion had too often permitted the excessive fear of the gods which nurtured superstition; deities, as friends of mankind, should be approached with great confidence. Atheism represented a mistaken attitude and an extreme reaction from superstition. In the golden mean Plutarch would have men find true religion.

The philosophers of the Mediterranean world were the most

persistent critics of both superstition and religion. They were themselves in search of the guiding principles of the universe; therefore they scorned the disorganized ideas of superstition and attempted to purify the concepts of religion. The sixth century before Christ saw the philosopher Xenophanes charge that the ancient gods bore unmistakable resemblances to their human creators. The gods were manlike because men had shaped them; had oxen, horses, and lions been able to mold gods for themselves, their deities would have been pictured as oxen, horses, and lions. Xenophanes would discard anthropomorphism entirely and see deity purely in terms of sight, mind, and ear, ruling all things by thought. The behavior of the Olympians excited further criticisms from Cicero and Lucretius. How could the Homeric mythology attribute deity to beings whose behavior was often immoral and scandalous, culpable even by the low standards men required of themselves?

Why, then, had ideas of the gods originated? Democritus found the answer in the fearful exhibitions of nature—phenomena which the common man could not explain under the science then available to him. Other thinkers believed the gods to have climbed from humanity to divinity on the ladder of legend, which glorified their natural lives and deeds until they were exalted above mortality. Great men had thus been distorted by time and fancy into gods. Damaging to the prestige of the Olympians, too, was the growth of comparative mythology during the Hellenistic age. Students of philosophy discovered that surrounding nations cherished beliefs in divinities whose form and function were strangely similar to their own. The result was to diminish the respect of each national group for its gods, as the sole guarantors of progress and governors of men. But if the gods were unseated for some of the populace, the need for reliance upon someone or something still had to be met. Life still needed some explanation; personalized forces, called Fortune, Fate, and Destiny, appeared to fill the gap.

The early Greek philosophers sought to organize the universe about one principle or cause. Beginning with researches in geography, geometry, medicine, astronomy, and natural history, they expressed their convictions in sweeping generalizations. Thales concluded that moisture was the origin of all things. Anaxagoras pronounced that "all things were together till Mind came and arranged them." Heraclitus saw in incessant change the key to understanding of the universe: "All things move, nothing stays; all things flow." Socrates turned away from the natural sciences to a piercing analysis of all generalizations and virtuous phrases, challenging speakers to define and illustrate in specific terms their talk of "justice" and "courage," their analysis of things as "beautiful" or "ugly." A critic of generalizations, Socrates himself probably left to his disciples a highly paradoxical teaching: virtue is knowledge, but it cannot be taught—no one willingly does wrong; through ignorance personal evil originates.

Plato was not a forgotten teacher in the Mediterranean world of the first century. Platonic idealism insisted that the only way to reach truth was to concentrate on the ideal world. In mathematics, one must begin with principles of arithmetic and then by reason deduce the whole world of number. The rules and principles are exactly true and always true; objects are fluctuating and imperfect. Principles and ideals are the real truth; objects in the external world are only images or imitations of reality. One cannot apprehend the truth about triangles by a study of existing triangles; instead, one judges each of these imperfect triangles in the light of the ideal triangle. Honesty and justice cannot be comprehended by observation of a thousand so-called "honest men"; degree of honesty must be assessed by comparison of each individual man with the ideal honesty. Sense perception and the world with which it deals fluctuate far too much to reach truth; instead, one must penetrate immediately to the ideal world through clear and strictly rational introspection. Just how one could be assured that he had penetrated through the haze of objects to ideal reality was not clearly stated by Plato. Perhaps intuition or introspection were to assist the thinker in his search for his "recollection" from a previous life.

Plato himself saw the dangers involved in this method. It could be perfectly demonstrated in an exact study, such as arithmetic; it fostered chaos when one sought to apply it in the realm of the conceptual or the aesthetic. One justice is not always equal to another; neither are "beauty" and "truth" to be taken in terms of two and four. But numbers of devoted adherents of Platonism were making the search for this ideal beauty and truth in the first-century world. Their influence upon the thinking of their day was not to be discounted; in fact, it left its ineradicable imprint upon early Christian thought.

Aristotle proved to be a good student of his teacher. He began as a Platonist but moved rather steadily toward an independent position. Induction was the keystone of the Aristotelian approach to "truth" and "beauty"; one discovered the meaning of general terms through observation of specific illustrations. The "form" is grasped by prolonged study of individuals, from them one may realize what the idea behind them must be. Truth is to be found in the characteristics of objects in the sensible world—in short, Aristotle denied the existence of Plato's world of ideas. Biology and the natural sciences dominated Aristotle's thought too much to permit his permanent identification with Platonism. He came to define the purpose of science as the classification and discovery of the attributes of objects. Plants and animals can be distinguished each from the other only by a minute study of individual characteristics, leading to classification by genus and species. This rigid study of variations and relationships led naturally to a firm development of the principles which controlled Aristotle's logic. Biology also convinced him of a perfect or characteristic form toward which all life moves, perfection being the ultimate end of every species. The influence of this dictum is still felt in circles where the teleological argument for the existence of God is used. The Mediterranean world of the first century cherished the intellectual heritage to which Aristotle had so largely contributed; later Christianity, under the guidance of men like Thomas Aquinas, made it the basis for a world synthesis.

But philosophy had not concluded its work when the great masters ceased to write and teach. Two other schools of thought dealt critically with the traditions and suggested ways to approach the universe with confidence: the Epicurean saw conquest in the cultivation of sweetness or pleasure; the Stoic found victory in the pursuit of virtue. Each formed an important challenge to the thinking of first-century searchers for truth.

Epicurus (d. 270 B.C.) was an Athenian of good birth who drank the dregs of poverty, defeat, exile, and distress, only to emerge convinced that life still held the possibility of sweetness and pleasure. Moderate and temperate living formed the key to happiness; its emotional color must be brightened by the absence of fear and the presence of love for one's friends. Sweetness or pleasure is the one good or aim of life; virtue is profitable only if it contributes to this supreme end. Epicurus dedicated his efforts to the defeat of false fears: fear of death, fear of the gods, fright at the contemplation of pain, uncertainty in the presence of the conventional world. He decried rank, power, and ambition as bitter delusions; learning and culture were encumbrances to be avoided. Courageous teaching was this, but not many adventurers were found. The work of Epicureanism was done when the educated Greek world was liberated from superstitious terrors. Two of its contributions made little impression until modern times: the atomic theory in physics and the utilitarian theory in ethics.

The Cynics and the Stoics did much to strengthen the moral fiber of the first-century world. The Stoics occupied a higher place on the social and educational ladder than did the Cynics, their brothers under the skin. The Cynic carried his doctrine to the street corner and into public places, claiming no advantages of dress or gold over the common man of the street. The Cynic-Stoic saw in virtue the supreme good; virtue, the direct relation of the naked soul to God. "Nothing but Goodness is good"; earthly pains and pleasures, sickness and health, poverty and wealth, have no importance whatever. Goodness is devotion to the purpose of God and identification of one's will with God's will, or complete co-operation with the cosmos. The world as a whole shows purpose, and the individual who is out of harmony with that purpose is wicked. Suffering results when one fails to perceive correctly the divine harmony or to attune one's self to it. The ultimate value in the universe is the willing fulfilment of the purpose of God. Our own efforts may be defeated, friends may die, and we may suffer great sorrows; ours is to accept the eternal purpose and be content. The Stoics refused consistently to narrow good to a far-off and divine future; the purpose is being fulfilled in the present, the cosmos is beautiful now—and always. Sufferings in themselves are of no importance; the way men face them matters tremendously. Stoicism taught men to adapt themselves to their universe, not to whimper and complain. From the lame slave Epictetus to the good emperor Marcus Aurelius it gave theoretical comfort in time of failure and inspiration to fulfil the divine purpose by governing well and justly.

In the exceedingly complex syncretism of the first-century Mediterranean world the nationalistic type of religion was not completely neglected. Imperial conquests had demolished many local governments; and with the downfall of petty states, their patron gods had become more personal and individual. The outstanding exception to this rule was Judaism, which maintained a highly nationalistic flavor within Palestine, even though it yielded slightly to the demands for personal comfort and adjustments outside its native home. Yet Jews were judged by surrounding peoples to be peculiar in their outlook. Far more natural was the latter's reliance upon a score of gods who had once belonged exclusively to one or another of the nations now a part of the great Roman melting-pot. Isis-Osiris assisted in the personal salvation of many people strange to their native Egypt; Mithras could no longer be confined to the land of Persia; Magna Mater promised to Romans rich blessings which had formerly been reserved for Phrygians; Demeter found Eleusis and Greece uncomfortably small. But the Jew in Palestine endeavored to stem the tide: to bask in the favor of Yahweh one must join the Jewish people. The force of the Jewish challenge to the syncretistic world has already been reviewed in chapter iii.

Another item in the complex religious environment was the merged form of the Olympian-Capitoline systems. A close inspection of the archeological and literary remains of the period shows that the ancient gods and goddesses were not simply outworn traditions or embellishments for public buildings. Although not in the flower of youth the Olympian-Capitoline religion commanded considerable respect from first-century worshipers. Augustus had revived the ancient Roman family religion to serve as cement for this primary social group. Olympian-Capitoline worship centered attention upon the temples, the city, and the state, as well as upon individuals. That these divine figures still gripped the imaginations and affections of men is shown by the Theodosian code of prohibitions, late in the fourth century after Christ, which under Christian pressure sought to suppress all activities in behalf of the ancient Greek and Roman deities.

The Olympian gods had grown with the changing fortunes of the Greek states. Although in origin each god had been associated with a specific function and locality, the crumbling walls of local independence had signaled a wider scope of activity for each deity. The social organization of the pantheon was modeled after that of the Greeks themselves. The Olympians rode into new fields of conquest with the victorious armies of Alexander; and long after the conqueror's death they came into Rome, there to effect something of a fusion with the Capitoline pantheon. The gods of Greece represented for the Hellenistic world the most concrete illustrations of Hellenic ideals, for they were the representatives and patrons of various departments in commerce and culture. The monopolies held by these gods were the envy of rival religions. The finest in literature and art gave praise to them. The most beautiful in architecture and sculpture was dedicated to their worship. Public festivals were held in their names. Because they helped to meet real social and community needs, these gods continued to be popular. Economic prosperity, health, and protection against the multifold dangers of life must be assured each city; each artisan must have his protective deity— and so the gods survived because they had functional value. Their power is better attested by the sharp rivalry which they furnished early Christianity than by the depreciatory writings which the Church Fathers hurled against them.

Closely related to the Olympian pantheon were the great heroes who had served humanity well and had been rewarded by elevation to divine status. These marvelous individuals were, at the same time, greater than men and less than the gods. Usually they were believed to have sprung from one divine and one human parent, thus blending the characteristics of divinity and humanity. Heracles, or Hercules, was one of the most popular of these heroic figures. Through twelve mighty deeds he showed himself to be a champion among men and a match for the gods; he was rewarded by a place among the immortal gods, there to serve as a mighty ally to oppressed humanity whenever it should call upon him. But, however admirable strength may be, the desire for health usually takes priority. So it was that, among the hero-gods, Asclepius took precedence in the affections of men; it was he who was the patron of the medical arts. According to the theories of the ancient world, illness resulted from divine displeasure or from the possession of one's body by supernatural beings called "demons." It was, therefore, the office of gods alone to assure health or cure infirmities. This was Asclepius' field of specialization, and his sanctuaries were crowded with the diseased and the disabled. Throughout the Greco-Roman world these sanatoriums could be found—at Pergamum and Smyrna, in Athens and in Rome, in addition to the famous shrine at Epidaurus. Recourse to the supernatural was an important part of the healing process, but the sane medical practices and healthful location of the sanctuaries were decisive factors in the record of cures which the shrines evidently established. At least, these sanatoriums passed the pragmatic test with flying colors.

The popularity of the hero-gods was largely attributable to the personal and individual character of their cults. Assistance of a given kind was directed toward the individual believer rather than toward a state or group. The hero-gods had been human themselves, therefore they could understand the frailties of supplicants and render proper assistance. The hero-god, by nature, training, and present position, was admirably adapted to the special task of assistance to struggling humanity. Divine parentage served to explain to followers the cause of exceptional ability. Tribulations and great deeds on earth gave them undisputed comprehension of human problems. Divine rating conferred the ability to render real assistance, not to be thwarted even by demons or malevolent spirits.

The genius of Rome found expression in its political use of the religious forms called "emperor-worship." Roman emperor-worship was a further development of the fusion of ideas which Alexander the Great had begun. The Persians had followed the oriental pattern, which deified a ruler because of divine parentage and kinship to the gods. The Greeks customarily apotheosized a citizen who had shown himself mighty in deeds or, occasionally, one whose near perfection in physique or countenance was common knowledge. Alexander accepted divine honors given him on both traditions. Prejudice against deification of the living on the part of the Greek successors of Alexander diminished gradually throughout the centuries succeeding his death, especially in the areas which later became Roman provinces. By the time of Augustus these provinces were including deceased heroes, such as Julius Caesar, among the gods and were openly according divine honors to the living emperor himself. The long and prosperous rule of Augustus encouraged emperor-worship; he became the patriotic symbol of the blessings which the empire afforded those within its protection. The decree, about 9 B.C., which made his birthday the official beginning of the year openly referred to him as "a god and a savior." After Augustus' death the Senate promptly elevated him to a place among the gods of the state. Tiberius approved apotheosization for Augustus, but he seems to have been rather modest concerning the divine honors which the provinces lavished upon him. Caligula, Nero, and Domitian were far less reserved in their expressed desire for divine honors.[1]

Emperor-worship in the Greco-Roman world of the first century was a blend of the religious and the political. The beneficent rule of men like Augustus evoked an appreciative response which could be interpreted only in terms of worship. Their deeds were of sufficient importance to suggest the powers of the hero-gods and to encourage reverence and gratitude. The political use-

[1] See, further, S. J. Case, *The Evolution of Early Christianity* (Chicago: University of Chicago Press, 1914), chap. vii.

fulness of such adoration or worship would at once be evident to the minds of administrative officials: it provided the adhesive force necessary to bind together peoples of varied traditions and races, all of whom found themselves in the melting-pot called the "Roman Empire." The imperial religion presented difficulties to many Christians late in the first century, but its main idea was highly useful in Christian missionary propaganda. Based in the cultural past of many of the peoples of the Empire was the strong desire for a heaven-sent helper to assist in ridding the world of its evils. Emperor-worship pointed to the imperial overlords as divine agents; Christianity saw that deliverer as its own cult-lord.

Of all the religious types present in the Greco-Roman world, the mystery religions were probably most responsive to human and personal needs. Yet, aside from cautious hints on the part of writers who had been initiated, little is known of the actual rites and promises that made them most attractive. The title "mystery" seems to have been well deserved, for conscientious silence was maintained both by the initiated and by outsiders. Of the effects and influence of these cults, contemporary writers are not hesitant to inform us; but the actual rites must be pieced together on the basis of fragmentary information. The popularity of the mysteries is corroborated by the testimony of contemporary writers and by archeological remains, which show that mystery chapels existed in cities all over the Roman Empire. Rome itself sheltered chapels ranging in importance from the temple of Magna Mater on the Palatine itself to numerous private shrines dedicated to the gods and goddesses of the mysteries. The disparaging remarks leveled against the mystery religions by early Christian writers form eloquent testimony to the keen rivalry which they furnished competitive religions in the Roman Empire.

What were the specific points of attraction offered to first-century worshipers by the mystery religions? First, the rites and guaranties were specifically directed toward individual and personal needs. In a syncretistic and rapidly changing world the individual often felt bewildered and in need of personal guidance;

the promises of the older and more nationalistic gods seemed weak in the face of shattered national boundaries. Definite help for specific individuals was needed. Second, the mysteries promised divine assistance in this world's difficulties and a blessed immortality after death. The lord of the cult had suffered severe injustices on earth; usually he had met death by foul means but had been resurrected in triumph over them all. Osiris and Attis are but two instances of divine beings who through their own experiences and trials could guarantee understanding of a person's hardships during life, and resurrection after death had temporarily triumphed. Third, the meaning and importance of the cult were impressed upon the neophyte by significant preparatory and purificatory rites. Denial of physical wants, rigorous self-examination and introspection, fasting, and supplication found important places in the preliminary ritual. Through these processes the candidate was instructed to prepare himself for the final rites or to withdraw before an irrevocable decision was made. Fourth, the inner meaning of the cult was revealed to the neophyte in a mighty dramatic performance based on the central myth and explaining the inner secrets of the group. The impression made upon the initiate was powerful enough to prevent his disclosure of it to outsiders and to substantiate his belief in the superhuman powers of the god.

Of all the mystery religions current in the first century of our era, none was more highly respected than the Eleusinian, so called because its first home was in the town of Eleusis, not a great distance from Athens. Originally a local agricultural organization under the divine patronage of the cereal-goddess Demeter, it had developed through several centuries to include peoples from every section of the Roman Empire, initiates as powerful as the emperor Augustus, and functions as wide as the ethical and religious realm. Although Augustus had been initiated in 21 B.C. and centuries later so distinguished an emperor as Marcus Aurelius was to become a neophyte, the moral regulations of first-century Eleusinianism proved too strict to encourage Nero to apply for admission. The high regard in which this mystery was held by intellectuals of the Greco-Roman world is attested by the commendations of Cicero[2] and Epictetus.[3]

The myth which grew up as an explanation of the Eleusinian rites found its classic expression in the Homeric Hymn to Demeter, although not all the details were there included. According to the myth, Demeter temporarily abandoned her usual role as guarantor of good crops when her daughter, Persephone, was whisked away to the underworld by Pluto with the full consent of Zeus. Abandoned by Demeter, the vegetation upon the earth scorched and died, men had little food, and the offerings to the gods were neglected. Finally Persephone was returned to her mother; but because she had eaten several pomegranate seeds while in the underworld kingdom of Pluto, it was agreed that she must return to the land of the shades for a visit of several months each year. In joy at the restoration of her daughter, Demeter caused vegetation once again to grow and gave to men the promise of new life or rebirth through eternity for themselves. In her sorrow each year for the temporary departure of her daughter the goddess allowed life to wither and die, but the pain was softened by the promise of renewed life in the ensuing spring. Thus the myth and the ritual of the cult sought to explain at once the rotation of the seasons and the pattern of human sorrow, suffering, death, and longed-for resurrection.

An analysis of the Eleusinian cult reveals four rather distinct stages: preliminary purification, preparatory rites and sacrifices, initiation proper, and highest grade of initiation.[4] Considerable testimony exists as to the nature of the first two stages, but the latter two were secret and must be pieced together through inference. The "great mysteries" were held in September, but the prerequisite or "lesser mysteries" were celebrated six months earlier at Agrae, near Athens. The earlier mysteries were evidently of a preparatory nature, looking forward to the major ceremonies which began on the thirteenth of September. The "greater mysteries" lasted over a full week and included a number of

---

[2] *De legibus* ii. 14.   [3] *Discourses* iii. 21.

[4] See, further, Harold R. Willoughby, *Pagan Regeneration: A Study of Mystery Initiations in the Graeco-Roman World* (Chicago: University of Chicago Press, 1929), chap. ii.

elements. (1) Near the beginning of the festival a warning to depart was issued to all who could not meet the moral and intellectual demands of the cult: purity of hand and soul, and Hellenic speech. (2) On the day following the assembly the candidates for initiation ran down to the sea, there to purify themselves in its salt waves. (3) Further cleansing was effected by sprinkling with pig's blood, each candidate having offered a suckling pig as sacrifice. These two rites were regarded as both cathartic and regenerative, as attested by the Christian writer Tertullian.[5] (4) On the nineteenth of September the solemn procession of purified candidates marched to Eleusis, performing ritualistic observances at the holy places along the way. (5) In the evening of the same day the neophytes engaged in a midnight revel, probably composed of dramatic attempts to experience the sorrow of Demeter through ritualistic use of the sacred monuments at Eleusis. (6) The initiation proper took place under the surveillance of the enlightened only, but evidently it was in the form of a passion drama re-enacting the main events of the central myth. Human emotions, stage settings, gongs, torches, and a number of other factors served to make a lasting impression upon candidates who had already experienced a long process of purification. It is probable that this stage of the initiation also included a symbolic ceremony of marriage and rebirth, indicating the initiate's newly enlightened state. Certain it is that the neophyte was no mere spectator; he was a full participant in the mighty drama. (7) Of equal importance with the passion play was the exhibition of sacred objects, only a few of which were shown the candidate for the grade of *mystae*. A year later, when the neophytes sought the final grade of initiation, the *epopteia*, they were shown the most sacred things of the cult and thus became *epoptae*. This, too, was done in dramatic ceremony. (8) Priestly exposition or verbal commentary accompanied most of the ceremonials. This was necessary to explain the significance of ritual or objects. (9) The password of the Eleusinian cult, according to Clement of Alexandria,[6] was as follows: "I have fasted, I have drunk the barley drink, I have taken things from

---

[5] *De Baptismo* 5. [6] *Protrepticus* ii. 21.

the sacred chest, having tasted thereof I have placed them into the basket and again from the basket into the chest." The fasting helped the worshiper to share the sorrow of the goddess. The barley drink, with which the goddess had broken her fast, represented for the participant attained fellowship with deity. Eating of food from the chest was, in all probability, a sacrament of communion, or indeed an operation marking realistic union with Demeter, the goddess of grain. Emotional union through the passion drama was succeeded by realistic union through the assimilation of food and drink.

That the emotional effect of these ceremonies was tremendous we cannot doubt. Contemporary writers affirm the joy of the initiated, the stirred feelings which resulted. The rites were so planned that the candidate himself believed that he followed the path of the goddess and shared her sorrows and joys. This emotion carried usually a salutary effect on practical living: it emphasized a purification and elevation of the present life. Not to be neglected, however, was the happy anticipation of a future life. The Homeric Hymn itself declared that a firm distinction would be maintained beyond the murky gloom between the initiated and those outside.

The Eleusinian cult furnishes but one illustration of the complex values offered by the mysteries. Many attractive features were offered by competing religions of this type: Orphism, the cult of Magna Mater, Mithraism, the Isis-Osiris mystery, and Hermeticism. The mysteries, in turn, were, as our study has indicated, but part of the complex religious world of the first century. The Christian movement was forced to find a place under the Greco-Roman sun in competition with superstition, the religion of philosophy, Judaism, the gods of Olympus and Capitoline Hill, the hero cults, emperor-worship, and the mysteries. It became more than a local cult because it creatively employed the values offered by its competitors, including Judaism, and adapted them to its own use. To that story we now turn.

V

LIFE AND LITERATURE IN THE NEW
TESTAMENT: A PREVIEW

THE New Testament was forged in the furnace of early Christian life. Its pages reflect the growing pains of several generations of people who became convinced of the special mission of Jesus and of its meaning for the eternal values by which men should live. The New Testament bears witness to the early Christian concepts of God; to the preaching by which they sought to win adherents in the Greco-Roman world; to the emotions which they experiences as they faced opponents, withstood persecution, and contemplated upon the fate of the dead. In short, the twenty-seven writings which in many Protestant circles so nearly determine the creed and thought of the group were themselves the products of the first Christian churches. They represent variety because the experiences of Christian churches and leaders were so varied. The New Testament was the literary record of the first churches.

We are prone to foist our own attitudes upon those whose experiences gave birth to gospels, letters, and apocalypses. We erroneously assume that early Christian writers were consciously producing "Scripture," that they were composing a "New Testament" to supplement and to supersede the Jewish "Old Testament." This assumption flatly contradicts the evident tone of all the earlier writings which were incorporated into the canon and disregards the purpose and occasion of the later ones. Paul's letters, for instance, are each directed to meet specific problems in particular church situations. They are occasional writings intended to be understood only by the people whose religious problems called them forth. In I Corinthians, Paul gives advice and warning on a number of problems which members of the Corinthian church have brought to his attention. Even the latest book of the New Testament, II Peter (A.D. *ca.* 150), does not claim for itself "scriptural" standing, although it refers to Paul and the gospel traditions as "Scripture."[1]

Members of the Christian cults during the first decades after the death of Jesus knew only one Scripture, the Hebrew Bible. Throughout Paul's letters, the gospels and Acts, Revelation, and the earlier General Epistles the quotations from Scripture are indubitably taken from the Jewish Bible. The gospels of Matthew and of Luke-Acts, for instance, take great pains to show that Jesus and his followers represented the fulfilment of the heritage and the promises of Jewish Scripture. Nowhere do they claim for themselves equal status or sanctity; Scripture is the authority to which they must appeal for their own validation. It was only the passage of time and the elevation of the early leaders to hero status, coupled with the popularity of certain books among the more powerful churches, which caused some of the early Christian documents to be placed alongside ancient Jewish Scripture and titled the "New" Testament.

Chronology is one of the most persistent problems in the study of the New Testament. If the student elects to proceed in strict historical fashion and thus to treat of the life and teachings of Jesus first, then he must use as his sources the Synoptic Gospels, the earliest of which was written some forty years after the crucifixion of Jesus. If, on the other hand, the student elects to employ the earliest literary documents of the Christian movement first, he will find himself delving into the activities of Paul, the apostle of Jesus Christ, who began his work several years after the lifetime of Jesus. Thus the earlier events are pictured in the later documents, while the later happenings are described by the earlier and more direct literary efforts. This book will utilize the former method: we shall attempt to follow the career of Jesus as it may be gained from the gospel materials; then we shall turn to the writings of Paul.

[1] II Pet. 1:17–20, 3:15–16.

A tabular chronological scheme will help to fix the main events of New Testament history in the correct sequence:

4 B.C.	Birth of Jesus
26 A.D.	Beginning of Jesus' ministry
29 A.D.	The crucifixion
50–63	Letters of Paul
70–110	Gospel-writing period
80–115	Ephesians, Hebrews, Revelation, I Peter, James
115–50	Letters of John, Pastoral Letters, Jude, II Peter

It will be kept in mind that each of these dates is approximate. The production of New Testament literature thus stretches over a period of one hundred years, even though the literature itself was not begun until approximately twenty-four years after the start of Jesus' career.

A large portion of the New Testament literature is composed of letters. Several of these letters are informal and highly occasional. They are directed to specific communities, churches, or individuals; and they deal specifically with issues which were of burning import for the particular group involved. Other New Testament letters are general in nature, treating problems which were current throughout a given area and directed often to no specific church.

Paul's letters are mainly of the former type. In every case except one he is communicating with a church whose problems he knew well. In fact, he could depend upon the friendship of these church members to the extent that he felt no hesitation in attempting to solve for them problems so personal as marriage and divorce, quarrels and bickering, incorrect sex relationships, improper conduct at the Lord's Supper, and treatment of slaves. In the Letter to Philemon intimacy reached the point that Paul was apparently unabashed to request that the guestroom be made ready for an impending visit. Paul's letters may be characterized as intimately personal and as highly pastoral.

The sole exception is his Letter to the Romans. This missive is, by contrast, a fairly formal document in which Paul seems to set forth for readers an explanation of the main beliefs and practices which he has come to regard as essential. It is in this sense "testamentary," but it is also "prophylactic" in its effort to prevent dangerous practices and errors from creeping into the congregation. Paul seems to know the church only by reputation; consequently his approach is more impersonal and his style slightly belabored. A false tone of intimacy is added to the letter in its present state by the array of personal greetings in chapter 16, but this section seems originally to have been addressed to Christian people in Asia Minor. It did not, therefore, form a part of the original Letter to the Romans.

Although Romans shows little trace of a specific situation, each of Paul's other letters flies straight to the heart of a crisis. The Thessalonians have been threatened by disaffection and troubled over the "day of the Lord"; the Galatians have been told that Paul is distinctly "second-rate" as an apostle and that all prospective converts must take upon themselves the obligations of Jewish Torah; the Corinthians have been torn by factions, unsettled by lawsuits, and weakened by divisive questions which none of their number can answer satisfactorily. Unacceptable religious beliefs and practices have developed among the Colossians; they speak of "aeons" and keep Sabbaths and new moons; in Philemon references indicate the return of a runaway slave at Paul's behest, and no one can accurately predict what the master's attitude will be; in Philippians a homesick assistant is being returned to his church, bearing a letter of gratitude for the kind attentions the imprisoned Paul has received. These letters of Paul come alive with burning issues and interesting side lights once the situations are clearly pictured.

The General Letters, or "Epistles," stand in sharp contrast to the Pauline missives. Where Paul was informal and direct, they are formal and circuitous. Where Paul concentrates his fire upon definite problems and specific individuals, they scatter their attention over a broad field of religious problems and a multitude of persons. Where Paul resembles the pastoral counselor of individuals, the General Letters read like sermons prepared for all types of people.

The General Letters are not all "letters" in the strict sense of the term. The Pastoral Letters are handbooks of rules and regulations meant to govern young church officials and to warn them against insidious heresies which were springing up. I Peter might well have been a sermon of encouragement and advice to candidates for admission to the church[2] or a circular address meant to be read aloud before all Christian churches in the provinces of Asia Minor in order that the influence of Revelation might be counteracted.[3] Certainly its contents indicate that it might well have applied to any church or individual disheartened by the gathering storm clouds of persecution in Asia Minor. The Letter of James is an excellent illustration of a sermon or teacher's address[4] meant to apply to Christian believers regardless of location or time. The work is filled with references to "the finely dressed man" and "the poor man," to "teachers," to the "tongue," and to "faith" as contrasted with "works." Typical of this general code is the well-known admonition, "Obey the message; do not merely listen to it, and deceive yourselves." Although most of these letters were written to assist churches in a given area to meet an impending crisis, their advice was so unspecific and miscellaneous that the term "general" has been well applied.

The second main type of literature, that which employs approximately three-fifths of the space in the New Testament, is the collection of traditions called "gospels and Acts." Casual examination of the gospels-Acts literature has led many readers to assume that they were "biographies" of Jesus and the early apostles, or that they were stenographic accounts of happenings in the early days of the movement, or that they were four mutually complementary accounts meant to be blended into one harmonious story. These assumptions, born of too cursory an examination of the evidence, have led to heated attempts to defend so-called "contradictions" in the gospel literature and to prove that every detail in each gospel represented an exact ac-

[2] B. H. Streeter, *The Primitive Church* (New York: Macmillan Co., 1929), pp. 121–41.

[3] Edgar J. Goodspeed, *An Introduction to the New Testament* (Chicago: University of Chicago Press, 1937), pp. 265–86.

[4] Donald W. Riddle, *Early Christian Life* (Chicago: Willett, Clark & Co., 1936), pp. 154–63.

count of a historical occurrence. Some readers have gone further, to the assumption that all of the main items in the life of Jesus could be found in the canonical gospel accounts. These assumptions stand squarely athwart the best in historical and literary study of the first Christian century.

Gospel literature represents a collection of the traditions which gathered about the early followers of Jesus. The literary student can readily trace the growth from tradition to gospel as the early stories of Jesus and tales about him were retold by Christian evangelists.[5] The geographical world in which Jesus lived determined not merely his physical movements but also the nature of the literary climate. It was not a world which wrote its religious precepts; rather they were memorized. Judaism had its basis in written Torah, but its teachings were rich with oral traditions and interpretations. For the rabbis, correct procedure dictated that everyday questions of religion and conduct be referred for an answer to the authoritative oral interpretation developed by the scribes throughout the centuries since Ezra. The Palestinian teacher was not encouraged to write down the oral tradition; he was distinguished because of his ability to remember and explain it.

How, then, did the gospel materials come to be written? The passage of time and the changing character of the Christian movement assured this literary activity. Living in the hope that Jesus would return for the final phase of his "kingdom," there was little need for written accounts; the main business of the moment was to prepare men for the approaching "end." As the years passed, however, this hope of immediate action began to wane, and the evangelists found themselves in need of supporting evidence for the authority of Jesus. Intense rivalries sprang up as the movement spread among Gentiles and differentiated itself from Judaism by its growing gentile religious characteristics. Oral traditions supporting Jesus' superiority over the Jews (and particularly their leaders, the "scribes and Pharisees") crystallized into written collections which the evangelists used as hand-

[5] Martin Dibelius, *From Tradition to Gospel*, trans. Bertram Lee Woolf (New York: Charles Scribner's Sons, 1935), *passim*.

books of the new movement. The gentile character of the developing religion can be seen in its adoption of the technique of written collections of collections (for this is what the gospels were) and in its lack of appeal for any significant number of Jews.[6] Its un-Jewish developments are directly attested in the vituperative attacks on the Jewish leaders.[7]

The gospels were produced because an intense need for them arose. The informal teachings of Jesus had at first been remembered by his intimate friends and disciples; these had been sufficient authority for their preaching and their behavior. But as time passed and the movement gained momentum, particularly among Gentiles, there was need for an authoritative handbook. Oral repetition became unsatisfactory, particularly for those who heard of the preaching of Jesus only at second or third remove. The evangelist needed a notebook for ready reference. And so it must have happened that the leaders in each community came to collect, to edit, and to write down the stories about Jesus. But oral tradition had done its work. By this time there were variations in details, additions of local color, and omissions of time and place.

The first written collections showed the imprint of many minds. Already the interpretation of Jesus had gone forward, and communities differed in their understanding of various utterances which had been bequeathed them. Parables identical in almost every detail were thought to illustrate different maxims or sayings. Healing stories varied, miracle stories exhibited different details, and genealogies and birth stories listed dissimilar characters.

The final stage in gospel production was reached about A.D. 70, with the compilation and editing of the Gospel of Mark. Highly dramatic and martyrological in character, it utilized earlier written collections and oral traditions to mold a story of impressive beauty. It was the dramatic presentation of a man of

---

[6] The scarcity of Jews in the Christian movement thirty years after the crucifixion can be clearly deduced from Paul's attempt to explain their "hardness of heart" (Romans, chaps. 9–11).

[7] Matt. 23:1–36; Mark 12:37b–40; Luke 20:45–47.

action who displayed a peculiar sense of mission and whose death on a Roman cross was but the prelude to a hint of glorious resurrection and regnant activity. The collector's purpose can be seen in his arrangement of the sources and in the introductory and transitional sentences. He wished to demonstrate that Jesus was the Christ, a tragic hero who marched through a brief time in history with the triumphant stride of the Greek immortals. This Jesus was enmeshed in the net of his enemies; but, even though he was killed, he triumphed. The lesson was obvious: Roman readers were encouraged to accept the responsibilities of the Christian movement, even though martyrdom be their lot.[8] Interpretation thus reached its third stage in the written gospel: first, the oral tradition, with its effects; second, the written collections, with obvious coloring; and third, the written gospel, arranged and planned for a given purpose.

The Gospel of Matthew illustrates compilation and planning of materials in order to picture Jesus as the great teacher, the successor of Moses. Matthew availed himself of written and oral collections not utilized by Mark, grouping many of these into five or six great sermons. Where Mark was primarily concerned with dramatic action, Matthew was careful to include the great mass of teaching material which supposedly indicated the norms by which the Christian community should live. The term "Jewish Gospel" has often been applied to Matthew because Jesus is there pictured as the fulfilment of scriptural "predictions" and because he is made to resemble the Jewish teachers and lawgivers. The Sermon on the Mount is an example of Matthean organization and planning. A birth story and a genealogy appear here for the first time in a canonical collection of Christian traditions. This gospel follows the order laid down by Mark.

In Luke-Acts appeared the first story of Christianity's rise and expansion. This two-volume work was separated early in the course of textual history and consequently has not been seen in its true light. It endeavored to carve for the emerging movement a place among the forces of the Roman Empire, to picture Chris-

[8] Donald W. Riddle, *The Martyrs: A Study in Social Control* (Chicago: University of Chicago Press, 1931), pp. 180–97.

tianity as a thoroughly patriotic growth.[9] The author-editor of these two volumes presented the Christian movement as the logical outgrowth of Judaism, utilizing all the values for which Judaism was noted and discarding some of its less attractive characteristics. The gospel volume traced the thread of growth from the familiar pattern of Judaism to the crucifixion and resurrection of Jesus, noting the promise of his ascension, which was to follow in the second volume. The Acts section continued the story of the earliest communities, noting the activities of selected leaders. With chapter 9 the deeds of the main character, Paul, began to dominate the story. The volume closed with veiled hints of Paul's death and an attempted explanation of the hardness of heart on the part of Jews; by this time, however, the movement had spread far beyond the bounds of Palestine.

This idealized story of Christianity's rise and expansion shows the author-editor's skill in welding the traditions around his central purposes. Luke-Acts is a planned collection and edition. The new movement is shown to be firmly rooted in the best of Jewish traditions, but the Jews consistently demonstrate their inability to grasp the meaning of their own religion: they hinder the work of Jesus and finally override the protestations of Pilate (the Roman procurator!) and cause the crucifixion of Jesus. They fail to appreciate the meaning of the resurrection, they persecute the early communities of Jesus' followers, and they blindly and obstinately cause trouble for Paul wherever he goes. The Jews, never the Romans, are to blame for uprisings and arrests.

The arrangement and "pointing" of the traditions indicates also Luke's preferences for the poor, for Gentiles, and for the women who identified themselves with the movement. Other interests appear after the more careful analysis to be given later. The diversity of the available tradition in the Christian communities at the time of Luke's writing (ca. A.D. 85–90) is attested by his use of a variant birth story, genealogy, list of resurrection appearances, set of beatitudes, Lord's Prayer, and others. Ideal-

[9] Henry J. Cadbury, *The Making of Luke-Acts* (New York: Macmillan Co., 1927), pp. 299–316.

izing and pointing are evidenced in the second volume by the "patterned" activities of the earliest communities and the incomplete, even contradictory, accounts of Paul when Acts is compared with Paul's own letters.

The Fourth Gospel stands apart from the three synoptic accounts by every criterion the scholars have been able to apply. It represents a re-writing and transmutation of traditions, the creation of new stories, and the planning of an entire narrative to meet the needs of the critical "intelligentsia" of about A.D. 110.[10] This writer eschews the main purposes of the synoptic collectors: he is an author where they were, in the main, compilers; he would depict Jesus as a theologian and a philosopher where they have him appeal to the masses; he would show that Jesus was neither a Baptist nor a Jew nor a magician,[11] where the Synoptics might leave the impression that he was all three. John, in fact, re-wrote the gospel to reach the educated groups, for which the Synoptics had little appeal. He used the old stories simply as springboards from which to plunge into his own thesis that Jesus was the incarnate Logos, the everlasting Word, through whom God's power and goodness were to be revealed. In short, the Gospel of John might be termed "Jesus as an Intelligent Second-Century Christian Saw Him."

The third main type of literature found in the New Testament is the apocalyptic, illustrated by the Revelation of John and sections of the gospels and Paul.[12] Apocalypses were not new to the Jewish religious atmosphere. The canonical Book of Daniel had helped to bolster religious faith in the dark days of the Maccabean era; and the uncanonical works, such as the Testament of the Twelve Patriarchs and the Assumption of Moses, had promised the triumph of God and his people. Apocalypses always conform to the following standards: (1) they contain symbols, "sacred" numbers, and secret meanings; (2) they are extremely

[10] Ernest C. Colwell, *John Defends the Gospel* (Chicago: Willett, Clark & Co., 1936), *passim*.

[11] *Ibid.*

[12] Mark 13:1–37; Matt. 24:1–36, 42, 25:13; Luke 21:5–36, 17:21, 23–24, 31, 37, 16:16, 12:38–40, 9:27; II Thess. 2:1–12.

pessimistic about "this present world"; (3) they promise the catastrophic intervention of God to remedy the situation in favor of his people; (4) they are "tracts for hard times." In addition, most apocalypses are pseudonymous or anonymous—a characteristic not true of New Testament works of this type.

The Revelation of John sought to encourage persecuted Christians in Asia Minor to hold on to the faith regardless of the consequences. Written about A.D. 95, it spoke in symbols of the suffering through which "the saints" were passing and promised that "Babylon" would fall. The saints would inherit the "New Jerusalem," and the "Lamb of God" would reign forever and ever. Unfortunately, this revelation written for the edification of believers in Asia Minor about A.D. 95 has been employed in practically every major crisis since that date as a predictive instrument. The testimony of history is against this practice, as is the discernible purpose of the book. Certainly it becomes under this influence "all things to all men" and loses its usefulness as the testimony of an early Christian to the fact of God in history.

Thus we have before us the panorama of New Testament literature and chronology. It is as varied as were the people and the times which produced it. Letters, gospels, apocalypses—but all primarily religious documents and only secondarily to be considered as history or literature.

VI

THE CAREER OF JESUS (A)

BOOKS on the life of Jesus are numerous. They vary from works of pious imagination to writings which deny the reality of Jesus as a historical figure, and from imaginative constructions which make of him a twentieth-century businessman to critical studies which look upon him as a loyal Pharisee of the first century. Verbal descriptions of Jesus and his mission are as diverse as the artists' conceptions of him. He has been seen as a fighter by the militaristic and as peacemaker by the pacifist; as conservative by the fundamentalist and as revolutionary by the radical; as emaciated by the ascetic and as vigorous by the athletic.

Christian people have been prone to judge a biography of Jesus entirely in the light of their own prejudices and preconceived notions of what Jesus must have been like. A "good" life of Jesus depended upon the religious tastes of the person passing the judgment. The primary principles of biography were forgotten: few people asked whether a given picture of Jesus was true to the primary sources, the Synoptic Gospels, or whether a critical study of these primary sources had preceded use of them. Consequently, most "biographies" of Jesus are worthless as historical pictures, for they are, rather, sermons based upon isolated quotations or feeble attempts to "harmonize" all of the sayings in the gospels, including John. The situation has been further complicated by deep resentment of honest attempts to understand the gospels as history and as literature—a feeling engendered by the conviction that biblical documents were handed down "from above" in such a way that critical study of them was taboo.

One of the vogues of a passing era of pseudo-scholarship was the denial that Jesus ever lived. Writers such as Arthur Drews[1] identified Jesus with the myths of the zodiac and attempted to discredit the gospels as historical sources. Much earlier the attempt had been made by David F. Strauss[2] and others of like persuasion to demonstrate that much of the gospel picture was dominated by mythological interests. Strauss himself did not doubt the existence of the historical Jesus, but he removed from the pale of historical reliability many stories and traditions which he declared to be dominated by the mythological concern of the early Christians.

That the categorical denials of Jesus' existence failed to meet the critical demands of the historian was clearly demonstrated by a succession of works firmly based upon reliable historical evidence. Jesus' existence as a historical person was shown to be a fact attested by writers both non-Christian and Christian. A host of reliable evidence was collected and conclusively interpreted by scholars such as Shirley Jackson Case[3] and Maurice Goguel.[4] The evidence indicated that references to the Christian movement by the Roman historians Tacitus[5] and Suetonius,[6] by the Roman-Jewish historian Josephus,[7] and by the Jewish Talmud[8] everywhere assumed the historicity of Jesus and nowhere reported doubt as to his existence. There is no reason to assume that any of these sources would have failed to report the Christian claim as mythological had they believed it to be so. In addition, there is the very powerful negative argument from the silence of the early Church Fathers. These leaders, who were so very careful to meet every argument against the growing faith, would cer-

---

[1] *Die Christusmythe* (Jena, 1909, 1910³; English trans., *The Christ Myth*, London and Chicago, 1911).

[2] *Das Leben Jesu, kritisch bearbeitet* (2 vols.; Tübingen: C. F. Osiander, 1835–36).

[3] *The Historicity of Jesus* (2d ed.; Chicago: University of Chicago Press, 1928).

[4] *Jesus the Nazarene: Myth or History?* trans. Frederick Stephens (New York: D. Appleton & Co., 1926).

[5] *Annals* xv. 44.   [6] *Claudius* xxv; *Nero* xvi.

[7] *Antiquities* xviii. 3. 3; xx. 9. 1.

[8] For a lucid discussion of the relevant passages see R. Travers Herford, *Christianity in Talmud and Midrash* (London: Williams & Norgate, 1903).

tainly have mentioned the charge that Jesus never lived had this accusation been made. This would at least argue for the silence of the opponents of the Christian movement on this issue. Even with the uncertainty concerning the passages in Josephus, the nonbiblical evidence for the historicity of Jesus is formidable.

The main evidence for the life and activity of Jesus rests, of course, upon a critical examination of the Synoptic Gospels, together with materials from apocryphal sources, "wild" traditions, the Fourth Gospel, and the writings of Paul. We must not assume that canonicity guarantees historicity, for the story of the early church shows all too well the human process through which the twenty-seven books of the New Testament were selected. Their popularity is to be taken as a valued sign of their usefulness to the early Christians.

The gospels are interpretations of Jesus. They represent in each case a compilation of traditions which were themselves the interpretations which various communities had placed upon Jesus. There is variety not simply because time and tradition had done their work but also because Jesus early became an object of faith —and faith is always individual. Thus we have at once in the gospels a picture of Jesus and a picture of the faith which the early communities had in him; the results are so interfused that the task of the historian is made most difficult. When one demands, "What, then, can we know definitely about the historical Jesus?" the historian's answer is usually disappointing to those whose faith is dependent upon the literal quotation of some teaching of Jesus.

We can know that Jesus lived, that he taught largely within the bounds of Palestine for a brief space of a few months to three years. His central message seems to have encouraged preparation for the Kingdom of God. He gathered about him a group of loyal followers and taught them in the simple and unadorned language of the artisan. In some way he brought down upon himself the crucifying arm of Roman law, but his devoted followers were convinced that he had been resurrected from the dead. The Christian movement sprang from the preaching of this conviction and the beliefs and practices which came to be associated with it.

The arrangement of full details into a "biography" of Jesus is beyond this point largely an eclectic matter. The writer must choose whether he will give one gospel precedence throughout his story or attempt the conflationary procedure of weaving together every possible biographical detail. The techniques of scholarship will greatly assist him to determine which of the stories or pericopes are consonant with the Jewish environment in which Jesus lived[9] and which stand the tests of literary form.[10] While these original stories tell us much about the character and emphasis of Jesus' teachings, they do not inform us with any exactitude as to *where*, *when*, and *how*—details which are extremely important if one is to write a "life" of Jesus. This information was early lost in the process of oral transmission because it was distinctly secondary in importance. Further, where these details are available, they differ from gospel to gospel. The early communities considered these of such slight importance that they wove the details of time and place to form a setting for the significant sayings and stories.

Illustrations of this lack of details, on one hand, and variety of explanatory matters, on the other, can easily be multiplied. Matthew's Sermon on the Mount is introduced by the words: "When he saw the crowds of people he went up on the mountain."[11] Note the inexactitude of the references to time and place. Further, the sermon closes with the descriptive sentence, "When Jesus came down from the mountain."[12]

A little more exact is the indication, "When he got back to Capernaum. . . . ."[13] A further reference gives the datum, "in the evening";[14] and still later the order is given to "cross to the other side," probably of the Sea of Galilee.[15] Typical is the reference: "Afterward, as Jesus was passing along, he saw a man called Matthew sitting at the tollhouse. . . . ."[16] A survey of the

[9] This method is exemplified in Shirley Jackson Case, *Jesus: A New Biography* (Chicago: University of Chicago Press, 1927).

[10] A full explanation of this method is given in Martin Dibelius, *From Tradition to Gospel;* the results may be seen in Dibelius, *The Message of Jesus Christ*, trans. Frederick C. Grant (New York: Charles Scribner's Sons, 1939).

[11] Matt. 5:1.   [13] Matt. 8:5.   [15] Matt. 8:18.

[12] Matt. 8:1.   [14] Matt. 8:16.   [16] Matt. 9:9.

succeeding sections, or of any portion of the gospels, will leave one in almost complete ignorance as to the length of time consumed, the exact location of the happening, or the stage in Jesus' ministry which it represents. This lack of information follows from an examination of any one of the gospels; picture the difficulties when one attempts to form a sequence for the events for all three of the Synoptics! The arbitrary character of the average "life" of Jesus can be seen if the reader attempts to follow the narrative with a harmony of the gospels, noting carefully use and omission of details.

Variety of details is evident in many well-known passages. The beatitudes not only differ within themselves from Matthew to Luke, but they are included in Matthew's Sermon on the Mount and in Luke's Sermon on the Plain.[17] This difference in allocation is true also of the sayings on judging,[18] on love of one's enemies,[19] on hearers and doers of the word,[20] and on many other topics. The rejection at Nazareth takes place first in his ministry according to Luke and late as viewed by Matthew.[21] The teaching of the Lord's Prayer occurs during the Sermon on the Mount as given in Matthew, but it is placed by Luke in his travel narrative.[22] The teaching that people should come from the east and the west to take their places alongside the great patriarchs and prophets while the heirs of the kingdom (or those present) should be cast into outer darkness is placed by Matthew early in the ministry at Capernaum, while Luke places it in another connection as Jesus journeys toward Jerusalem in the last days of his life.[23]

Thus the gospels serve as poor sources for a biography of Jesus, even though they fulfil admirably their primary aim, namely, to serve as handbooks for the preaching and government of the new religion. The compilers and editors of these traditions were chiefly interested in the religious effects which

---

[17] Matt. 5:3–12; Luke 6:20–23.

[18] Matt. 7:1–5; Luke 6:37–38.

[19] Matt. 5:43–48; Luke 6:27–28.   [20] Matt. 7:24–27; Luke 6:47–49.

[21] Matt. 13:53–58; Mark 6:1–6; Luke 4:16–30.

[22] Matt. 6:9–13; Luke 11:2–4.   [23] Matt. 8:11–12; Luke 13:29–30.

would be produced in readers and hearers; therefore, they are valuable for us today largely in that same area.

If, then, an exact biography of Jesus is impossible because of a dearth of specific references to time, place, and sequence and because of confusion in the data which are given by the gospels, what can be known about specific acts in the career of Jesus? Can an outline of his preaching and teaching ministry be given? Can we be assured that we have extant most of his teachings? Can the details of his life prior to the beginning of his public work be recovered with any degree of certainty? Let us examine the evidence on these questions.

There has been intense interest in the details of Jesus' birth, boyhood, and youth since the appearance of the Gospel of Mark about A.D. 70. This earliest gospel contained no details about Jesus prior to his ministry, which, according to all traditions, began at thirty years of age. Interest in the manner of Jesus' birth was manifested by the inclusion of two different traditions of his miraculous nativity in the gospels of Matthew and Luke. Although conflated by many interpreters of the New Testament, these two narratives were originally separate and mutually exclusive.[24] The Matthean narrative responds to the Christian demand for additional knowledge about the infancy by a citation of the tradition of the flight into Egypt,[25] the slaughter of the innocents,[26] and the return to Nazareth,[27] each of which is constructed about an Old Testament citation. Luke's response to the growing demand for knowledge of the birth, infancy, and boyhood is more exhaustive in its collection of traditions. A lengthy group of traditions about the birth of John the Baptist precedes those concerning Jesus and helps to root the movement-to-be more firmly in Jewish soil.[28] Luke alone records the tradition of Jesus' circumcision and presentation at the Temple, with the attestations of certain worthy figures.[29] This work further employs the tradition of Jesus' visit to the Temple at the age of twelve—

[24] Matt. 1:18–2:12; cf. Luke 2:1–20.
[25] Matt. 2:13–15.
[26] Matt. 2:16–18.
[27] Matt. 2:19–23.
[28] Luke 1:5–80.
[29] Luke 2:21–40.

already the tendency of the traditions to attribute miraculous thought and action to Jesus is in evidence.[30]

The canonical gospels, however, still leave much to be desired concerning Jesus prior to thirty years of age, even if these traditions could be trusted implicitly. This gap the later uncanonical gospels sought to fill. Following the lead given by the publication of the Fourfold Gospel about A.D. 115, leaders with Gnostic leanings compiled about A.D. 150 the little-known Gospel of Thomas.[31] If versions of that gospel can be trusted, it contained stories about Jesus between the ages of five and twelve. These traditions are so late and so indicative of the tendency to push Jesus' miraculous powers back into his boyhood that they are generally discarded as unhistorical. They picture Jesus as the wonder-boy of the carpenter shop, a person who resorts to miracles to remedy errors of workmanship. He employs punitive miracles against those who annoy him, while he exerts curative powers for those to whom he is attracted. To the delight of his playmates, he is able to bring life into clay sparrows and to confound his teachers with his wisdom.

Indicative of the work of the tradition-makers in the late second century was the Protevangelium of James,[32] which further expanded the collection of infancy narratives. Modeled after the scriptural story of the birth of Samuel, it told of the birth of Mary in answer to prayer and of her stay in the Temple from the age of three to her marriage at the age of twelve to the widower Joseph. At the birth of Jesus she was found still to be a virgin. All nature did reverence at the moment of Jesus' birth by a temporary but complete transfixion. Every characteristic of this narrative leads scholars to the conclusion that it is completely fictitious. Its obvious purpose was to push back the miraculous ele-

---

[30] Luke 2:41–52.

[31] See critical treatment in Edgar J. Goodspeed, *A History of Early Christian Literature* (Chicago: University of Chicago Press, 1942), pp. 80–83; for critical treatment and translation of the fragments, see M. R. James, *The Apocryphal New Testament, Being the Apocryphal Gospels, Acts, Epistles and Apocalypses, ... Newly Translated* (Oxford: Clarendon Press, 1924), pp. 14–16, 49–70.

[32] Goodspeed, *op. cit.*, pp. 89–92; James, *op. cit.*, pp. 38–46.

ment as far as the mother of Jesus and to amplify tremendously the wonderful "attestations" to the nativity.

The evidence thus indicates that few details of Jesus' life prior to the age of thirty can be recovered. The earliest and most reliable traditions contain no information on this portion of his life, and the farther one proceeds from these traditions the more miraculous and predetermined the later narratives become. An object of faith and worship because of the work of his later years, it was assumed that Jesus must have experienced a wonderful boyhood and that his birth was an event of world-shaking proportions. This tendency to glorify the boyhood, the birth, and even the ancestry of religious figures is observable in Confucianism, Taoism, Buddhism, Mohammedanism, and other of the world's religions.

The canonical gospels could not possibly contain all of the teachings which Jesus gave during the course of his career. Even if Jesus' ministry lasted several months only, the volume of things he must have taught would far exceed the limits of the Synoptic Gospels or even of the Four Gospels, as the last verse of John suggests.[33] Further, we have the assurance from at least one of the leaders of the early church that there were those who still valued the oral tradition, even in preference to the written gospels. Papias of Hierapolis, writing about A.D. 140, indicates his feeling that what "was to be got from books was not so profitable to me as what came from the living and abiding voice."[34] The context of the reference indicates that he must have known the Fourfold Gospel, which began to circulate about A.D. 115; but he clings to the belief that greater value may be gained from traditions circulating orally. It is a safe surmise that many of these oral traditions had not been used by the compilers of the Synoptic Gospels because they were not adaptable to their main purposes or because of unavailability, but to conclude that they were therefore worthless is unsound. On the contrary, many seemingly authentic traditions, some of them closely parallel to gospel contents, have been found in collections such as the Oxy-

[33] John 21:25.
[34] Papias, Frag. I, in Eusebius *Church History* iii. 39. 15.

rhynchus Sayings[35] and the fifth- or sixth-century Codex Bezae.[36] These sayings, called "wild" because they circulated apart from the standardizing effects of written form for so long, must represent the merest fragments of a once extensive literature. Not any great proportion of them will ever come to light, and our knowledge of the early church's impression of Jesus is that much poorer.

Can we make an outline of Jesus' preaching and teaching ministry, and can that outline be illustrated by specific acts? The answer here depends upon one's view of the character and purpose of the gospels, particularly of the Gospel of Mark. In the main, Matthew and Luke follow the order of events set down by the earliest gospel. It serves as their pattern, except when they wish to insert additional materials. There are variations in details of chronology and place, but the skeletal events follow Mark's arrangement. Where Mark has no parallel material, Matthew and Luke differ tremendously.

Mark's primary purpose was to present a dramatically effective arrangement of the traditions concerning Jesus. The passion narrative, which told of Jesus' suffering and death, he evidently found in rather fixed condition. It had been the earliest preaching material of the Christian movement, if Paul's letters are any indication. The remainder of the traditions were arranged for dramatic effect, with the passion story and the resurrection promise as a mighty climax. If through the decades which had intervened since the crucifixion some semblance of a chronological scheme remained, preference was probably given it. That such an authoritative scheme was in existence is doubtful. The available traditions and the purposes of the compiler were undoubtedly primary considerations in the arrangement of the complete narrative; chronological order was secondary—even if it were possible for the editor to have such a scheme at hand.

We are thus largely at the mercy of the Gospel of Mark if we attempt an outline of the main events in the ministry of Jesus.

[35] See Introduction and translations in James, *op. cit.*, pp. 25–30.

[36] See particularly the pericope concerning Jesus' words to the man whom he found working on the Sabbath.

The statement of Clement of Alexandria to the effect that Mark wrote after consultation with Peter[37] and that of Irenaeus which indicated that the earliest gospel was written when Mark realized that Peter's death had closed a chapter in the oral testimony[38] have been too heavily relied upon for proof of the accuracy of Mark's order of events.[39] Neither does triple attestation (where the Synoptic Gospels agree) constitute proof of correct order, for scholarship long ago established the dependence of Matthew and Luke upon Mark for order of events. We are faced finally by the question: "What facts in an outline of Jesus' ministry would be least affected by the aims of the compiler Mark?" This is to ask, of course, what items would be least subject to change at the hands of the compiler.

The early relationship of Jesus' movement and that of John the Baptist is quite certain, although its exact nature is far from clear. Jesus evidently accepted John's baptism of repentance—an act which caused Matthew and some of the apocryphal gospels no little concern.[40] That John, in his preaching and in the founding of his movement, was less subservient to Jesus than the gospels picture is certain: the crowds who heard John did not immediately accept Jesus, neither did John's disciples immediately go over to the new teacher—years later they are mentioned as a rival movement in Asia Minor.[41] The natural supposition is that Jesus for a time identified himself in some way with the program of John and later began his own movement. John's popularity is attested by the numerous attempts of the gospel writers to show that he sanctioned the deeds of Jesus.

There is no reason to doubt the tradition that Jesus' early ministry was spent in Galilee announcing the coming Kingdom of God and attempting to prepare men for it. The exact nature of this Kingdom is difficult to determine, as succeeding sections of this book will show. Men must be made ready for this reign of

[37] *Hypotyposes*, in Eusebius *Church History* vi. 14. 5–7.

[38] *Against Heresy* iii. 1. 1., in Eusebius *Church History* v. 8. 2–6.

[39] See more complete discussion of this point below, in chap. xiv.

[40] Matt. 3:14–15; Gospel of the Hebrews, cited in James, *op. cit.*, p. 6.

[41] Acts 18:25, 19:1–6.

God, and Jesus himself was both an instrument and a signal of its coming.

The spontaneous nature of Jesus' teachings attracted men to him. Many of the traditions show the simplicity of the language and the religious concepts which he used. As was the case with many great religious teachers, cures attended his ministry—healings largely dependent upon faith on the part both of the healer and the patient. These the traditions tended to magnify into mighty miracle tales.

After a career of several months, at least, Jesus moved toward Judea and Jerusalem. His popularity with groups of people who knew him already must have agitated against him in the minds of political leaders, both Jewish and Roman. Fear of rebellion was sufficient cause in those troubled days to bring any popular leader under the surveillance of authority. As in the fear-bringing days of modern war any extraordinary thought or action brings suspicion, so the Romans disposed of leaders first and asked questions afterward. It was a Roman cross upon which Jesus died: it was a crime before Rome which must have brought his crucifixion.

The crucifixion of Jesus brought in its wake the strong conviction on the part of some of his followers that he had been resurrected from the dead. The preaching of this conviction brought into form the telling of stories concerning his suffering, death, and resurrection: the passion narrative took form first. A natural interest in Jesus as a person plus a desire for norms for living brought forth the recollections of his teachings and the traditions of his life. These earliest teachings attributed to Jesus will be our next concern.

VII

THE CAREER OF JESUS (B)

THE gospels have long served as norms for Christian behavior. The teachings of Jesus have to many persons represented the great moral peaks toward which men should strive. Great emphasis has therefore been placed upon their interpretation either by churches or by individuals. Protestantism particularly has prided itself upon the belief that the Bible is an open book and that all men may learn for themselves correct standards of religious belief and behavior. With the growing understanding that the gospels represent interpretations of Jesus by early evangelists and that many of his utterances were considerably colored by the process of transmission, renewed interest has arisen in the search for the authentic (uncolored) sayings of Jesus.

Our closest approach to these actual teachings of Jesus lies down the trail which leads back from the gospels to the sources or collections behind them; from thence one must push on to the individual stories and sayings as they first circulated in Christian communities. There the trail ends, and we can glimpse the teachings of Jesus as his earliest interpreters saw him. We must constantly remember that the probability of coloring and interpretation is not thus completely removed but may be considerably lessened.

Recent scholarship has perfected two techniques for the discovery of this trail back to the original pericopes, or early stories and sayings. The first is the test of environment rigidly applied: those elements in the tradition which fail to harmonize with the Jewish environment in which Jesus operated are to be labeled as secondary additions, constructed by the evangelists to adapt the message to gentile ears.[1] The main problem involved in the use of this method is the identification of normative Judaism of the first century. The second technique requires the close examination of gospel materials to discover the *forms* which are more primitive in nature; these are to be separated from the secondary editorial and transitional material. This method, commonly called "form criticism," was developed in Germany by Martin Dibelius[2] and Rudolf Bultmann.[3] Its proper use demands a keen sensitivity for literary form and history as well as the knowledge of environment required for the first technique.

Dibelius has endeavored to pierce through the coloring of the gospels and the underlying sources to provide a clear picture of these earliest stories as they were circulated by preaching. We shall view several of his reconstructions in each of the literary classifications. These items represent Professor Dibelius' own fresh reconstructions of the Greek stories as he believes they first circulated. They bear the marks of translation from the Aramaic oral form into which they were first cast by Jesus and his Palestinian associates. The demand for wider circulation put them into Greek, the common language of the Mediterranean world. Dibelius translated his own reconstructions into comparable German, from which the English rendition was made. It is from this English translation[4] that the following quotations in this chapter are taken, unless otherwise noted.

The gospels were compiled from collections made by and for the early evangelists. The individual pericopes are therefore shaped by the needs of preaching. Several small sections bear the characteristic form of an early Christian sermon, and "we may infer that it was more or less in this way that the Christian missionaries spoke of the life of Jesus."[5] Secondary details have been

---

[1] This method is fully illustrated in Case, *Jesus: A New Biography*.

[2] See *From Tradition to Gospel* and *The Message of Jesus Christ*.

[3] *Study of the Synoptic Gospels*, in F. C. Grant, trans. and ed., *Form Criticism: A New Method of New Testament Research* (Chicago: Willett, Clark & Co., 1934), pp. 7–75; *Jesus and the Word*, trans. L. P. Smith and E. Huntress (New York: Charles Scribner's Sons, 1934).

[4] *The Message of Jesus Christ*. Cited by permission of Charles Scribner's Sons.

[5] *Ibid.*, p. 129.

omitted, since they probably did not belong to the earliest form. One of them read as follows:

> Here begins the Message of Salvation through
> Jesus Christ the Son of God:
> As it is written in Isaiah the Prophet—
>
>> A voice resounds in the wilderness:
>> Prepare the way of the Lord,
>> Make his paths smooth,

so John the Baptizer appeared in the wilderness and announced a baptism of repentance for the forgiveness of sins. And he preached as follows: "After me comes one who is mightier than I, and I am not worthy to stoop and loose the latchet of his shoes.

>> I have baptised you with water;
>> he will baptise you with holy Spirit."

Now after John was cast in prison, Jesus appeared in Galilee and proclaimed the Message of God:

>> "The time is fulfilled, the Kingdom of God is at hand;
>> repent and believe in the Message of Salvation."[6]

Another of the early sermons is taken from the second volume of Luke-Acts. It was, according to the editor, a sermon delivered in the house of Cornelius the Centurion. While these words, as quoted, may never have been given in the form and place suggested, Professor Dibelius feels that they represent a logical type for an early sermon:

> You know what took place in the land of the Jews: how following the baptism, which John had preached, the Gospel began in Galilee with Jesus of Nazareth. God anointed him with holy Spirit and with power. And he went about the country and did much good, and healed all that were in the devil's power, for God was with him. And they hanged him on a tree and put him to death.
>
> God awakened him on the third day, and let him appear visibly, not before all the people but before those witnesses whom God had previously chosen. And he bade us preach to the people and to proclaim: He is the one whom God has ordained to judge the living and the dead. All the prophets bear witness to him, that everyone who believes in him shall through his name receive forgiveness of sins.[7]

---

[6] Mark 1:1-4, 7-8, 14-15.   [7] Acts 10:37-43.

Other sermons may be seen in sections of Acts where Luke felt that a speech was in order and therefore composed one for the occasion, using the familiar materials at his disposal.[8]

Of interest is a sermon from the earliest writer in the New Testament, Paul. This "christological" passage states more of the actual life of Jesus than any other section of Paul's writings:

> He lived a divine existence,
> but thought nothing of grandeur
> nor of the glory of divine nature;
> he gave up glory and grandeur,
> taking a poor existence in exchange,
> became humanlike in form,
> and humanlike in bearing.
> He chose renunciation,
> obedient to death,
> to the death upon the cross.
> Therefore God exalted him to highest glory
> and gave him the name above all names.
> Now at the name of Jesus
> let every knee bow, of all that live and move
> whether in heaven or earth or the under-world,
> and let every tongue confess
> that Jesus Christ is Lord—
> to the honor of God the Father.[9]

From the Fourth Gospel's attempt to harmonize developing Christian concepts with prevailing philosophical thought in the Hellenistic world comes this sermonic presentation of Jesus as the Logos. It does not represent the thought of the earliest communities, but it reflects the intellectualizing tendency of approximately A.D. 110. Professor Dibelius' reconstruction of sections from the Prologue reads as follows:

> In the beginning was the everlasting Word
> and the everlasting Word was with God
> and of godlike nature was the everlasting Word,
> hence it was in the beginning with God.
> By its activity all things came into being
> and naught that exists came apart from its activity.

---

[8] See, e.g., chaps. 2, 3, 10, 13. [9] Phil. 2:6–11.

And the everlasting Word became man upon earth
and sojourned in our midst
and we beheld his glory—
glory given an only begotten by a Father—
full of grace and truth.

And from his fulness have we all partaken:
grace upon grace.
For Moses gave the Law,
but Jesus Christ brought grace and truth.

No one has ever seen God;
the only-begotten Son,
who was in the Father's bosom,
he has made him known.[10]

The second type of tradition which assumes an identifiable form in the gospel literature is described by Dibelius as "old stories." In these stories may be found direct evidence of their relationship to the early preaching. They make little or no use of detail; they are brief, artless, vigorous. Their purpose is simple: they "provide the setting for Jesus' word and saving deed."[11] Sometimes they grow to some length, especially when two become intertwined; but as a rule, they are simple illustrative anecdotes which the evangelist may use in his sermon. Stripped of the transitional and editorial materials of the gospel writer, their meaning becomes more clear. Often the details are added simply to provide a situation for the saying or to make the story move from one tradition to another.

A story which Mark incorporated into his narrative with few changes is that of Jesus' cure of the demoniac in the synagogue at Capernaum:

And they came to Capernaum. Then on the Sabbath he went to the synagogue and taught. And they were astonished at his teaching, for he spoke not like the scribes but as one who had authority and power. Now right in their synagogue was a man who was possessed by an evil spirit, who cried out at him: "What do you want with us, Jesus of Nazareth? You have come here to destroy us! I know you well enough!

---

[10] John 1:1–3, 14, 16–18.

[11] Dibelius, *The Message of Jesus Christ*, p. 136.

You are the Holy One of God!'' But Jesus sternly commanded him, ''Keep still, and go away!'' Then the evil spirit shook the man violently and threw him about, and roared loudly, but came out of him. They were all amazed, and asked one another, ''What does this mean? What new teaching! What wonderful power!''[12]

This story of Jesus' curative power would readily impress listeners as proof of his peculiar relationship to God and would fit nicely the dramatic purposes of the gospel editors. A similar story, but one which emphasized even more the unique relationship of Jesus to God, was that of the healing of the paralytic.[13]

The calling of Levi the taxgatherer formed an excellent vehicle for the aphorism concerning the nature of Jesus' ministry:

Again he was walking along the lake; and as he went by he saw Levi, the son of Alphaeus, sitting at the toll-booth, and he said to him, ''Follow me.'' And he arose and followed him. But certain scribes, who belonged to the Pharisee sect, took notice that he [Jesus] went about with sinners and publicans, and they asked his disciples: ''Does he mingle like this with publicans and sinners?'' When Jesus heard it, he answered:

''It is not the healthy who need a physician, but the sick. I came to call sinners, not the righteous!''[14]

The contribution of Jesus to the much-discussed question of ''work'' on the Sabbath was believed by the early communities to have been a decidedly liberal one:

It happened that once he was going through the fields on a Sabbath, and his disciples picked off heads of grain as they went along. And the Pharisees said to him, ''See, how they do what is forbidden on the Sabbath!'' He replied to them, ''Have you never read what David did when he was in need, and he and his men were hungry?—how he went into the house of God when Abiathar was high priest, and ate the show-bread, which it is unlawful for anyone but the priests to eat—and even gave some to his men?'' And he said to them:

''The Sabbath was made for man, and not man for the Sabbath. So the Son of Man is lord even of the Sabbath.''[15]

---

[12] Mark 1:21–27.   [14] Mark 2:13–17.

[13] Mark 2:1–12.   [15] Mark 2:23–28.

The phrase "Son of Man" acquired special significance for the early Christian communities when applied to Jesus; its clear interpretation here should be in the original Aramaic sense of man or mankind.

The common brotherhood of men under their father God was emphasized by Jesus' aphorism placed in a family setting:

And his mother and brothers came, and stood outside; they sent word, and asked for him. But around him was gathered a crowd of people. Someone said to him, "See, your mother and your brothers and sisters are outside, looking for you." And he replied, "Who are my mother and my brothers?" Then looking around upon those who sat about him he said, "These are my mother and my brothers! For anyone who does the will of God is my brother and sister and mother!"[16]

This pericope reflects the early communities' assumption of a natural family relationship, indicating nothing of the adoration of Mary which later developed. The family relationships are employed once again, together with the home-town setting, to provide a vehicle for the aphorism which Dibelius completes from the Oxyrhynchus papyri:

"No prophet amounts to much in his own country,
And no doctor can heal his own kin."[17]

Sometimes the purposes of the gospel writer lead him to make editorial additions or explanations which were not a part of the original story. Thus the story of the rich young man who asked how to obtain eternal life[18] was associated by the compilers with the explanatory section which now follows it; this prevented any misunderstanding of the figure of the rich man, the Kingdom of Heaven, the camel, and the eye of the needle. Likewise, the gospel writers made an addition to the following story, which proves its point when altogether alone:

Some of the Sadducees came to him—those who maintain that there is no resurrection; and they laid a question before him. They said, "Master, Moses gave us a law that when a man's brother dies leaving

[16] Mark 3:31–35.

[17] Mark 6:1–4; see Dibelius, *The Message of Jesus Christ*, pp. 14, 139.

[18] Mark 10:17–25; Matt. 19:16–24; Luke 18:18–25.

his wife childless, the man must marry his brother's widow and raise up children to his dead brother. Now there were once seven brothers. The first took a wife and died without issue; the second then took her, and he too died childless. The same thing happened with the third, and finally with all seven—none of them had a child. At last the woman herself died. If they are to rise again, to whom shall the woman belong then?—for all of them had her as wife!" Then Jesus said to them, "Little you know of the scriptures, or of the power of God! For when the dead rise they neither marry nor are given in marriage, but are like angels in heaven."[19]

The additional reference to Scripture which follows in the gospels is not applicable enough to prevent the feeling of anticlimax.

Some of these old stories seem to suffer from incomplete reporting on the part of the gospel writer. For one reason or another details or sayings have been omitted which must have contributed real meaning to the original story. Thus, Mark never gives the reader Jesus' reply to the disciples' statement that he is the Messiah;[20] instead, he dramatically moves his hero toward his death. Incomplete also is the Lucan story of the inhospitable Samaritans:

In their journeying about they came to a village of the Samaritans, but the villagers would not admit him, since he was on his way to Jerusalem. Then his disciples asked him, "Lord, shall we call down fire from heaven to burn them up?" But he turned and forbade them. And they went on to another village.[21]

In the form which the story takes in Luke "the reply of Jesus to the disciples is obviously crowded out to make room for the names of the two disciples, James and John, who come forward with a request and in their excess of pious zeal get thrust into the foreground."[22]

These identifiable old stories, of which the foregoing are but a sample, indicate that verbatim reports were required of the teachers of the churches only when quoting the decisive sayings of Jesus; each evangelist could describe the occasion in the man-

[19] Mark 12:18–25.
[20] Mark 8:27–29.
[21] Luke 9:52–56.
[22] Dibelius, *The Message of Jesus Christ*, p. 137.

ner which best suited him. Illustrations of this can be multiplied by contrasting the same story from gospel to gospel: the point is the same, but the details vary. The story of the centurion at Capernaum,[23] of the message from John the Baptizer,[24] of the men who wished to follow Jesus,[25] and of the Phoenician woman[26] attest to this rule.

Another salient characteristic of these stories is their unequivocal witness to the conception of Jesus as redeemer and teacher which prevailed in the early communities. They picture Jesus as he touched the common man, helping and rebuking, proclaiming the coming Kingdom and the necessity of preparation for it. Healing is never seen in these old stories simply for healing's sake: the miracle attests to the greatness of the healer. The question of forgiveness of sins assumes importance because God alone was believed to have that power; if Jesus demonstrates it, the conclusion will be hard to avoid.

The longest single narrative in the gospels, and that which first took permanent form, was the passion story. The narrating of these events in the suffering, death, and resurrection of Jesus formed the content of the earliest preaching. This demonstration of the power of God through Jesus served as the nucleus for the message of the earliest evangelists; its order and form vary only slightly from gospel to gospel, so well-established were its various items in the oral tradition. The passion narrative was, in reality, the story of redemption; and, as the first concern of the early evangelists, it came into existence before the Gospel of Mark was written. Although many of the details are not narrated with documentary exactness but are stylistically treated with a view to the history of redemption, one need not discard the general narrative as unhistorical. The passion narrative was very old, and it plainly relied upon eyewitnesses for some of its events.[27]

[23] Matt. 8:5–10, 13; Luke 7:1–10.

[24] Matt. 11:2–6; Luke 7:18–23.

[25] Matt. 8:19–22; Luke 9:57–62.   [26] Mark 7:24–30; Matt. 15:21–28.

[27] Dibelius, *The Message of Jesus Christ*, pp. 144–47; *From Tradition to Gospel*, pp. 178–217.

The parables form the third literary type in the gospel collections. These illustrative stories are at the same time well known and thoroughly misunderstood. Jesus, in common with all oriental teachers, employed parables to clarify his meaning. Usually the point of the parable stands out in sharp outline once the details of the story are completed, and the hearer or reader is able to complete the analogy and perceive the lesson without difficulty. Parables were not employed to mystify people; statements to that effect in the gospels (e.g., Mark 4:11–12, 33–34) were later additions to the tradition meant to explain the Jewish rejection of Jesus. This particular section (Mark 4:1–34) must have circulated in the early communities as a separate tradition; its conclusion that Jesus spoke in figures to hide his meaning from the populace would have sounded logical for the separate tradition, but it cannot apply to the remainder of the traditions.[28] Parables and figures made clear the points of Jesus' teaching.

Jesus' stories used the materials at hand to bring home to his listeners a lesson in religion and morals. Thus the story of the Pharisee and the publican[29] impresses hearers with the lesson of humility before God. The parable of the lost son and of the elder brother[30] teaches the love and mercy of God which often takes precedence over strict justice. The unavoidable impression which the story of the unmerciful servant[31] made upon hearers was the necessity of forgiveness of one's fellows under the reign of a forgiving God.

Parables teach a single lesson; they make one clear point. The details of a parable serve simply as background for the point of the story. Thus the parable and the allegory differ: in the parable the details are unimportant, while in the allegory each item is important for the correct interpretation. Injury is often done parables by forcing them to become allegories, thus burying the intended lesson beneath a mass of subjectively imposed materials. A reading of Jesus' parable of the unscrupulous steward will illustrate the point:

[28] Donald W. Riddle, "Mark 4:1–34: the Evolution of a Gospel Source," *Journal of Biblical Literature*, LVI (June, 1937), 77–90.

[29] Luke 18:10–14.   [30] Luke 15:11–32.   [31] Matt. 18:23–35.

Once there was a rich man who had a steward, who was accused of wasting his property. So the man had him called in and said to him, "What is this I hear about you! Close up your accounts, for you cannot be steward any longer." So the steward thought to himself, What shall I do, now that the owner is taking my position away from me? I cannot dig; and I am ashamed to beg. I know what I will do: and they will take me in, after I lose my position! So he called in each of his lord's debtors, and said to the first, "How much do you owe my master?" "A hundred measures of oil," was the reply. He said, "Here, take your note, sit down at once and make it fifty." Then he asked the second one, "What do you owe?" "A hundred bushels of wheat," he replied. And he said, "Here, take your note; make it eighty."

And the Lord Jesus praised this wicked steward, since he acted prudently; for, as he said, the children of this world manage their affairs more cleverly than the children of light![32]

The point of this parable is obviously Jesus' praise of prudence, foresight, and preparation on the part of the steward and his fear that the children of light would not show the same preparation for the coming Kingdom of God. The main character of the story was a rascal; Jesus certainly did not challenge men to emulate him in his business practices but rather in his prudence. The parable of the wicked judge[33] likewise cannot, by any stretch of the imagination, be made to teach a lesson in each of its details without doing injury to the character of God. The brief parable of the hidden treasure[34] tells of a man whose business code was thoroughly unethical but whose determination to get the treasure he desired was unsurpassed. This determination could be recommended to persons who valued the Kingdom of God. Thus the parable, whether lengthy or brief, drives home only one point; the tendency to allegorize should be resisted, even when precedent is set by the gospel writer himself.[35]

Occasionally the form of a story which the gospel compiler included as an incident in the life of Jesus gives evidence of its original status as a parable. Thus Professor Dibelius reconstructs the parable of the widow's mite to read as follows:

[32] Luke 16:1-8.
[33] Luke 18:2-7.
[34] Matt. 13:44.
[35] Mark 4:13-20; Matt. 13:18-23; Luke 8:11-15.

One day, when the people were bringing gifts to the temple-treasury, and the rich were offering large sums of gold, there came a poor widow who dropped in two tiny coins, worth about a quadrans. Verily, I tell you, this poor widow brought more than all the others who contributed to the treasury. For they all gave out of their surplus, but she in her poverty contributed all she had, even her very living.[36]

Some of the parables have a very brief setting for the analogy; the entire story may be given in a single sentence. Thus the parables of the man who does not expect a thief in the night,[37] the fig tree which indicates the coming of summer by the growth of new leaves,[38] the Kingdom of God like leaven,[39] the pearl of great price,[40] and many others are extremely concise in form. The effectiveness of the parable does not depend upon the amount of detail but upon the accuracy of the analogy.

Of extreme importance to the early communities was the fourth type of literature found within the gospels, the "sayings." Since these were thought to be the direct pronouncements of Jesus himself, double precautions would operate to keep them free of accretions. These sayings served as the norms of conduct and thought, however; and the need for new interpretations as problems arose brought changes both conscious and unconscious. Thus, opposing forces operated upon the traditional norms: one to conserve the sayings unaltered, the other to adapt them to changing needs.

These sayings are presented in various forms from gospel to gospel. The Matthean compilation gathers many of them into six great "sermons," arbitrarily located so far as time and place are concerned. Luke sometimes tries to bring these deliverances into suitable historical settings, although often he succeeds in complicating the obvious interpretation by too much detail. Fortunately, many of these sayings appear in two or more gospels, affording the opportunity to observe the utterance itself

[36] Mark 12:41–44.
[37] Matt. 24:43; Luke 12:39.
[38] Mark 13:28.
[39] Matt. 13:33; Luke 13:20–21.   [40] Matt. 13:45–46.

against the background of its explanatory details. It is possible
to present only a few of these sayings as Dibelius has reconstructed them.[41]

The Lucan form of the beatitudes shows characteristics more
primitive than those in Matthew:

> Hail, you that are poor—for yours is the Kingdom
>   of God!
> Hail, you that are hungry—for you shall be filled!
> Hail, you that weep—for you shall laugh!
> Hail to you, when they put you to shame, and speak
>   evil about you!
> Rejoice and exult! A great reward awaits you in heaven!
> For just so they dealt once with the Prophets.[42]

Extremely varied are the prophetic sayings about the Kingdom
of God:

From the days of the Baptiser up to the present time, the Kingdom of
God suffers violence, and all the violent are taking it.[43]

When a cloud rolls up in the West, then you say, It is going to rain—
and so it does. When the wind blows from the South, then you say, It is
going to be hot—and so it is. You know how to read the signs of the
weather, but do the signs of the times mean nothing to you?[44]

> No trace of God's Kingdom shall they find, who seek
>   it by reckoning,
> Nor a trace they who say, Here it is—or, It is ·
>   there;
> For behold, God's Kingdom is to be sought in your very
>   midst![45]

Two men will be toiling afield:
One will be accepted, the other refused!
Two women will grind at the mill:
One will be accepted, the other refused![46]

[41] *The Message of Jesus Christ*, pp. 61–87.

[42] Luke 6:20–23.

[43] Matt. 11:12.   [45] Luke 17:20–21.

[44] Luke 12:54–56.   [46] Matt. 24:40–41; cf. Luke 17:34–35.

Of interest is the tradition of the Lord's Prayer, which was current in the early communities:

> You shall pray as follows:
> Father, hallowed be thy Name!
> Let thy Kingdom come;
> Give us this day our bread, until the morrow,
> And forgive us our offences
> As we also forgive them that offend against us;
> And lead us not into temptation.[47]

Many of the sayings bring home their lesson by the use of forceful similes:

> Are not two sparrows sold for a penny?
> And yet not one falls to the ground, unless God
> wills it.
> And you too!—the hairs of your head are all counted![48]

> From the fruit one knows the tree—
> Or can one pluck grapes from thorn-bushes or figs
> from thistles?[49]

> No one sews a patch of new material on a torn coat.
> If he does, the new piece tears away some of the old,
> And the hole is bigger than ever.
> No one pours new wine into old wine-skins.
> If he does the wine bursts the wine-skins,
> And the wine is lost, and the skins as well.[50]

> A good man from his good treasure can bring forth
> only good things,
> An evil man from his evil treasure only evil.
> Even so your mouth speaks only from what fills your
> heart.[51]

As one would expect, a number of these traditional sayings were in the imperative:

> Judge not, lest they judge you!
> For the judgment you pass applies to you as well,
> And the measure you use will be the measure for you.[52]

---

[47] Luke 11:2–4; Matt. 6:9–13.
[48] Matt. 10:29–30; Luke 12:6–7.
[49] Matt. 7:16; Luke 6:44.
[50] Mark 2:21–22.
[51] Luke 6:45; Matt. 12:34–35.
[52] Matt. 7:1–2.

When you bring your offering to the altar and even
there remember that your brother has something against
you, leave your offering there before the altar, go,
reconcile yourself first with your brother, and then
come and present your offering![53]

A group of narratives called the "great miracle tales" composes the fifth type of literature in the gospels. These stories
arose to show the "mighty works" of Jesus, demonstrations of
power which would validate the claims of the early evangelists
that Jesus was peculiarly related to God. In the old stories the
details were relatively unimportant; they served only to provide
a setting for Jesus' saving word or deed. In the miracle tales,
however, the details are important. Each item in the story was
calculated to center attention upon the wonderful power of Jesus.
These tales have their parallels in the oriental stories of prophets,
wise men, and performers of marvels. The narratives were de-
signed to create effect, to awaken interest, to be heard for their
own sake. They are not primarily concerned with preaching the
Kingdom of God but with attestation to the power of Jesus over
nature, disease, and enemies.

These principles are illustrated directly from the miracle tales.
In the Marcan story of the curing of the leper[54] no teaching is
given, but the reader is impressed by the power of Jesus over disease. No particular lesson is to be drawn from the calming of the
storm on the lake[55] except the power of Jesus over nature. There
are a number of colorful details in the Marcan story of the ex-
orcism of the legion of demons and their damage to the herd of
swine,[56] but there is no pronouncement or teaching at the end.
Two miracle tales have grown together in the story of the healing of Jairus' daughter and the woman with an issue of blood.[57]
Other stories which attest to the miraculous powers of Jesus with
no effort to set forth a "teaching" are the great feeding,[58] the
journey across the lake,[59] the healing of the deaf and dumb,[60]

[53] Matt. 5:23–24.
[54] Mark 1:40–44.
[55] Mark 4:35–41.
[56] Mark 5:1–17.
[57] Mark 5:22–43.
[58] Mark 6:34–44.
[59] Mark 6:45–51.
[60] Mark 7:32–35.

the blind man at Bethsaida,[61] the epileptic boy,[62] the young man at Nain,[63] the marriage at Cana,[64] and the healing at the pool of Bethzatha.[65]

The final literary type discernible in the gospels is the "legend." The legend is not to be taken as completely fictional, with no basis in fact. It is the *legenda* (what is to be read) to bring hearers to emulate the good deeds of the person described. This hero or saint must be shown to be so holy that he could control his surroundings, and it must be demonstrated that from the very first this individual was under the special care and direction of God.[66] Legends are "pious tales of pious persons."

The legends in the gospels, for the most part, give some pious insight into the nature of Jesus and his work. The details included are in each case those which would edify the early communities and strengthen their faith in the mission and the person of Jesus. Their primary aim is religious edification, not historic occurrence.

The legend about the Virgin Mary[67] brings a heavenly message and concentrates attention upon the nature of Jesus. Likewise the heavenly messengers appear again in the legend about the shepherds[68] to bring further attestation to the nature of Jesus. The legend of Simeon is a pious attempt to relate Jesus to the Temple and its vision of the future,[69] while the story of Jesus at the age of twelve[70] emphasizes not only Jesus' peculiar relationship to the Temple (his Father's house) but also his gifts of wisdom in things religious. Exemplifying the characteristics of the legend were the stories of the temptation,[71] the transfiguration,[72] and the entry into Jerusalem.[73] Out of the wealth of materials attesting to the divine nature of Jesus the legends of the empty tomb[74]

[61] Mark 8:22–25.

[62] Mark 9:14–29.

[63] Luke 7:11–16.

[64] John 2:1–3; 6–10.

[65] John 5:2, 3, 5–12, 15, 16.

[66] Dibelius, *The Message of Jesus Christ*, p. 174.

[67] Luke 1:26–35, 38.

[68] Luke 2:4–20.

[69] Luke 2:25–35.

[70] Luke 2:41–49.

[71] Matt. 4:1–10; Luke 4:1–12.

[72] Mark 9:2–9.

[73] Mark 11:1–10.

[74] Mark 16:1–6, 8.

and the walk to Emmaus[75] were constructed. The pious character of the stories of the baptism of Jesus,[76] the great catch of fish,[77] and of Zaccheus[78] signifies their use as legends.

These were the six types of literature found imbedded within the gospels. Painstaking research has assisted us to wind our way up the trail toward the actual teachings of Jesus through an examination of their descriptions of environment and by an analysis of their form. This study takes us to the sermons, old stories, parables, sayings, miracle tales, and legends as they circulated in the early communities. Upon the accuracy of the first witnesses we must still depend.

[75] Luke 24:13–21, 25–32.

[76] Mark 1:9–11.

[77] Luke 5:3–6, 8–10.

[78] Luke 19:1–9.

VIII

THE CAREER OF JESUS (C)

WHAT were the main emphases of Jesus' preaching? What was meant by Jesus' preaching of the Kingdom of God? In what sense do the gospels picture Jesus as employing the term "Son of Man"? What was Jesus' relationship to the Kingdom of God? Did he believe himself to be the expected Messiah, in whatever sense that term was understood by Judaism of his day? An attempt must be made to steer a course through these troubled waters before any understanding of the career of Jesus is possible.

Jesus definitely preached the coming Kingdom of God, if the combined testimony of the gospels can at all be trusted. Further, he pictured that Kingdom as consonant with the reign of God, a state where righteousness should prevail. All sections of the gospels likewise attest to the conviction of Jesus that he was himself somehow connected with the approaching Kingdom and that its coming was related to his activities. The exact nature of this Kingdom, however, presents a problem. The solution cannot be guaranteed by the simple expedient of harmonizing the gospel sources, for a difference of testimony exists from section to section within the same gospel. Neither can the harmonizing method solve the question of Jesus' relationship to the Kingdom, for the gospel sections vary in their picture of his work.

Again we face the attempt to delineate the later attitudes of the gospel collector and his generation from the information which the earliest stories might have given. It must be the constant aim of the careful reader to distinguish the viewpoint of Jesus from the viewpoint of his first interpreters, if that distinction is possible. The procedure should follow the techniques illustrated in the last chapter, namely, the test of environment and the examination of literary form.

In what sense would the hearers of Jesus understand the phrase "the Kingdom of God"? Writers upon this problem have often assumed that there was one prevailing concept of the Kingdom of God among Jews of the first century after Christ, namely, the lively expectation of a messianic agent of God who should restore Israel to her former position of political power. This oversimplification fails to take into account many of the sources of Judaism; it disregards the belief and practice which in the eyes of many scholars was "normative" for Jews of the first century. What views, then, were held about the Kingdom by the Judaism of which Jesus was a part?

1. Many Jews thought of the Kingdom in largely political terms. God's favor would be shown by the rise of the Jews to political dominance and the return to power of the house of David. This group conceived of God's rewards largely in materialistic terms. The "chosen nation" was primarily designated to reach political supremacy, although through this supremacy the reign of the God of Israel and Judah was to be spread. The scion of the house of David was not otherworldly in character, nor is there a necessary relationship to a Messiah.[1]

2. A few decades before the birth of Jesus the apocalyptic traditions were gathered by two Jewish writers about a messianic figure variously titled the "Righteous One," the "Chosen One," and the "Anointed One."[2] The Psalms of Solomon draw a composite portrait of the "son of David" who shall be the "king of the golden age," utilizing items from the whole range of Old Testament literature. This righteous king, guided entirely by God, shall rule over Israel in the days when unrighteousness shall cease to exist and all shall be holy: "the Lord's Anointed" shall reign. Enoch emphasizes the power and the glory of this rule: kings and potentates fall never to rise again,

[1] Isa. 11:1; Jer. 23:5, 33:15; Zech. 3:8, 6:12.

[2] Ps. Sol. 17:21–46 (*ca.* 50 B.C.); I En., chaps. 37–71 (*ca.* 50 B.C.).

"because they denied the Lord of Spirits and his Anointed."[3] The "Son of Man," here used with special messianic significance, is equated with the Anointed One, who has been with God in heaven since before creation. The work of this Anointed One is chiefly in the line of judgment: the destruction of the evil and the heathen, the deliverance of the righteous. Heaven and earth will be transformed under the reign of the Lord of Spirits; the righteous will enjoy table companionship with the Son of Man, the elect will all be clad in glorious raiment.[4]

This idea of a sudden deliverer or agent of God did not engage the attention of many Jewish leaders prior to the fall of Jerusalem in 70 A.D. The very scarcity of references to any such figure is adequate attestation that this concept was not in the main current of Jewish thought. There is no reference to it in the Apocrypha, in the Testaments of the Twelve Patriarchs (excluding Christian interpretations), in the Book of Jubilees, in the Assumption of Moses, the Jewish Sibylline Oracles, the Wisdom of Solomon, or anywhere in Philo. After the disastrous occurrences of A.D. 70, supernatural interference in the mundane political order became more prominent in Jewish apocalypses. Even so great a religious leader as the Rabbi Akiba supported the messianic claims of Bar-Koziba in the revolt against Hadrian. But the period of Jesus saw the vast majority of Jews loyal to a third concept of the reign of God.

3. The average Jew of the first century saw in the Torah the laws of the Kingdom of God. When all men should come to obey these divine rules, then should the Kingdom come. In the Jewish liturgy, prayers for the appearance of the descendant of David are distinguished from those for the Kingdom. The universal reign of the God of Israel was the main concern of the first-century Jew in his prayers for the coming of the Kingdom; all else was secondary. Many loyal Jews doubtless believed that the Kingdom must come through political means, as we noticed under the first viewpoint. A small proportion during Jesus' day, losing both their hope in normal political means and their con-

---

[3] I En. 48:10.   [4] I En. 45:36, 42:14–16.

fidence in purely spiritual force, fixed their trust in a heaven-
sent figure. Most of Jesus' compatriots, however, believed in the
sufficiency of their revealed teachings; to that law they would
give their allegiance. This viewpoint has, by the most competent
scholars in recent years, come to be called "normative" Judaism.[5]
Extreme apocalypticism, with its hope for catastrophic intervention through God's messianic agent, was but a side eddy, apart
from the current that was Judaism.

These viewpoints, then, must have been represented in the
groups to which Jesus spoke. His terminology was interpreted
by his listeners in the light of their own understanding of religion. If Jesus was the religious child of Judaism, we shall expect his own preaching to grow normally from the prevalent
Jewish concepts of the Kingdom. What is the evidence from the
gospel narratives?

Contrary to one's expectation after a close study of Judaism,
the gospels picture Jesus as proclaiming, in the majority of his
teachings, a sudden and apocalyptic coming of the Kingdom of
God.[6] In some of the sayings attributed to Jesus he speaks of the
"new age," as contrasted to the present one, and of the "signs"
which will presage the advent of the "Son of Man," who will
inaugurate the great era.[7] There are, to be sure, several sayings
which describe the Kingdom as of slow growth[8] or as "within
one,"[9] but these are far outnumbered by the sudden and apocalyptic type. The Synoptic Gospels contain within themselves a
small but complete apocalypse, embracing all the traditional
elements.

[5] Consult, e.g., the scholars acceptable to both Jews and Christians: G. F. Moore, *Juda-
ism in the First Three Centuries of the Christian Era, the Age of the Tannaim* (3 vols.; Cambridge:
Harvard University Press, 1927–30); R. T. Herford, *Judaism in the New Testament Period*
(London: Lindsay Press, 1928); I. Abrahams, *Some Permanent Values in Judaism* (Oxford:
Clarendon Press, 1924), pp. 30 ff.

[6] A partial list of these references includes Mark 13:5–37; Matt. 24:4–36, 25:1–13;
Luke 12:36–40, 45–46, 17:23, 24, 31, 34–35, 21:8–36.

[7] An incomplete list of these references includes: Mark 13:5–37; Matt. 13:37–38, 41, 49,
24:4–36; Luke 11:30, 13:25, 17:22–31.

[8] Mark 4:26–29, 30–32; Matt. 13:31–33; Luke 13:18–21.

[9] Luke 17:21.

Is the conclusion unavoidable, then, that Jesus adopted the apocalyptic and messianic concept of the Kingdom of God? Before the answer to this question can be given, one must recall the character of the gospel records and analyze the beliefs of the Christian communities during the gospel-writing period. The gospel pericopes do not represent verbatim accounts of the preaching of Jesus, but rather the early communities' interpretations of him. Unavoidably, their own conclusions and beliefs about the Kingdom of God and about the person of Jesus colored the traditions of his sayings. The "modernizing" of Jesus began with the preaching of his first followers, long before gospels were thought of. Part of this modernizing and adaptation was along the line of apocalyptic belief, for the early evangelists looked forward to the early end of the age. Even a cursory reading of the earliest New Testament literature, the letters of Paul, shows the fervent hope and expectation of the return of Jesus to inaugurate the blessed age.[10] This conviction on the part of the first interpreters of Jesus undoubtedly heightened the apocalyptic effect of Jesus' teachings on the Kingdom of God.

But how can one explain the contention that Jesus was less apocalyptic in his expectation of the Kingdom than were his early interpreters? From whence did their apocalypticism stem? Just as the disastrous events of the Jewish rebellion of A.D. 68–70 were later to stimulate the apocalyptic hope in Judaism, so the blackness of utter defeat in the crucifixion of Jesus, coupled with the faith in his resurrection, awakened apocalyptic hopes among the associates of Jesus. The entire drama of Jesus' life and death was placed upon an apocalyptic stage. As they looked back upon the events in his career, it seemed to these early interpreters that each thought and deed must have significance with reference to an apocalyptic framework. The entire trend of his life and teachings then seemed obvious: hints which Jesus had given were developed into full and positive statements, inferences became factual information.

The gospel traditions are uniform in their testimony that

---

[10] I Cor. 7:26, 29, 31, 11:26; Phil. 4:5; I Thess. 3:13, 4:16, 5:1 ff., 23; II Thess. 2:1–12.

Jesus taught the nearness of the Kingdom of God and the necessity that men should prepare themselves for it. His connection
with the movement of John the Baptist suggests that judgment
was an important element in the announcement of the Kingdom; men must prepare themselves to meet the rigorous requirements which God's reign would demand. The laws of
righteousness were much more exacting than even the leaders
of the religious groups suspected; the Matthean traditions pictured Jesus as the giver of a new law which was more demanding than the Mosaic regulations.[11]

The surpassing worth of this Kingdom of God Jesus never
doubted. It demanded of each the full use of his capacities.[12] It
was so valuable that a man should gladly exchange all else that
he possessed in return for it.[13] Its characteristics were familiar to
the first-century Jew: devotion to a common Father-God, humility, love of one's fellows, purity of heart and motive, and
complete obedience to God's will as seen in revelation (chiefly
Torah). So identical were gospel interpretations of righteousness and those of the Jewish teachers that Jewish scholars have
been able to find rabbinical parallels for every important teaching in the Matthean Sermon on the Mount.

In addition to the commonly accepted Jewish teachings on
the nature of the Kingdom, Jesus must have intimately connected his own ministry with its approach. Already were the
signs of the Kingdom manifesting themselves through him.
It was by no means yet complete: the reign of God was break-
ing in upon men, but its full force was to be felt in the not-too-
distant future. The bud was now faintly visible, the full bloom
could be envisioned but was not yet realized. Only in this light
can Jesus' references to the Kingdom as a present reality be
understood.[14]

Interpreters of this difficult problem of Jesus' teaching on the
Kingdom of God have unfortunately adopted the "either-or"
attitude: either the gospel traditions indicate that Jesus was a

[11] Matt. 5:17-48.
[12] Matt. 25:14-30; Luke 19:12-26.   [13] Matt. 13:44-46.
[14] See, e.g., Matt. 11:11-12 and Luke 17:21, 11:20.

thoroughgoing eschatologist[15] or his position was that of realized eschatology.[16] Either Jesus fully indorsed the completely apocalyptic expectation of a catastrophic end of this present age and advent of the new era or he believed that the new age had already arrived in its fulness. To adopt either of these mutually exclusive positions is to deny the ever present possibility of variation within the thought of an individual Jewish teacher and to necessitate a thorough explanation for all contradictory traditions.

Briefly, then, the variety of Jesus' teachings on the Kingdom of God may be resolved into a workable unity, provided that the environmental tests are rigidly applied. Jesus taught the tremendous value of the reign of God and the necessity of preparation for its coming. The requirements for admission to that Kingdom he defined in the familiar Jewish pattern, the demands for righteousness were articulated in the light of the high concept of God. But Jesus added more: he stated that his particular mission was the inauguration of that Kingdom. It had already begun; since the days of John the Baptist men had been forcing their way into it. It would continue to grow slowly, progressing in the hearts of men like leaven, growing as the mustard seed. The beginning was visible; the consummation might come suddenly—with such rapidity, in fact, that men engaged in their daily occupations might have no time to make an additional move. Since this Kingdom was righteous in nature, it would involve a sorting of the good from the evil, the wheat from the tares, the desirable from the undesirable fish. An intensive period of preparation was necessary before men would be fit candidates for admission to this reign of God—to this preparation Jesus came to call men. A review of the events of his life by evangelists of the gospel-making period heightened the impression of the suddenness with which Jesus had said that the Kingdom would

---

[15] Consult Albert Schweitzer, *The Quest of the Historical Jesus: A Critical Study of Its Progress from Reimarus to Wrede* (2d Eng. ed.; London: A. & C. Black, Ltd., 1911), pp. 222–68, 293–401.

[16] So C. H. Dodd, *The Parables of the Kingdom* (3d ed.; New York: Charles Scribner's Sons, 1937).

be consummated. The apocalyptic convictions of the evangelists were read back into the teachings of Jesus. Consciously and unconsciously the words of and about Jesus were adapted to the apocalyptic hopes of his early followers. Gradually a concept of the Kingdom of God as the spread of righteousness became molded into an apocalyptic hope involving a heaven-sent messianic figure.

This tendency to read back the experiences and beliefs of the early evangelists into the life of Jesus is evident in the attitude of the gospels toward Jesus' claims to be "Messiah" and "Son of Man." The gospels use the term "Messiah" exclusively in the sense of the divine agent whose coming should signalize the advent of the new age. This was not the common Jewish understanding of the term in Jesus' day. Scholars such as Klausner[17] have indicated that the Messiah was always thought of in political terms: he should be an anointed king who should reign over a restored Israel in God's name. To the majority of Jews an angelic, otherworldly, and purely supernatural Messiah such as that pictured in the Enochic Similitudes was beyond the realm of belief. This supernaturalistic concept dominates the gospels' use of the term, but it is probable that Jesus understood it in the common Jewish sense derived from the Law, the Prophets, and the Psalms of the Old Testament. Thus Jesus' "theology" would stem not from the small and visionary apocalyptic circles but from the great trunk that we know as normative or legalistic Judaism.[18]

The term "Son of Man" in the Greek is a direct translation of the common Semitic expression meaning "man" or "mankind." Its first special usage in the apocalyptic sense occurred in the Similitudes of Enoch, written about 50 B.C., where the Son of Man appears to bring in the new era of peace and prosperity. The Enochic Son of Man was also the agent of God's justice. This is

---

[17] Joseph Klausner, *Die Messianischen Vorstellungen des jüdischen Volkes im Zeitalter der Tannaiten* (Berlin, 1904); also *Jesus of Nazareth: His Life, Times, and Teaching*, trans. Herbert Danby (New York: Macmillan Co., 1929), pp. 199–202.

[18] A clear discussion of this point may be found in F. C. Grant, *The Gospel of the Kingdom* (New York: Macmillan Co., 1940), pp. 111–35.

the concept which predominates in the gospel pictures of Jesus wherever the term "Son of Man" is applied to him. In some pericopes, as has already been indicated, the simpler meaning of the term would more closely approach the original intent of Jesus.[19]

Even the earliest gospel represents a fairly well-developed theology about Jesus. Part of this theology treats of the growing convictions about his "messiahship" and his filial relation to God. Mark pictures the baptism of Jesus as a meaningful experience in which a keen realization of his sonship is derived. The experience is a private one: Jesus alone sees the heavens torn apart, perceives the Spirit coming down like a dove, and hears the voice attesting: "You are my Son, my Beloved! You are my Chosen!"[20] From this time the conviction of an especial relationship to God is pictured by Mark as growing in Jesus. Foul spirits, being of the supernatural sphere, at once recognize Jesus' true character and attest to his unique relationship to God.[21] Healings and miracles mark his pathway, thus proving that he is of supernatural caliber.[22] He heals through the forgiveness of sins, which astounds the scribes, and justifies himself through appeal to the authority of the Son of Man.[23] His pronouncements are brilliant; in controversies he silences his opponents with an analogy or an aphorism, oftentimes successfully appealing to Scripture.

Thus far, Mark has not stated the exact character of Jesus. This is given to the disciples alone in the recognition scene at Caesarea Philippi, where Peter dramatically states: "You are the Christ."[24] It is at this point, approximately halfway through the gospel, that Mark begins to turn Jesus in thought and movement toward the climactic events at Jerusalem. Predictions of the crucifixion and resurrection are frequent; demonstrations of Jesus' power are equally numerous. The phrase "Son of Man"

---

[19] Mark 2:28.

[20] Mark 1:9–11.

[21] Mark 1:23–27.

[22] Mark 1:40–45, 4:36–41.

[23] Mark 2:1–11.

[24] Mark 8:27–29.

takes on the unmistakable characteristics of the apocalyptic and Enochic pictures mingled with the distinctively Christian ideas of the suffering Messiah. The needs of early Christian preaching are becoming most evident in the coloring of the dramatic narrative. The events of the last few tragic days in Jerusalem were already fairly fixed in order and form when Mark found them: they suited the apocalyptic trend without further adaptation. The "Small Apocalypse" (chap. 13) illustrates the high doctrine of the Christ or Messiah and the Son of Man which represents the farthest departure from normative Judaism.

Throughout the passion narrative are numerous stories or incidents constructed upon the basis of Old Testament citations. These represent the conscious attempt of the early evangelists to relate the strange apocalyptic teachings of their own developing groups to the stream of typical Judaism. In this narrative occurs the direct statement of Jesus to the effect that he is the Christ and the Son of Man.[25]

Thus the testimony of the earliest gospel—and the others follow suit—indicates that the Christian communities of the gospel-making period were developing an apocalyptic and otherworldly doctrine of Jesus as the Messiah and Son of Man. That they heightened the messianic element in Jesus' own teachings concerning himself there can be little doubt. Fully persuaded that Jesus had been a Messiah on the order of the Enochic Son of Man, the Christian communities interpreted the traditions to mean that Jesus had made those claims for himself. By the time the gospels came to be written the oldest traditions could be fitted into an apocalyptic framework.

The final answer to our question concerning Jesus' personal claims to messiahship must take into account the fact that he died upon a Roman cross. Jesus' preaching of the coming Kingdom of God and of his own mission to inaugurate its beginnings on Palestinian soil must have aroused the suspicions of the Romans. Ever on the alert for incipient rebellions, Roman officials must have seen in the movement of Jesus signs of approach-

[25] Mark 14:61–62.

ing trouble. Their answer was speedy and final: the cross and the ensuing faith of Jesus' followers. The first phase of the movement had closed; the religion of Jesus was a matter of history, but the religion about Jesus became the Christian faith. When the nature of the gospel records is considered, it is little wonder that students of Christianity confused the apocalypticism of the early communities with the more normal religion of Jesus.

IX

THE RISE OF CHRISTIANITY

WHEN some of the devoted followers of Jesus became convinced that he had been resurrected from the dead, "Christianity" began. Throughout the career of Jesus all that was done and said would leave the movement still within the pale of Judaism. Perhaps in some respects Jesus and his followers were considered strange or atypical, but the main current of their activities still moved within the broad limits of Judaism. It was the beliefs and practices which developed after the resurrection experiences that distinguished the movement from Judaism.

Belief in the possibility of a general resurrection of the dead (sometimes the "righteous dead") was not strange to Judaism. The Pharisees had espoused that point of view with growing conviction against their rivals, the Sadducees; and the masses of the people seemed willing to follow their leadership. But the belief that any one person could be resurrected from the dead *here and now* was not held by any first-century Jew. This conviction about Jesus his followers began to preach. The traditions of the gospels, including Luke-Acts, indicate that action based upon that belief separated the followers of Jesus from their Jewish compatriots. Sufficient resurrection "appearances" were cited by the traditions to guarantee belief on the part of anyone who was willing to believe. That disbelief in the resurrection was common among Jews is shown by the brief story of the guard around the tomb, doubtless intended by the Matthean compiler to contradict the common Jewish explanation that Jesus' body was removed from the tomb by his disciples.[1]

[1] Matt. 27:62–66.

Although the vast majority of the Jews never seriously considered belief in the resurrection of the person Jesus, a loyal group of followers began vigorously to proclaim the resurrection appearances and their tremendous significance for mankind. It became for these convinced few the central fact of history and religion. The early "sermons" composed by the author of Luke-Acts for the first apostles, the general content of which stands the environmental test, lay stress upon the resurrection as their chief emphasis.[2] The evidence from Luke-Acts is substantiated by the straightforward statements of Paul, who declares the evangelistic effort to be in vain "if Christ is not risen from the dead."[3] There can thus be little doubt that the content of early "Christian" preaching centered about the resurrection appearances and their significance.

This, then, constituted one of the points at which most violent disagreements would arise between the normal or typical Jew and the follower of Jesus. The typical Jew denied the possibility of the resurrection of any person here and now; the loyal believer in Jesus not only accepted the resurrection appearances as positive proof that God had raised him from the dead but considered this belief necessary to a correct pursuit of Judaism. The resurrection, he now believed, had been predicted by Scripture, it had been foreseen by Jesus in his teachings: it had now become the central fact in religion.

Chronology is difficult when one comes to consider the development of the beliefs about the resurrection. Very early, however, the Messiah and Son of Man theology came to incorporate the resurrection belief as its guarantee par excellence that Jesus had been a combination of these mighty figures. The Synoptic Gospels show this integration of beliefs already completed. Very early, also, the preaching began to emphasize belief in the resurrection as necessary for "salvation,"[4] since it must also be understood that this particular belief was a necessary part of the general requirement to "believe in the Lord Jesus."[5] The proclama-

[2] Acts 2:24, 32, 3:15, 4:10; see also above, chap. vi.

[3] I Cor. 15:13–18.

[4] Acts 4:10–12; I Cor. 15:12–19.

[5] Acts 2:38, 16:30–31.

tion of this belief would still further alienate the typical Jew, for "salvation" was not a normal Jewish concept in the sense in which it is here employed. Historians in the field of religion have insistently averred that Judaism was and is a religion of attainment, identifying goodness and righteousness before the Lord with obedience to his revealed will in the Torah. No one was "lost," according to the concepts of Judaism; instead, one might fail to attain to the high demands of God. The early preaching of the followers of Jesus identified them immediately with the religions of redemption, whereby the assistance of a redeemer was necessary to rescue them from their "lost" state. The resurrection of Jesus certified him as this redeemer to all who would "believe on him." This concept was essentially un-Jewish.

A second belief which early distinguished the followers of Jesus from typical Jews was the conviction that Jesus had been exalted to the right hand of God. The essential doctrine of Judaism was thus challenged: the point from which all other beliefs radiated was the firm conviction that God was one. The Shema, which Jews recited each Sabbath in solemn convocation, gave voice to their most prized possession: the knowledge, born of the centuries of experience, that God was indivisible. Contradicting this central doctrine (for so the Jew must have regarded it) was the developing belief that after the resurrection appearances Jesus had been exalted to equality or near-equality with God. Each of the formulas or sermons in the early sections of Acts infers this belief.[6]

A third factor which operated to distinguish the early believers from typical Jews was their insistence that the crucifixion of Jesus had proved his messiahship.[7] The Messiah concept in Judaism was normally associated with the resurgence of political power, as the foregoing chapter indicated. By a very small group he was understood in apocalyptic terms; he should be the agent of God's justice and power who should inaugurate the new era. Both of these concepts involved power; neither of them permitted the disgrace and failure of a cross. Yet it was this cross and

---

[6] Acts 2:33, 3:20–21, 5:31, 10:42.

[7] Acts 2:36, 3:14, 15, 5:30–32, 7:52, 10:40–43, and *passim*.

this physical failure which the early evangelists emphasized, increasing the breach with the Jews.[8] The apocalyptic tendency of the developing movement readily adapted the crucifixion of Jesus to the believers' faith in his continuing existence. The elements in the developing "Christian" apocalypticism represented an extreme advance on the already egregious Enochic point of view, making strange, indeed, the sound of their preaching upon Jewish ears.

Ecstatic activity was an additional characteristic of the early believers which divorced them from Judaism. Luke-Acts records several instances of this phenomenon, often with a notation as to its strangeness in the eyes of observing Jews. The earliest direct references to this practice among believers are the numerous instances in the letters of Paul. We should expect pronounced pneumatic behavior on the part of Paul and his converts, for Paul's Christ-mysticism led him to count ecstatic behavior normal, even though he did not rate it as most important in his list of functions. The testimony of Paul is particularly important with reference to the various resurrection appearances, for he lists his own vision of Jesus (mystical in nature) alongside the appearances Jesus made to the witnesses before him.[9] By this statement Paul certainly infers that his own experience was of value equal to the others; it is possible that he means to indicate the similarity of method by which the appearance came.

An idealized account of an ecstatic experience shared by a number of believers occurs in the Luke-Acts description of the Pentecost, or Harvest Festival, just after the ascension.[10] This was evidently a manifestation of the glossolalia, or speaking with tongues, common to the ecstatic experiences of many religions. This effervescence of language, springing from an overpowering emotion which the subjects cannot adequately express in understandable phrases, proceeds sometimes from the religious experience of mystics. It is explained in this particular instance as the result of the believers being "all filled with the holy Spirit." This, too, was believed to be a frequent and natural phenomenon

[8] E.g., I Cor. 1:23.

[9] I Cor. 15:3–8.

[10] Acts 2:1–42.

for followers of Jesus. Jesus himself had acted all through life on guidance from the Holy Spirit; he had conferred upon his followers the right to cure diseases and drive out demons through the investiture of that same power—it was but natural that Paul and others should identify possession by Holy Spirit with authorization to religious action. The gift of the Holy Spirit was the signal of acceptance into the circle of believers, although there was no set procedure for obtaining it. As already indicated, a great number were reported to have received the Holy Spirit at Pentecost; according to the Fourth Gospel, the disciples received it on the evening of the resurrection by having Jesus breathe upon them;[11] some received the gift through baptism,[12] others by the laying on of hands.[13] A number of instances show spiritistic gifts falling upon those who hear the preaching of the gospel.[14]

First-century Jews objected to these practices primarily because they seemed to be a usurpation of the place of the great prophets of the past. The "sons of the prophets" had exercised these gifts, perhaps to excess;[15] even a king of Israel had been caught up in the spirit of ecstasy,[16] and the prophet Ezekiel had made full use of this method,[17] but contemporary Judaism was a religion of obedience to the Torah. The era of prophetic revelation was believed to have closed. The ancient prophets had further explained the Law, but the canon of the prophets had been closed for over a century. The Torah was complete in every respect, it needed only explanation; therefore, the first-century Jew might well have laughed "derisively" and remarked that "they have had too much new wine."[18] The ecstatic behavior of the early believers further widened the breach with Judaism.

A fifth factor which aided in the separation of the followers of Jesus from Jews was the use of the miraculous element in such a way as to appear magical. Cautiously using the material from

[11] John 20:22.

[12] Acts 2:38.

[13] Acts 8:14–17, 9:17, 19:2 ff.

[14] Acts 10:44–48, 11:15; I Thess. 1:6; Gal. 3:2.

[15] I Sam. 10:10–11, 19:20–24.   [17] Ezek. 2:2 ff., 3:12, 24, 8:3 ff., 11:1, 5, 24.

[16] I Sam. 10:10–11, 19:23–24.   [18] Acts 2:13.

the Acts volume, we may infer that opposition arose to the various miracles because it was thought that the Deuteronomic prohibition against magic was being violated.[19] Although the importance which miracle assumes in the Acts volume is only a continuation of the miracle-filled gospel section, it is logical to assume that zealous Jews would readily suspect anyone who claimed exceptional powers as availing themselves of forces prohibited by law. Again the history of Judaism indicates that by the first century the age of God's manifestation through miracles was believed to be past; the loyal Jew avoided any such activity which would suggest syncretism with gentile religious and curative procedures.

 A final force which drove a wedge between Jews and the early believers was the evangelists' constant use (to the Jews, misuse) of the Scripture. The earliest preaching materials, which came to be collected in the passion narrative, placed their structural foundations upon citations from the revered Hebrew Bible. These quotations were "pointed" to prove the truth of the believers' contentions, namely, that Jesus had suffered and died in accordance with God's plan for "salvation" and that God had raised him from the dead to an exalted position on his own right hand. Thus the Scripture, which to the Jew was the story of monotheism and of the Torah, was used to contradict the validity of both concepts. A human being was raised to equality with God, and belief in the messiahship of this individual was made the first principle of "salvation": Torah was thus effectually relegated to a thoroughly secondary position. This theology and the resultant practices were highly objectionable; to base them upon honored Scripture proved infuriating.

The sections of the Hebrew Bible used to prove the contentions of the new movement are too numerous and too familiar to warrant citation. They came from all sections of Scripture, as a perusal of Paul and the gospels-Acts literature will verify. A number of the substantiating citations are taken from the Psalms; others from the Pentateuch and the historical books; and a large percentage from the prophets. Of these last, by far the most popular

[19] Deut. 18:9 ff.; Acts 3:6, 12–16, 4:7 ff., 5:16–18, 40.

were the satire on the dulness of the people in the story of Isaiah's call[20] and the Suffering Servant passages[21] composed by a
later writer. The Jews correctly interpreted these scriptural citations with reference to the historical situations of each, while
the early evangelists used one to explain the "hardness of heart"
on the part of typical Jews and the other to "prove" the messianic mission of Jesus.

These were the six main factors which forced a separation of
the first believers from the fold of normative Judaism; they are,
in fact, the principles which today distinguish Christians from
Jews. These distinguishing characteristics give us a clue to the
content of the early preaching. The testimony of the earliest
writer of "Christian" literature accords fully with this conclusion. A study of Paul's letters will yield little about the life of
Jesus: his repeated emphasis was upon the suffering, death, and
resurrection of Jesus, with their consequences for the "salvation"
of the believer.[22] The sermons which Luke places in the mouths
of the evangelists in Acts make these same emphases. Professor
Dibelius has concluded that, although these are obvious editorial
compositions, they represent the elements which must have been
continually emphasized by the evangelists in the period immediately following the resurrection appearances.[23] These idealized
sermons[24] show profuse references to scriptural supports for the
message about Jesus; they picture Jesus as the crucified Messiah
who had been resurrected from the dead and exalted to the right
hand of God; and they connect all of these happenings with
the outpouring of the Holy Spirit and the miraculous occurrences which were taking place in the name of Jesus.

Thus the earliest sermons had as their main concern the story
of redemption. This story of redemption was essentially un-Jewish, for it centered upon the power of a resurrected Lord to bring
believers to "salvation." It is directly cited and indirectly as-

[20] Isa. 6:9–10.

[21] Isa., chaps. 49–53.

[22] See, e.g., Rom., chaps. 5–8; I Cor. 1:18, 11:23–27, 15:1–58; Phil. 2:6–11.

[23] Dibelius, *The Message of Jesus Christ*, p. 129.

[24] E.g., the sermons in Acts, chaps. 2, 3, 10, and 13.

sumed in the writings of Paul; it took shape as the earliest of the continuous narratives which were incorporated into the gospels, the passion story; and its idealized contents were reproduced in the "sermons" of Acts.

Of tremendous interest to every reader of the New Testament is the question: "When was the gospel transferred to gentile soil?" A careful study of Luke-Acts will show that it was written to give an idealized and telescoped picture of Christianity's rise and expansion. It conceives of the movement as beginning in Palestine, with its roots firmly implanted in Judaism; it is first preached to the Jews, who reject it; then, having acquired all of its essential characteristics, it is taken to the Gentiles, finally reaching even Rome itself. The entire plan is ideally conceived by the compiler of Luke-Acts; its schedule of operations is over-simplified and foreshortened; and its omissions are numerous, as a comparison with the letters of Paul will show. It is unfortunate that this idealized work, admirable as it is, has been taken as a complete description of the progress of the early "Christian" movement.

An examination of the factors which helped to distinguish the early believers from the Jews will at once indicate that these characteristics would prove attractive to Gentiles. Those beliefs and practices which would alienate Jews from the movement would demand the attention of their gentile contemporaries. For, indeed, many of these beliefs and practices were familiar to Gentiles from various religions current in the Hellenistic world.

The resurrection, exaltation to equality with the highest gods, and belief in the power of a "lord" or god to bring salvation to those who believed in him were familiar concepts in the gentile world. Neither would death at the hands of debased men by the use of despicable methods prove a stumbling-block, for this framework, too, was a common one in contemporary cults. The Isis-Osiris cult, for instance, emphasized the goodness of Osiris, his death by foul means at the hands of his brother Set, and his restoration to life by the kindness of the goddess Isis. Osiris was believed to have become the king and chief judge of the dead. Membership in the Isis-Osiris cult brought guaranties as to future happiness. Similar characteristics could be found in the cults of Magna Mater, Mithras, and Demeter.

Ecstatic behavior was no novelty to Gentiles. A long schedule of purificatory and dramatic ceremonies prepared the neophyte in the mystery religions for communion with his god. In many instances ecstasy was the accepted means for divining the will of the gods. The famous Delphic Oracle relied upon ecstatic interpretations. The Sibylline Oracles of Hellenistic times were the interpretations given in ecstasy by selected "old women" whose reputation in this line had been established.

Miraculous and curative powers were common manifestations for first-century Gentiles. The tales of the hero-gods, such as Herakles (Hercules), related the marvelous deeds of mighty men who had been elevated to divine status. Shrines of the physician-god Asclepius were well known over the Hellenistic world, and piles of discarded crutches attested the curative powers of the god. Magical control over the elements or the gods raised an individual in the estimation of witnesses. That which constituted an offense in the eyes of the first-century Jew raised the status of a religious figure in the eyes of the Gentile.

Where the careful Jew would strenuously object to the use of his Scripture to prove theology contradictory to the main tenents of normative Judaism, the Gentile would regard reference to the Jewish Scripture as excellent validation for the believers' point of view. Regardless of his attitude toward the strange regulations of the Torah, the thoughtful Gentile respected the antiquity of Hebrew Scripture. Exegesis not acceptable to the Jew might pass his inspection and bring the influence of Scripture to bear upon acceptance of the "Christian" point of view.

Thus the very distinctive characteristics of the new movement were gentile in nature or attractive to the gentile way of life. It might well be said that in so far as the developing movement embraced gentile values it became distinct from Judaism. Its appeal from the first was almost exclusively gentile. About thirty years after the resurrection appearances Paul bemoans the fact that there are so few Jews in the church. The movement gained power outside Palestine; it is not to be overlooked that Luke-Acts indicates that it was in gentile Antioch that the disciples were first called "Christian." The distinctive characteristics of the movement thus developed in gentile circles of influence and often on gentile soil.

The answer to our question is then clear: the new movement effected the transition to gentile spheres of influence almost immediately. It never threatened normative Judaism on its native soil. Its adherents were regarded as atypical to the point that opposition developed against them. Pressure exerted upon them drove the movement immediately outside dominantly Jewish circles. Growth continued, but the bond with Judaism had been severed. The powerful churches which were distinctively "Christian" developed upon gentile soil. No problem exists on the score of availability of Gentiles in Palestine: contemporary history indicated the large number who actually lived in Palestine, and others, also, had commercial and personal relationships with the residents.

Misunderstanding has often arisen concerning the so-called "Jewish Christians." Strictly speaking, this phrase represents a contradiction of terms. Anyone who espoused the principles which marked the early Christian believers could not, in the religious sense, be called a Jew. He remained a member of the people called Jews, but he had placed himself outside the pale of Judaism. Even those whom Paul and Luke-Acts indicate as endeavoring to keep the prescriptions of the Torah[25] would, by their espousal of the beliefs about Jesus, separate themselves from typical Jews.

In studies of the beginnings of Christianity great injustice has been done those early evangelists who left no letters to posterity and for whom no interested "biographer" appeared. It has consequently been assumed that Paul, almost single-handedly, founded the gentile churches. The incompleteness of this view will be immediately apparent to the careful reader of the sources. Luke-Acts mentions Philip's work in evangelizing the Samaritans,[26] the labors of Barnabas as associate of Paul,[27] and the brief

[25] Gal. 2:3–5, 11–14; Acts 15:1.

[26] Acts 8:5–13.   [27] Acts 12:25—15:39.

work of John Mark,[28] and infers the missionary labors of others in connection with Gentiles.[29] The list of these early evangelists will, of course, never be complete. The church at Rome was founded by some other evangelist; tradition attributes it to Peter. The strong churches of the Lycus Valley, at Colossae and Laodicea, were reached by evangelists unknown to us. Before the crisis experience of Paul, beginnings had been made in Damascus. Thus, in the early years the movement spread, through the efforts of people now unknown to us, largely because its appeals were predominantly gentile in nature.

[28] Acts 12:25, 13:5, 13, 15:37–39.   [29] Acts 13:1.

X

PAUL AND THE EARLY EXPANSION
OF CHRISTIANITY

THE emerging Christian movement had been under way for
some time when Paul appeared. The early messengers of the
new faith of Jesus had proclaimed their messages throughout
Palestine, and the believers were now to be found in some of the
cities of the gentile world. Already Antioch had become a new
point of dissemination of the new faith. In the gentile cities both
Jews and non-Jews were numbered with those who accepted the
messages of the early heralds, and certainly in Antioch (and very
probably elsewhere) Jews and Gentiles had common fellowship
in their new way of life. It is the natural inference of Paul's own
words[1] that his first contact with devotees of the faith of Jesus
was in the thoroughly Hellenized region of Syria and Cilicia.

It was mentioned earlier (p. 7) that Hellenistic Judaism has
been characterized as a bridge between Judaism and Christianity.
Paul was one of the Hellenistic Jews who formed that bridge.
The tradition that he was a native of Tarsus in Cilicia is borne
out by the facts of his life that can be gleaned from his letters.
Certainly his native tongue was Greek, and his idiom betrays no
influence of the community use of a Semitic tongue; the familiar
figures of his speech are thoroughly Greek.

It was as no friend of the new faith that he first encountered it.
By his own word he "persecuted" its adherents. By his own
word, also, his background was that of the ardent, devoted—
even fanatical[2]—Jew. He had been brought up according to a
strict Pharisaic code; and, according to its standard, his achievement of the religious life within it was without fault.

[1] Gal. 1:21 f. [2] Gal. 1:14.

106

Yet it is plain from Paul's letters that in this ancestral religion he had found no peace, no satisfaction of his inner, emotional life. It appears that his sense of the contrast between the satisfactions and the outwardly praiseworthy result which he found led him to strive the harder according to the pattern which he knew and valued. The outcome was greater and greater struggle.

It is thus an easy inference that one way by which Paul strove the harder to achieve a satisfying religious life was by "persecuting" these religious folk of another cult when and where he encountered them. It is of the highest probability that these persons whom he persecuted were, like himself, Hellenistic Jews. Obviously, Paul would have had no right, whatever was his negative evaluation of the contemporary gentile religions, to oppose members of gentile cults except by debate and disputation. It was different, however, with people of his own religion; Judaism had a legal system, and this system had certain provisions for the discipline of its people. Whatever was the type of Paul's activity as a persecutor, it involved coercion and the use of physical force. It is a plausible inference that the first adherents of cults of Jesus whom Paul encountered were Hellenistic Jews, and these he opposed with considerable vehemence.

By a strange transformation Paul's conflicts were resolved unexpectedly through an experience which he later interpreted as a revelation from God: God revealed his Son to Paul, who from that moment became an advocate of the movement which he had opposed. He now believed that Jesus was God's Son, God's Anointed—the Messiah. Significantly, Paul also applied to Jesus the familiar term of the gentile cults: Jesus was his Lord.

From Paul's own statements about this revolutionary experience[3] it appears that Paul had some kind of a cataleptic vision. Obviously, his statements about it come from a time long subsequent to the event and are interpretations rather than descriptions. However, what can be determined fits into the total picture convincingly. Paul had been a zealous Jew, and by an extreme rigorism he had achieved in external behavior the high standard of the Torah. But his experience with the Law had been

[3] Gal. 1:11 f., 13–24; II Cor. 12:1–4.

an unhappy one.[4] Thus one may sketch the probable picture: by further effort, which involved deeper repression, Paul struggled the more valiantly to find the religious life which eluded him. Ultimately he went so far as to persecute fellow-Jews who, in his judgment, were unfaithful to their ancestral religion. This only intensified the conflict, until it was resolved in the visionary experience which transformed his life.

It is not to be thought that Paul's "conversion" was from Judaism to Christianity. This point is obvious, for there was not, as yet, any "Christianity" to which he might have become "converted"—the emerging Christian movement was as yet too inchoate, too lacking in self-consciousness of its distinctiveness, for this to be possible. Further, Paul never regarded himself as aught but a loyal Jew. Late in his experience[5] he felt his close relation to fellow-Jews. So far as can be determined, he understood his new way of life to be Judaism in the pure form that God desired and intended Judaism to be. He continued to use the old Scriptures; the religious terms of Judaism were, of course, appropriated and applied to his new faith. Apparently Paul continued to follow some of the ancestral customs; others he modified; some he abandoned.[6] In his preaching he evinced the same horror of idolatry that was fundamental in Judaism, and his arguments against it were always Jewish. His messages were colored by the Scriptures from which they were ultimately derived; many of his ideas reflected Judaism in the same way.

Paul's experience is rather to be understood and characterized as a transformation of the direction of his religious life, especially in the emotional aspects. It was indeed revolutionary. It was, to use a psychological term, a redintegration. For subsequently the same zeal, the same herculean capacity for effort, the same devotion that had formerly been put to the service of legalistic Judaism were now applied in his new, reorganized, redintegrated life.

Paul had been somewhere in the neighborhood of Damascus

---

[4] Rom. 7:7–25. Whether this passage is quasi-autobiographical or not, still in it Paul characterizes an experience of Torah *as though it were his own.*

[5] Rom. 9:1 ff.   [6] I Cor. 9:20–22.

when the unexpected experience had come to him. He "went into Arabia," a short distance eastward, and presently returned to Damascus. Here, if he had not done so before, he threw himself into active propagation of the new way of life. This brought him into conflict with his former group, the strict Hellenistic Jews; and in his turn he suffered "persecution." The situation was so fraught with danger that he had to escape from Damascus by stealth.[7]

His own statement indicates that he engaged in evangelistic activity in Damascus for three years before Aretas undertook to bring him to book. He then made a brief visit to Jerusalem, following this with evangelistic activity in Syria and Cilicia; some of this work was done in Antioch.[8]

This phase of Paul's work does not seem to have had particularly fruitful results. There is no extant letter from him to a church in these localities; nor is there tradition of his having founded churches there. However, this period was doubtless important to his development. Here he was in contact with fellow-workers of the rapidly expanding cults of Jesus. What he learned from others—he insists that it was little—was learned here. One negative result may be perceived. In his subsequent work Paul interpreted his revolutionary experience as his divine commission to evangelize non-Jews. He says that it had been his ambition to proclaim the good news only where it was unknown,[9] thus not building upon another worker's foundations. During this early period Paul seems to have discovered that his talents were not best suited to work with Jewish co-religionists or with other heralds of the good news of Jesus.

At all events, Paul found his conspicuous success in the West, and it is probable that his decision (later interpreted as the leadership of Holy Spirit) to go as a herald of the good news to the West was formed in this negative experience in Syria (which included Damascus and Antioch) and Cilicia (which included Tarsus, his traditional home). He turned to the West and took his good news to many a city there, founding several churches

[7] Gal. 1:15–17; II Cor. 11:32 f.

[8] Gal. 2:11–14.   [9] Rom. 15:20.

and bringing many people into the rapidly growing Christian movement.

On the basis of reports in the second volume of Luke-Acts, it is customary to define Paul's subsequent activities in terms of several "missionary journeys." These cannot be as sharply distinguished on the basis of Paul's letters, which contain certain semi-autobiographical statements. The arbitrary and incomplete character of these "journeys" can be seen by comparison with the list of stonings, beatings, shipwrecks, and other of his experiences which Paul himself catalogues in correspondence written several years prior to his death.[10] Luke-Acts does not hesitate to idealize and telescope available materials. Since correct biographical procedure dictates that preference be given the primary sources, Paul's own letters will be used as the basis for inferences concerning his activities.

This enables the reader to perceive that Paul was twice in the region which he calls Galatia. Since Paul elsewhere uses Roman provincial nomenclature, it is probable that he here refers to the province of Galatia. This includes the towns mentioned as visited on the "first missionary journey."[11] Paul also labored in several cities of the Greek Peninsula and spent a fruitful period of time in the province of Asia, centering in Ephesus. During this time he made an important visit to Jerusalem. His own summary of his travels and labors states that he had preached the good news from Jerusalem to the environs of Illyricum (Dalmatia).

Although the statistical aspects of Paul's accomplishments are remarkable, the qualitative aspect is more so. The most significant single element in Paul's work is its documentation of one of the types of the religious life in emerging Christianity. Further, Paul's work demonstrates, in the fullest possible detail, the transition in the nature of Christianity from its beginning as a religious group within Judaism to a thoroughly gentile movement.

Emerging Christianity, or Christianity when it may properly be called such, was never homogeneous. There was never any one

[10] II Cor. 11:24 ff.   [11] Acts 13:4—14:28.

single type of Christianity. What became Christianity was, in the beginning, the experience of those who declared that they had "seen" Jesus subsequent to his death. In short, Christianity had its beginning in the "resurrection experiences" of certain persons. These persons told their experiences. Some of their hearers believed their stories; others did not. Those who believed were the nucleus of beginning Christianity. The spread of the movement was in the proclamation of the good news that God had raised Jesus from the dead, together with the various interpretations of the nature of Jesus which his "resurrection" naturally involved.

One of these who had such an experience was Paul. This occurred in his so-called "conversion." He lists his experience with those of others.[12] Like others, Paul immediately told of it, and launched upon his career as an evangelist. He was by no means the first; several others besides those mentioned in I Cor. 15:3 ff. preceded him—he mentions two[13] as of note among the apostles and as having been "in Christ" before he was.

As has been pointed out, the emerging Christianity embraced the two major types of the religious life, Jewish and non-Jewish, before Paul came into the movement. He was by no means the creator of gentile Christianity; he was more its product than its initiator. Not only did gentile "Christianity" exist before Paul, but non-Pauline types of it are to be observed during and after his career. It has been pointed out that he shared in the community at Antioch, which was already racially inclusive when he came to it. Alexandrian Christianity, although its early history cannot be determined, is a notable example of non-Pauline Christianity. It will be remembered that "Acts" mentions believers in Damascus and in Ephesus preceding Paul's advent to those places.

Nevertheless, Paul's work and writings illustrate the transition of Christianity from a movement within Judaism to a dominantly gentile movement more fully and completely than any

[12] I Cor. 15:3 ff.   [13] Rom. 16:7.

available source. Thus an understanding of his career is invaluable for the study of Christian beginnings.

One perceives from the observation of these processes that Paul, strict Jew though he was, recognized from what he saw (both as persecutor and as evangelist) that non-Jews were capable of a valid religious experience. He therefore made the sensible conclusion that in the new way of life which he was advocating non-Jews might properly be received without requiring them to become circumcised—i.e., without requiring them to become Jews.

This illustrates the adoption of that fundamental element of Hellenistic culture which was emphasized in the beginning chapters of this book: thoroughgoing individualism. The religious life which Paul (and others) lived and proclaimed was a religion of individual salvation. A person was confronted with the good news of Jesus; he believed or disbelieved; if he believed, he confessed his belief (that God had raised Jesus from among the dead and that Jesus is Lord Messiah)[14] and his nature was changed— he was "pronounced acquitted"; he was saved. Once sinful, he was now spiritual; formerly the old creature, he was now the new creature. He was then baptized, and as a member of the community he was expected to live in a way that exhibited the fruits of his new life. This is the religion of a salvation cult, not essentially different from many others current in the Hellenistic world.

This represents an aspect of Christianity's adaptation to its environment; and, as has been insisted, the processes are fully illustrated and documented in Paul's life and work.

Although Paul apparently regarded himself as a strict Jew, he took a radical position on the relation of non-Jews to the movement as a whole. He declared that these were under no obligation to become Jews; further, they must not do so. For them to accept circumcision (his Letter to the Galatians details this position) would mean that they had forfeited, broken, and canceled their

---

[14] I Cor. 12:3; Phil. 2:11; Gal. 2:16.

relation to the Lord Jesus; if they accepted circumcision, Christ profited them nothing.[15]

Paul was able to do this and still maintain his own viewpoint as a strict Jew by making a certain interpretation of Jewish Scripture. This plainly reflects his own religious experience in Judaism. His had been an unhappy experience with the Torah; consequently, it is the easier to see how he made the distinction between the Torah as law (which he regarded as valid only until the coming of Jesus) and the Torah as promise—the promises which God had made to Abraham were eternally valid. But Paul interpreted these in his own way. He reasoned that, when God promised Abraham that his descendants should be as numerous as the sands of the sea, he meant that all who would ultimately believe in Jesus were to be children of Abraham. Paul concluded that gentile believers were thus children of Abraham, even though they were born Gentiles. Consequently, his recognition of their valid religious claims made him insist vigorously that they need not and must not take upon themselves the observation of the Torah as law. Every element of the Torah as statute, he insisted, was only of temporary validity, pending the arrival of Christ.

This was the intellectual statement of his experience. It illustrates the manner in which one early Christian leader functioned in the transition of Christianity to the inclusion of Gentiles, to the propagation of the faith in gentile territories, and to the point at which it became dominantly gentile. This was simply the adoption of the social attitude of thoroughgoing individualism so characteristic of the Hellenistic age.

A distinctive way of life grew up in the dominantly gentile Pauline communities. In general, Pauline Christianity was a salvation cult. The content of the teaching was largely derived from Judaism:[16] belief in Jesus as Messiah, ideas of life after death, the apocalyptic world view and expectation, concepts of God, attitude toward idolatry. But in behavior the Pauline com-

[15] Gal. 5:2–4.

[16] Note, e.g., such a summary as Paul gives in I Thess. 1:9 f.

munities were quite un-Jewish; indeed, they were radically individual. What may be called "spiritism" (for want of a better English word for the Greek terms) was characteristic of all these communities; people uttered ecstatic prophecies (sermons), they healed the sick and performed other "miracles," they used the unintelligible gibberish of "speaking in tongues." If the modern reader thinks that the Corinthians in their avidity for this were untypical, he may remind himself by reading I Thess. 5:19 that Paul wanted no one to "quench the spirit," however praiseworthy it was to "test the utterances it inspires." One cannot correctly picture Pauline Christianity without perceiving that this aspect was of high importance and was given a prominent place.

Paul's expectation of the imminent end of the age is likewise of focal importance. His work cannot be understood without recognizing it, nor can the type of the religious life in the communities be understood without an appraisal of it. This was an aspect of his preaching which was received with great enthusiasm; some people ceased to work because they expected the end immediately.[17] Paul's apparently strange advice to the Corinthians that it was not worth while to marry was doubtless projected upon his belief that the end of the age would come very soon.

Paul insisted upon a high ethical standard in the lives of the people of his churches. The content of this ethic was conventional, largely Jewish in derivation, but inclusive also of Hellenistic teachings (e.g., Col. 3:18—4:1 is closely parallel to Stoic ethical teaching). The distinctive aspect of the Pauline ethic is its dependence upon Paul's fundamental recognition of the place of the spirit in the religious life; people whose natures had been transformed so that they were now "spirit-persons" were expected to live as "spirit-persons" should, not like "flesh-persons."

Whether by design or chance, Paul founded churches in various parts of the middle-north Mediterranean world; and some of

[17] II Thess. 3:6–12.

these were in cities of strategic importance for the subsequent development of Christianity. Thessalonica, Philippi, Corinth, and Ephesus are the most significant of these. In the places (obviously, there were more than these which were listed) where he planted the Christian movement, a considerable number of people were brought into the new communities. It is of secondary importance that Christianity in these places changed after Paul went from the scene; the point is that from these places Christianity continued to spread and to grow. This aspect and result of Paul's work is of obvious significance and importance.

In all of Paul's work he encountered conflict. His early experience had been one of conflict, and the conflict did not cease when his personal problems were resolved in a revolutionary experience. His understanding of his "call" and his interpretation of the religious life involved him in controversy and dispute.[18] Perhaps experiences such as this led him to transfer his activity to the West. But here, too, he encountered struggle, as is to be perceived in his letters. Of especial significance is the long series of tribulations and dangers which he had endured for the sake of Christ.[19] Just as he had been forced to leave Damascus by stealth, so he left Thessalonica under pressure.[20] The Corinthians, or at least some of them, became disaffected; and a violent turmoil ensued.[21] Paul argued, sometimes vehemently and passionately, in writing to the Romans,[22] a church which he had not founded. His rigid insistence upon the validity of his understanding of the religious life led him to a serious discussion with the leaders in Jerusalem.[23] Paul's life was a constant struggle.

It is not surprising, then, to find in what is apparently the latest of the "autobiographical" passages of his letters[24] that Paul anticipated grave opposition and trouble on what proved to be his last visit to Jerusalem. Acting upon the counsel which he and Barnabas had accepted in the important earlier Jerusalem confer-

---

[18] E.g., Gal. 1:11–14.
[19] II Cor. 11:23 ff.
[20] I Thess. 3:4.
[21] II Cor. 10:1 ff.
[22] Rom. 2:1 ff.
[23] Gal. 2:1–10.
[24] Rom. 15:14–33.

ence, Paul had collected money for the poor in Jerusalem. He had been highly conscious of the churches in Judea[25] and recognized his obligation to them. Certain Jewish leaders, however, had been of great trouble to him, chiefly in Galatia and in Corinth. At all events, he expected more opposition from "those who were disobedient" in Jerusalem. The latter sections of Luke-Acts charge that trouble was instigated and fomented by Asian Jews who had followed him there. Even though there is every reason to follow the general outlines of the story there chronicled, one must question certain details. Tradition agrees that Paul died a martyr in Rome. Whether his death was by beheading, as general tradition has it, or by exposure to wild beasts, as may have been the case, Paul's meteoric career was brought to an end all too soon for the welfare of the movement which he had done so much to further.

[25] I Thess. 2:14.

XI

PAUL'S LETTERS: THE BEGINNING
OF EARLY CHRISTIAN LITERATURE

AS ONE of the means of control over the people of the churches which he founded, Paul wrote several letters. He ventured also to write to two churches which he had not founded, to people with whom he was not personally acquainted. Some of the letters which he wrote survived and have become a part of the New Testament. This aspect of his work constitutes Paul's most direct memorial. The letters are of the greatest value, however, for their picture of Paul's influence upon expanding Christianity and of the religious life which he propagated.

The occasion of writing and the time, place, and destination of the letters, and thus the stages in the growth of Christianity which the letters reflect, should be determined from the letters themselves. In this, fortunately, Paul furnishes an essential clue. In writing to the Corinthians[1] Paul mentions an experience of his which had occurred "fourteen years ago." In his letter to the Galatians,[2] which internal evidence shows to have been written at about the same time, he refers to what is doubtless the same event in dating an experience which occurred "fourteen years later." The earlier experience was his so-called "conversion"; the later one was an important visit to Jerusalem, at which the persistent problem of the reception of non-Jews into the movement was discussed. Thus Paul's letters, all of which reflect various stages of his evangelistic activity, were written before, at the time of, and subsequent to, the crisis which occurred during this visit to Jerusalem.

The application of this criterion of sequence to the letters de-

---

[1] II Cor. 12:2.   [2] Gal. 2:1–10.

termines their relative dates and enables the student to see that I and II Thessalonians, Philippians (except the section 3:2–16), Colossians, and Philemon do not reflect the crisis; this fact and other considerations require the judgment that they were written before it occurred. I Corinthians reveals certain phenomena which exhibit an early stage of the crisis. Galatians, that part of II Corinthians which constitutes chapters 10–13, and Philippians 3:2–16 reflect the crisis at its height and heat. Chapters 1–9 of II Corinthians reflect the crisis in retrospect, and Romans can readily be seen to have been written after it had occurred.

Since all of Paul's letters came out of his evangelistic activity, they are human documents of his work in the expansion of Christianity. From them certain details of his travels can be perceived, but not in such detail as is sketched in Acts, chapters 13–20. On the other hand, details in the letters cannot be accounted for by reference to the schematic stories in Luke-Acts. The proper procedure is to follow the information which is derived from the letters themselves.

The letters to the Thessalonians do not reflect the crisis; and their evidence throughout indicates that they are early, as compared to other letters. They obviously assume the evangelization of people of Thessalonica and therefore are the first memorial to an event of decisive importance. As Philippi and Thessalonica lie across the upper Aegean from the continent of Asia, Paul's first letter is a witness to the transplantation of emerging Christianity from the continent of Asia, where it was born and received its early growth, to the continent of Europe. This act, of momentous importance—although it is not to be supposed that it was done by conscious design—caused that union of Christianity with Western civilization which has had such far-reaching implications.

Paul had evangelized people in Thessalonica after having founded a church in Philippi, which lay to its east. Trouble had developed,[3] and Paul had left after an all too brief effort of evangelism. His messages had been eagerly received.[4] He had presented to the Thessalonians the good news of Jesus, and the people

---

[3] I Thess. 2:14 ff., 3:4.   [4] I Thess. 1:5, 9.

had absorbed his teachings with lasting result. They had accepted Paul's warnings that this was an evil age which they must forsake for the age to come; they had turned from their former idolatrous religious ways of life and now lived the highly spiritistic[5] life of people whose natures had been transformed. Their expectation of the soon-to-come end of the age was vivid and realistic,[6] although in this item of their new faith they needed further instruction.

On his part, Paul had been highly pleased with the results of his work at Thessalonica.[7] But naturally he felt no little anxiety for the welfare of those whom he had to leave so soon. He had gone on (doubtless stopping at other cities for evangelizing) to Athens.[8] By this time his concern for the welfare of his early followers in the good news was so great that he could contain himself no longer. He had wished many times that he might return to them,[9] but his sense of compulsion did not permit it. At Athens he determined upon the next best plan; he sent Timothy, one of his trusted helpers, to Thessalonica to find out how his own converts were doing. Timothy made the journey and returned to meet Paul (perhaps in Athens, very probably in Corinth) with his report of the eminently satisfactory condition of the people. Paul thereupon wrote I Thessalonians, the first item of early Christian literature, in response to the news brought by Timothy.

The point of his letter, aside from the personal references already noted, was to encourage the Thessalonians. In the main, their achievement in the new religious life had been satisfactory; and Paul desired to give them the further counsel and instruction, which it appeared that they needed.

One major question was their achievement in the moral aspect of the new religious life. The primary factor was that these people had changed: they had undertaken to live a new kind of religious life. As modern Christians say, they had been converted from "paganism" to Christianity. This oversimplification is cor-

[5] I Thess. 1:5, 4:1.

[6] I Thess. 1:10, 5:1.

[7] I Thess. 1:2, 2:7–12, 19 f.

[8] I Thess. 3:1.

[9] I Thess. 2:17 f.

rect in its emphasis upon contrast. The problem arose when Thessalonian converts attempted to carry over into the new life certain elements from the pattern of behavior in their old life. Thus Paul's advice is upon the elementary levels of sexual behavior.[10] Otherwise, in matters of their relation as fellow-members of a new religious society, their behavior left nothing to be desired.[11] The only point at which they were open to exhortation was that some, at least, were inclined to resent their leaders.[12] Paul urged them to keep on as they were and to surpass their current standard in the orderly way in which they made their livings and participated with the common life outside the church relationship.[13] Some of the people, naturally, were not up to the standard of others; some were idlers, discouraged, and weak. Paul counseled those whose lives were satisfactory to work with these. Some general advice with reference to cheerful demeanor, non-retaliation, prayer, thankfulness, and the giving of free expression to ecstasy applied to all.[14]

Additional instruction was needed concerning the expectation of the end of the age. The Thessalonians eagerly believed in it. And they had shaped their religious lives with reference to their eager expectation. But a problem had arisen: the end had not come as soon as it had been expected (a fact, incidentally, which conclusively proves the immediacy with which Paul preached the early end of the age), and some of the believers had already died. Did this mean that these believers would have no part in the joyous event when it came?

When Paul discussed this question,[15] he was glad to assume their acceptance of the basic belief and complimented the Thessalonians that in certain items he had no need to instruct them further; they had learned their lessons well.[16] He had only to give them further detail. This was that the end of the age would come when the archangel calls and the trumpet speaks; Jesus would come from heaven, and the dead who believed would rise

---

10 I Thess. 4:3–8.

11 I Thess. 4:9 f.

12 I Thess. 5:12 f.

13 I Thess. 4:11 f.

14 I Thess. 5:15–22.

15 I Thess. 4:13—5:11.

16 I Thess. 5:1 f.

and be the first to meet him. After them the surviving believers would be caught up into the air. But as to its time, no one could say, except that it would be soon. One thing was certain: it would be sudden. Therefore, people must be ready at any and all times.

This particular factor seems to have brought forth a second letter to the Thessalonians. Paul had directed[17] that the first letter be read publicly. But a confusing factor had arisen: letters forged in Paul's name, with contents out of harmony with Paul's other teaching, had also been circulated.[18] Apparently, some persons who did not follow Paul's leadership had propagated contradictory teachings about the end of the age—some had taught that the general resurrection had already occurred.[19] Thus Paul had to exercise control at this point. He disavowed all forged letters and oral messages and called attention to what would be his custom from now on: that of writing the subscription of his letters in his own hand (the letters were written by public writers at Paul's dictation).

The Thessalonians illustrate that which has been found in groups of Christians ever since: people who emphasize the coming of Christ and the end of the age always disagree as to details, especially the timetable. Paul had written in I Thessalonians to correct misapprehensions, and now some people had misapprehended his corrections. He had made the point that, while the end would come soon, it was not proper for people to try to calculate the date. The result was that some people thought "soon" meant sooner than Paul had had in mind. In II Thessalonians he writes to explain the delay that was bound to be involved, whatever the time eventually proved to be. Here, as is characteristic of teachers of the end of the world, Paul uses figures of speech.[20] These figures were doubtless meaningful to the Thessalonians, so that it was unnecessary for him to explain their content. At all events, he expected this to be a corrective.

Some modern scholars doubt the authenticity of II Thessalonians, especially on the ground that the teaching about the end

[17] I Thess. 5:27.

[18] II Thess. 2:2.

[19] II Thess. 2:2.

[20] 2:3.

of the age disagrees with what Paul writes elsewhere, especially in I Thessalonians. But he says in II Thessalonians that he had taught the same things when he was with them.[21] And it is the very nature of apocalyptic teaching that it uses protean figures; in many an apocalypse they change in apparently contradictory disagreement. Many Jewish apocalypses illustrate this, as does the great Apocalypse of the New Testament. The personal details of II Thessalonians are indubitably authentic.

In this letter, too, Paul expresses confidence and general satisfaction with the Thessalonians; he warns only those who had taken his teaching about the end too literally and had ceased work to await it. These must get to work.[22] Others are commended,[23] and Paul has confidence in them;[24] he expresses the hope that they will go on and on in their excellent progress.[25]

The three letters, Philippians, Colossians, and Philemon, show in their internal evidence that they were written when Paul was in prison. Until recent days it was generally concluded that they were written from Rome when Paul was in prison there toward the close of his life. But this is an unsatisfactory judgment; they appear, on their face, to have been written in the very midst of Paul's active work of evangelization. Some have attempted to show from their thought and teaching that these letters reflect a late stage in the development of Paul's thought, especially in such "doctrinal" matters as the conception of Christ and the end of the age. But no such development can be shown; none occurred. Paul insisted that he had his message from the time of his revolutionary experience;[26] it was, he insisted, a revelation from God—certainly he would have repudiated any "development" of it.

In any case, it is proper to seek for another, an earlier, prison experience. Paul says[27] that he had experienced "far more imprisonments" than the opponents whom he was then castigating. Acts specifies two—one in Philippi, one in Rome. Paul refers

[21] 2:5.
[22] II Thess. 3:6–12.
[23] II Thess. 1:3 f.
[24] II Thess. 3:4.
[25] II Thess. 2:15, 17, 3:5.
[26] Gal. 1:12.
[27] II Cor. 11:23.

to an experience in Ephesus in which he "fought with wild beasts."[28] There is a tradition, with certain archeological detail, that he was imprisoned during his activity in Ephesus. Thus there has been a growing tendency to utilize the tradition of the Ephesian imprisonment as the time and place of the writing of these letters. That view will be followed in this book.

Perhaps the strongest argument in favor of it is geography. Ephesus was more accessible for communication from Philippi than was Rome; the Philippian correspondence involves threefold communication: news of the imprisonment reached Philippi; the Philippians sent Epaphroditus with a gift of money to Paul, the messenger fell ill and nearly died; Paul sends Epaphroditus back to Philippi with the letter. This is much more understandable from Ephesus than from Rome.

Similarly, Onesimus, a runaway slave, comes under Paul's influence. Onesimus is from either Colossae or Laodicea. It is much more likely that a runaway slave would find his way from either of these towns to Ephesus than to Rome. Paul says[29] that he hopes to see the people of the church addressed; evidently he expects to visit them soon. An early visit to that church, presumably in Laodicea, would be much easier from Ephesus than from Rome.

At all events, Philippians was written from prison.[30] The latter is plainly composite, made up of fragments of several letters. The lack of transition is a revealing evidence of this—note the abrupt breaks after 3:1 and 4:3. There is no connection between 3:16 and what follows, or between 4:9 and what follows. The passage 3:2–16 is completely out of adjustment, and also out of harmony, with the remainder of the letter. The salutation appears to have been supplied by an editor; in referring to "superintendents"[31] (usually translated "bishops") a word is used which does not occur save for this reference in the authentic letters of Paul. There is, indeed, no evidence that the official was known as *episcopos* until considerably later.

Philippians is then to be understood as an editorial organiza-

[28] I Cor. 15:32.
[29] Philem. 22.
[30] Phil. 1:13, 17, 2:23, 4:22.
[31] Phil. 1:1.

tion of parts of several letters which Paul wrote. Some of these parts are obviously early; some may be relatively later, and 3:2–16 certainly comes from the time of the great crisis in Paul's work.

The letter plainly reflects the most cordial relations between Paul and the Philippians. Paul praises them and mentions their unfailing helpfulness at various times. They are commended for their achievements in the religious life; their behavior leaves little to be desired. Thus the letter is like other Pauline letters: it reflects the result of successful evangelizing activity.

The sections[32] which reflect the imprisonment situation reveal Paul's condition at the time. He was in prison (one of the several times mentioned later in II Cor. 11:23) for the sake of preaching the good news.[33] A striking fact is the clear indication of opposition to Paul from other leaders.[34] Evidently this was a constant factor in Paul's life. The issue was doubtful,[35] but Paul was courageous. The Philippians had sent Epaphroditus with a gift of money, which Paul writes to acknowledge gratefully.[36] Epaphroditus had fallen ill, and Paul writes to explain this.[37]

As to Paul's teaching, aside from such matters as minor bickering between Philippian church people,[38] Paul has nothing but praise for the Philippians. He exhorts them, not with special reference to their deficiencies, but as to general ideals, to increasing expressions of their fruitful way of life. In so doing he is led to articulate one of his noblest passages of writing in his paean on Christ's example.[39] In this early letter one sees Paul's high conception of the nature of Christ; in this passage one sees an expression of his teachings in perfect correspondence with the contemporary gentile world view—especially in his faith that demonic creatures will all pay their homage to Christ:[40] heavenly spirits, spirits in the earthly realm, and even spirits of the under-

---

[32] Chiefly Phil. 1:12–20, 2:23–30, 4:10–20.

[33] Phil. 1:13.

[34] Phil. 1:15 ff.

[35] Phil. 1:20.

[36] Phil. 4:10–20.

[37] Phil. 2:25–30.

[38] Phil. 4:2 f.

[39] Phil. 2:5–11.

[40] Phil. 2:10 f.

world. This passage is a striking illustration of Paul's world view.

Philippians, then, is to be regarded not as a single letter but as a composite formation from several parts written by Paul to the Philippians. Some of these, certainly the prison parts, were written early; one[41] was written later. Probably the letter in its final form was put together by the Christian leader who collected Paul's letters and published them as a corpus. In this process a certain amount of editing was necessary, and some examples of it are to be seen here.

Colossians, too, was written from prison.[42] Paul had not founded the church in Colossae, a city of minor importance in the Lycus Valley east of Ephesus. Presumably it had been founded by Epaphras.[43] Paul had been informed of the particular problem in evidence there; the Colossians were being attracted to a quasi-philosophical, highly mystical way of life which was hardly similar enough to the other types of the religious life in emerging Christianity to be regarded as one of them. The religion which was attracting them away from their earlier way of life was highly syncretistic, composed of Jewish, other oriental, and certain Greek aspects. It was ascetic.[44] It included angel-worship and other occult elements.[45] The feature which was proving most dangerous for the Colossians, however, was the emphasis upon philosophy. As shall be pointed out in discussing I Corinthians, Paul had a place for philosophical reflection of a mystic type. Colossians shows how far he could go in stating his ideas in a kind of philosophical language and form. But Paul was negative to philosophy as it was used and practiced by professional philosophers. Paul's way of life was mystical, not "rational." He had basic religious assumptions which came by revelation and were not to be obtained by philosophical reflection. Therefore he proceeded, in this case, to make his point by setting forth certain aspects of his religion in quasi-philosophical terms of his mystical type. His plan was to lead the Colossians, who were being at-

[41] Phil. 3:2–16.

[42] Col. 1:24, 2:1, 4:3 f., 10, 18.

[43] Col. 1:5–7.

[44] Col. 2:16, 20–23.

[45] Col. 2:8, 18, 20–23.

tracted *away* by this sort of thing, to stay within the sphere of the common church relationship.

The reader has only to study Colossians, noting the metaphysical language and imagery (wisdom, knowledge, light and darkness, "likeness"—i.e., image, seen and unseen, the divine fulness, mystery, philosophy, etc.), to see how far Paul had gone in adopting values from contemporary Hellenistic culture. Many of the ideas of Colossians are so similar to those of the mystery religions[46] that many scholars can only conclude that Paul was directly influenced by this part of his environment. The metaphysical elements of Colossians are so similar to the teachings of later Gnosticism that, although this movement was only in its incipiency during Paul's time, direct influence upon him was possible. Colossians 3:18—4:1 cites a table of the duties of the members of the household (in the Greek conception of the family); this is closely similar to conventional Stoic ethics and may have been derived from that popular movement.

Colossians is an example of Paul's use of letter-writing to exercise control over a group which he had not founded. Yet it is not without personal elements.[47] The references to Onesimus and Archippus[48] link the letter to Philemon. The direction to exchange letters with Laodicea is especially interesting, as shall be pointed out.

The relationship of these two letters is closer than appears on the surface. Onesimus is mentioned in Colossians[49] as a member of the Colossian church. He is the major subject of the Letter to Philemon. Although this letter is printed under the title of "The Letter to Philemon," the salutation shows that, like all Paul's letters, it is written to a church: it is addressed to Philemon, Apphia, Archippus, "*and to the church* that meets in your house."[50] Whose house is meant? Since Archippus is the last individual mentioned, the grammar indicates that it was in his house. Does the reference to Archippus in Col. 4:17 tie up with this letter? What is the "service" to which Paul there refers?

---

[46] Most striking of all is the figure in 2:11–13; cf. Rom. 6:3–11.

[47] Col. 4:7–17.

[48] Col. 4:9, 17.

[49] Col. 4:9.

[50] Philem. 2. (Italics ours.)

Perhaps, this, too, had to do with Onesimus. The general situation is plain. Onesimus was a slave who belonged to Archippus or to Philemon—again the grammar points to Archippus—who had run away and had come under Paul's influence while he was away. This influence led him to become a convert to the good news, and Paul here takes the daring step of sending him back to his master.

Under the Roman law this was potentially dangerous to the returning slave. But Paul ventures to anticipate this danger by recommending him to his owner on the basis of his new status as a child of the good news—he and his master are now brothers. This does not cancel their relation as master and slave—Paul says nothing which would disturb that relation—but he expected what he said to affect it. Indeed, he seems to have had more than that in mind. He expects—and all but demands—that the slave's owner will not only receive and treat the runaway kindly but will return him to the writer. Is this the "service" which the Letter to the Colossians calls upon Archippus to do?[51] Probably the exchange of the Philemon and Colossian letters was to exert pressure to insure that Onesimus would not be punished.

Some decades later there was a bishop of Ephesus whose name was Onesimus. One scholar[52] believes that this bishop was the former slave—the same person who is mentioned in Colossians and is the subject of Philemon. It is at least an interesting possibility.

Philemon is commonly regarded as a merely personal letter of minor importance. It is much more. When it is seen to be a letter to a church, when its connections with Colossians are recognized, and when it is related to the contemporary developments in Paul's life, it does not seem strange that so small a letter should have found its way into the New Testament.

[51] Col. 4:17.

[52] John Knox, *Philemon among the Letters of Paul* (Chicago: University of Chicago Press, 1935).

XII

PAUL'S LETTERS: CONFLICT AND CRISIS

PAUL'S letters fall into four groups. The first consists of I and II Thessalonians, which reflect the phenomena of evangelistic activity. The second group is made up of the three letters written from the Ephesian imprisonment: part or parts of Philippians, Colossians, and Philemon. The documents making up the second group exhibit particular problems which had emerged in Paul's further work. It is interesting to discover that in Philippians and Colossians opposition to Paul is clearly indicated. As was remarked, conflict was continuous in Paul's experience.

Conflict is even more readily observed in the letters forming the third group, for in the Corinthian correspondence and in Galatians the great crisis which marks the watershed of Paul's labors presently appears as a major phenomenon. The fourth group expresses calmness after a storm successfully weathered, even though Paul is still concerned with detailed guidance of his Christian friends. The Letter to the Romans and II Cor. 1–9 thus complete Paul's extant correspondence.

Chronological data are noteworthy in the third group of letters. Paul was no longer a prisoner when he wrote I Corinthians.[1] He was engaged in collecting money;[2] presumably this was in response to the obligation referred to in Gal. 2:10. Thus I Corinthians is related to this cluster of letters around the crisis.

I Corinthians, however, was not the first letter actually written by Paul to the Corinthians, for in it[3] he refers to a letter written earlier. II Corinthians gives every evidence of composite

[1] See 15:32.
[2] I Cor. 16:1–9. [3] I Cor. 5:9.

128

character, and it is possible that it contains a fragment[4] of this earlier letter.

At all events, the Corinthian correspondence reflects the evangelization of people in Corinth (a large and important commercial city near Athens) and the foundation of a church predominantly gentile in constitution. Sometime after the founding of the church Paul undertook his long and effective work in Ephesus. In Ephesus he heard through two sources distressing reports of the church at Corinth: (1) "Chloe's people"[5] (probably slaves who were transferred from Corinth to Ephesus) indicated several problems which had arisen; (2) a letter from the Corinthians to Paul[6] set forth several questions. This letter may have been delivered by Stephanas, Fortunatus, and Achaicus.[7] The letter mentioned in I Cor. 5:9 and the canonical I Corinthians were written in response to the conditions thus disclosed. These conditions in part also occasioned the further correspondence.

These conditions were anything but desirable; for, while Paul began (as he does in all letters except Galatians) with a thanksgiving and with compliment, he immediately passed to serious criticism. One unfortunate development was that the Corinthians had divided themselves into cliques and factions: there was a Cephas party, an Apollos party, a Paul party, and a Christ party. Paul could only deprecate this with the utmost sternness.

Second, litigious Corinthians, instead of settling differences privately and peaceably among themselves, thus keeping their quarrels within their religious relationship, were suing each other in the civil courts. Since this involved certain "pagan" religious ceremonies, Paul must sternly forbid it.

Some of the Corinthians, like the Colossians, were going too far in philosophical speculation. Paul reminds these that his own way of putting his messages, which was quite different from the philosophical, was by deliberate choice. He insists that he was capable of putting it in that form if he chose, and he did so when he was with people who were capable of following him. He had refrained from this method in evangelizing the Corinthians be-

[4] 6:14—7:1.   [6] I Cor. 7:1.
[5] I Cor. 1:11.   [7] I Cor. 16:17.

cause they were not capable, and he reminds them that their behavior proves that he was correct in his estimate of them.

Paul does not permit them to play him and Apollos over against one another. He insists that he and Apollos are fellow-workers, not vying with each other for prestige.

Gross immorality among the Corinthians is treated strictly and harshly. This must be viewed as meeting a situation in which former "pagans" experienced problems when their old patterns came into conflict with the standards of their new lives as spirit-persons. Paul is uncompromising here; he goes so far[8] as to have performed some kind of mystical ceremony in which a man living in incest has his body delivered to Satan.

When we come to the questions which the Corinthians had asked in their letter,[9] interesting situations are discovered. Some of the married people in Corinth were living apart, since they understood that their lives as spirit-persons meant that they must not indulge in physical passions even within the conventions of marriage. Others wondered whether they should marry. Married persons whose partners were "pagans" wondered whether they should continue to live with these unregenerate husbands or wives. Paul counsels that, while ideally the celibate life (such as he lives) is best, many persons find it impractical. Since it is dangerous to suppress sexual desire, it is more practical, Paul says, to express it within the conventions of marriage. He advises married people not to leave a "pagan" husband or wife; his reasoning here is highly mystical: the union blesses the other person and consecrates the children. Obviously, Paul's teaching in this passage is conditioned by his expectation of the imminent end of the age—that is why there is little or no use to marry, since there will not be time to bring up families of children. The responsibilities of marriage, further, are time-consuming and permit only divided attention to the Lord's work.

Other problems, also, are discussed. The Corinthians were doubtful about eating meat which was offered for sale after having been slaughtered for sacrifice in the "pagan" temples. Paul sensibly told them that nothing had happened to the food; their

---

[8] I Cor. 5:3 ff.   [9] See I Cor., chaps. 7 ff.

guide should be whether any conscientious scruples were involved; if so, they should refrain from eating such food.[10]

This matter, discussed in other relationships in chapter 10, shows further effects of the gentile environment upon Paul. The figures in these passages[11] are all from Hellenistic life and show thorough familiarity with Hellenistic institutions.

In I Corinthians, chapter 11, Paul discusses two more unsatisfactory features of the Corinthian community: women have been taking too prominent a part in the church meetings; and the observance of the Lord's Supper has been grossly perverted—gluttonous people have overeaten and some have become drunk. With the same sternness evinced elsewhere in the letter, Paul strictly charges the Corinthians to correct these abuses. He would have no confusion of this Christian celebration with gentile revels.

Chapters 12–14 give the classic references to the spiritistic practices integral to Paul's conception of the religious life. The Corinthians were too fond of the least valuable of the spirit manifestations—speaking in a tongue. Their meetings became so disorderly, with several people speaking at the same time in unintelligible gibberish, that outsiders coming into the meetings could only draw the conclusion that they were crazy.[12] Paul desires only that order be secured. He does not deprecate this ecstatic behavior, not even speaking gibberish; he thanks God[13] that he does this more than the Corinthians do! But he does it in private. So he insists that in the meetings for common worship there must be "prophecy"—inspired ecstatic preaching that is intelligible, reading of Scripture, singing, prayer, and a certain amount of gibberish (but this latter only by two or three, one at a time, and only if someone is inspired to "interpret" the unintelligible message of the Spirit[14]).

A further problem of the Corinthians was the resurrection of Jesus, with its implications for the resurrection of believers. These Greek-thinking people could not understand how a spirit

[10] I Cor. 10.

[11] I Cor. 2:6–16, 4:9, 9:24–27.

[12] I Cor. 14:23.

[13] I Cor. 14:18.

[14] I Cor. 14:26–33.

could have a body. Paul "explains" this by pointing out that there are spiritual bodies as well as physical bodies. In this section he gives the valuable reference to the list of the resurrection appearances,[15] citing his own as the final one. The letter closes with instruction about collecting money and with personal references and greetings.

I Corinthians shows that Paul had met much opposition in Corinth. At one point[16] Paul's language becomes very strong; he gives the Corinthians their choice. He expects to come to them. Shall he come in a spirit of love and gentleness or with a club? Some of the Corinthians were suspicious of him.[17] It is easy to see that the incestuous person so straightforwardly condemned[18] would not be kindly disposed to Paul. The people of the Cephas and Apollos parties were presumably critical of him. At all events, a serious situation developed in Corinth, and Paul had to meet it without compromise. For a time it looked as though his control would be lost. This condition, bad enough in itself, was the more critical when it became a part of the great crisis which now appeared.

Chapter 9 of I Corinthians seems to reflect a developed stage in this conflict over Paul's authority; its stage is below that of II Cor. 10–13 but higher than that of the remainder of I Corinthians. Since, as shall be seen, II Corinthians has to be partitioned to understand its parts, it seems necessary to regard I Corinthians, chapter 9 (at least 9:1–18, but perhaps also vss. 19–27), as the fragment of a letter written between the canonical I Corinthians and II Corinthians, chapters 10–13. Perhaps Timothy's mission[19] was a failure, so that upon his return he brought further bad news of an already difficult situation. Paul had said[20] that he was coming to Corinth again; some had thought that he was not, and were boasting about it. Grimly Paul says that he is coming and that he leaves it to the Corinthians whether he shall come with a spirit of gentleness or with a club. In II Cor. 13:1 he says that his next visit will be his third. When had the second one

---

[15] I Cor. 15:3–8.
[16] 4:21.
[17] I Cor. 4:3.
[18] I Cor. 5:1 ff.
[19] Referred to in I Cor. 4:17.
[20] I Cor. 4:18–21.

occurred? Was it after the second visit that the heated words of I Corinthians, chapter 9, were written?

At all events, in I Corinthians, chapter 9, Paul is on the defensive. Apparently, his freedom to do as he did was questioned;[21] certainly, his apostleship was doubted.[22] Some wanted to investigate him.[23] His good faith in money matters was impugned[24]—with irony Paul reminds the Corinthians that he took no other pay than the satisfaction which came from his efforts. He insists upon his rights, even though he does not exercise them.[25] Evidently his way of life was called into question; he had to explain why he seemed to be inconsistent as he dealt with Jews and with non-Jews.[26]

This may furnish the key to the understanding of the whole situation; for, when the next item of the Corinthian correspondence is examined (II Corinthians, chaps. 10–13), the tension has increased and its focus is narrowed. The instigators of the trouble are plainly Jewish opponents ("If they are Hebrews, so am I! If they are Israelites, so am I! If they are descendants of Abraham, so am I!"[27]).

The tenor of this entire section is bitter. It begins in sarcasm and rises soon to anger. The criticisms of his opponents appear: Paul is humble in the face-to-face relationship and bold at a distance.[28] His letters are impressive, but his personal appearance is unimpressive and he is a poor speaker.[29] He is inferior to other apostles.[30] Again the money question is referred to (apparently some accused Paul of subterfuge); he accepted no money from the Corinthians and then used for himself the money which was contributed by them for the poor—at all events, Paul cites the claim made by his opponents that he took the Corinthians in by a trick.[31] That the money question was important appears from the fact that Paul repeatedly states his honesty and insists that

[21] Vs. 1.

[22] Vs. 2.

[23] Vs. 3.

[24] Vs. 18.

[25] Vss. 5–15.

[26] Vss. 19–23.

[27] II Cor. 11:22.

[28] II Cor. 10:1.

[29] II Cor. 10:10.

[30] II Cor. 11:5.

[31] II Cor. 12:16.

he wants not the Corinthians' money but themselves,[32] and he declares that neither Timothy nor any other helper had accepted any money.

Paul takes the offensive in the bitter argument, and here his tone rises to invective. He admits that he is not impressive physically and that he is a poor speaker, and he points only to the spiritual power of his preaching and his deeds.[33] He points out[34] that, at all events, it was he who had first come all the way to Corinth to evangelize them, not these opponents who came only after he had prepared the way. He insists upon his possession of knowledge, whatever may be his lack as a preacher.[35] He explains why he has accepted no money.[36] He declares that he is in no degree inferior to these opponents who think so highly of themselves;[37] indeed, he savagely returns their claims—they are sham apostles, dishonest workmen, only pretending to be apostles.[38]

Then Paul reluctantly meets them on their own ground and compares his record with theirs.[39] However disinclined to descend to this level, he moves to accept their challenge; and in a deeply moving flight of language he tells his readers more about himself than the heroic narrative of Luke-Acts contains. In brief, this is the picture of an ardent worker utterly expending himself in the discharge of spiritual energy to accomplish a work which is the dearest value of his life.

Then Paul, still on the offensive, raises the question of spiritual experiences.[40] Which of these opponents has shared his visions of the exalted Christ? Who among them has been caught up into the third heaven? Who has had comparable revelations from God? This proves that he is in no degree inferior to these "super-apostles," as they think of themselves. With withering sarcasm Paul closes this part of the argument by citing again the question on which he was so sensitive; he begs the Corinthians to forgive

[32] II Cor. 12:14–18.

[33] II Cor. 10:3–11.

[34] II Cor. 10:14.

[35] II Cor. 11:6.

[36] II Cor. 11:7–10.

[37] II Cor. 10:12, 11:5.

[38] II Cor. 11:12, 13 f.

[39] II Cor. 11:16–33.

[40] II Cor. 12:1–13.

him for the wrong he has done in not accepting money from them!

He proposes a third visit.[41] Having brandished a club before[42] and wielding it verbally here, it is made plain that on the third visit no one would be spared.

As has been pointed out, the only rational understanding of the Corinthian correspondence is to read it as partitioned. The whole may be listed as follows:

1. The letter referred to in I Cor. 5:9; perhaps a fragment of this is found in II Cor. 6:14—7:1.

2. The Corinthians wrote a letter to Paul (I Cor. 7:1).

3. The canonical I Corinthians, minus chapter 9.

4. A letter, a fragment of which is I Corinthians, chapter 9.

5. A letter, a fragment of which is II Corinthians, chapters 10–13.

6. The letter which consists of II Corinthians, chapters 1–9 (minus 6:14-7:1).

The Letter to the Galatians is the key to the whole situation. It reflects conflict and opposition from beginning to end. Its tone is indicated in the fact that this is Paul's only letter in which he has no thanksgiving for the attainment of the recipients; there is nothing for which he congratulates the Galatians.

They had been evangelized by him and had received him and his message warmly.[43] They had accepted his gospel and had accepted the way of life which he taught.[44] Paul had been with them twice.[45] Recently, however, some evangelists with a different good news[46] had appeared among the Galatians and had completely unsettled them. These people were extreme legalists —obviously they were Jewish propagandists who represented to the gentile Galatians that they must accept the obligations of the Jewish Torah to be pronounced acquitted (justified, made upright). These people denied Paul's apostleship; that is why he defends it.[47] True, he had not been one of the associates of Jesus, but he had "seen" the risen Lord. They accused Paul of incon-

---

[41] II Cor. 12:14, 13:1.

[42] I Cor. 4:21.

[43] Gal. 4:14.

[44] Gal. 1:6, 3:2–5, 5:7, 13.

[45] Gal. 4:13.

[46] Gal. 1:6 ff.

[47] Gal. 1:11–24.

sistency: he preached freedom from the Law, but he had some people circumcised.[48] Apparently it was alleged that Paul's teaching of the futility of the Law led to licentiousness.[49]

The Galatians had been convinced by these propagandists. They had already begun to keep the Sabbath and other religious special days;[50] they were at the point of accepting circumcision and becoming Jewish proselytes—joining the Jewish people.[51] It was to forestall this that Paul wrote the letter. He could not come to Galatia, although he wished very much that he might:[52] it fits perfectly at this juncture to picture Paul with his hands full in a desperate attempt to maintain control over the Corinthians while he did his necessary work in Ephesus.

Paul attempts to meet the situation by answering the arguments of his opponents and by convincing the Galatians that his way of life is the right one. He reviews his own case: how he used to be an opponent of the members of the Christ cults—how, as a fanatical Jew, he was a persecutor of the church. He tells how God had reversed all this by revealing his Son to him. This, he insists, was the source of his good news—he did not acquire it from any man! He recounts his visits to Jerusalem—only two; and in these he was not "taught" anything. He reminds the Galatians how they were evangelized to the good news of freedom and the life of spirit. Do they now wish to go back to the old life, to become enslaved again?

The crux of the whole matter was that the Galatians were almost convinced that to achieve the highest religious life they must become circumcised, keep the Jewish Law, and thus join the Jewish people. Against this Paul is fighting.

His logical arguments[53] are less convincing than his arguments from experience. His logic requires dubious interpretation of Scripture.[54] Yet Paul has an effective figure—the Law being, in God's purpose, the slave (*paidagogos*) who conducts the pupil

---

[48] Gal. 5:11.

[49] Gal. 5:13, 16–24.

[50] Gal. 4:10, 11.

[51] Gal. 5:2–6.

[52] Gal. 4:20 f.

[53] Gal. 3:7—4:31.

[54] Note the allegory in 4:22–31 and the irrelevant fact of the singular number of a noun which obviously has the collective meaning in 3:16.

to his master.[55] He has the noble statement of utter individualism: in Christ it does not matter whether one is Jew or non-Jew, slave or freeman, man or woman. This is, indeed, the simplest putting of Paul's good news.

As in Corinth and elsewhere, there were people in Galatia who had the wrong conception of the relation between spirit and flesh. Taking Paul's antipathy to the Law at its face value and having become spirit-persons, they lived as though the body did not matter, and thus they were led into licentiousness and libertinism.[56] Paul reminds them sharply that spirit-persons must live according to the spirit—live on the spirit level of life, not as flesh-persons on the level of flesh.

The whole situation is related to what Paul recounts in Gal. 2:1–10. He tells the Galatians how, fourteen years after his conversion,[57] he had made his second visit to Jerusalem, going by spiritistic direction.[58] The point at issue was this same problem: the relation of non-Jews and Jews in the cults of Christ. Paul had laid his "good news" before a formal conference, telling what he had been doing all these years. Titus, a Greek, was a sort of "Exhibit A" of the non-Jew who was having the worthiest possible religious life—thus evidence of Paul's point that the non-Jew did not need to become a Jew (specifically, submit to circumcision and keep the Torah) to be pronounced acquitted. The point was bitterly argued. People whom Paul designates as "false brothers"—i.e., not really brothers at all—had been "smuggled" into the meeting, there to "spy out" the freedom that the non-Jews and all people of Paul's churches enjoyed. These rigorous people insisted upon the necessity of non-Jews becoming Jews. Paul defended his good news tenaciously, and he insists that he won his point. The leaders—James, Cephas, and John—accepted his case without reservation; they had nothing to lay upon him and Barnabas, and they pledged their co-operation.[59] They agreed that Paul and Barnabas were to continue their work with non-Jews, while they would evangelize Jews (Peter is especially

[55] Gal. 3:23–25.
[56] Gal. 5:13–24.
[57] See II Cor. 12:2.
[58] Gal. 2:2.
[59] Gal. 2:7–9.

mentioned; since he is spoken of in the same sentence in which Cephas is named,[60] it appears that Peter and Cephas were not the same person). Thus an agreement, a working policy, was reached.

But an analysis of the Corinthian correspondence and Phil. 3:2–16, the writings which reflect the great crisis, indicates that this agreement was not kept by certain Jews. In spite of their pledged word, these emissaries of the "different good news" had come to the Galatians and to Corinth (had they visited Philippi also?) and had represented their position. It has been shown how this complicated the already bad situation in Corinth; Galatians shows how critical the outlook was in Galatia. Probably at this time Paul wrote Phil. 3:2–16 as warning. The defection of the Galatians was threatened; further loss of control in Corinth was a strong possibility; and it looked as though much of Paul's work would be nullified and wrecked. This explains the heated tones of Galatians and II Corinthians, chapters 10–13.

Nowhere else in his letters does Paul exhibit such extreme emotion of this kind. Anger is plain in II Corinthians, chapters 10–13; contempt, in Philippians 3:2 ff.; and in Gal. 5:12 Paul does not hesitate to become coarse. He insists not only that the Galatians need not become Jews but that they must not, telling them that, if they do, they will lose their relationship with Christ.[61]

This was the great crisis. What was its outcome? The further Corinthian correspondence enables an answer as far as the Corinthians were concerned, but one can only guess about the Galatians. This much can be said: Since Paul in subsequent letters does not mention what would have been to him a tragic loss if the Galatians had failed to heed his words, it may be inferred that, like the Corinthians, they were convinced by his letter.

The significance of the crisis for Paul's total work cannot be exaggerated. He had proclaimed a good news which was not merely a supplement to Judaism but a different way of life. Paul continued to regard himself a Jew. Being a follower of Christ did

60 Gal. 2:7 ff.   61 Gal. 5:2–6.

not de-Judaize him or any other Jew. But it created for Paul a new life, a different way of life. It was freedom—freeing the spirit, satisfying the whole life, giving assurance of guiltlessness as it gave certainty of salvation. This was what he had offered to all, Jew and non-Jew alike. Experience had taught him that life according to Jewish Law did not give this freedom. It was to be in only one way: by belief, faith, in Jesus. When one believed that Jesus was Lord and Christ, that God had raised him from among the dead, when one confessed that Jesus was Lord Christ, his nature was changed—whether he were Jew or non-Jew. He was a new creature, a spirit-person. Paul could not allow that in this he had been mistaken and wrong. He insisted that he was right, and he fought vigorously for his conviction. Whether he won or lost the single battle in Galatia, he won the final victory.

XIII

PAUL'S LETTERS AND PAUL'S RELIGION

THE crisis in Paul's work was at its height when he wrote II Corinthians, chapters 10–13; Galatians; and Phil. 3:2–16. The outcome—at least in Corinth—can be seen in I Cor. 1–9.

Paul had been in an agony of apprehension as soon as his fourth letter to the Corinthians had been sent on its way. He had been so crushed that he had despaired of life.[1] He had written with many tears;[2] he knew that his harshness would cause pain.[3] But the critical situation had demanded stern measures. However, Paul had been afraid that he had been too severe, had gone too far. He could not contain himself where he was; he therefore decided to go to Corinth. Apparently he had sent his harsh letter by Titus and had arranged to meet the returning messenger. To give Titus time to take the letter and handle the situation, Paul took the long route, going first to Troas. It was his plan, after crossing the upper Aegean, to go through Macedonia to Corinth.

But at Troas he suffered the same agony of apprehension, particularly over the fact that Titus, whom he had hoped to meet there, had failed to come.[4] He therefore went on to Macedonia,[5] where it appears that Titus met him with the good news that the Corinthians were entirely amenable to his control.[6] Paul thereupon dispatched his final letter to the Corinthians[7] and timed his own arrival sometime after it.

This final communication is as emotional as the three docu-

[1] II Cor. 1:8.

[2] II Cor. 2:4.

[3] II Cor. 2:4, 5, 7:8–11.

[4] II Cor. 2:12 f.

[5] II Cor. 2:13.

[6] II Cor. 7:6 ff.

[7] II Cor. 1–9.

ments of the crisis, but in this case the emotion is that of joy. He now praises the Corinthians, counsels them not to be too hard on the men who had caused the trouble,[8] and in the tenderest and most beautiful passage which he ever wrote (II Corinthians, chaps. 4–5) he unveils his heart. 'He expresses complete satisfaction with the manner in which the Corinthians have followed his instructions.[9]

Lastly, in II Corinthians, chapters 8 and 9, Paul gives final instruction concerning the collection of money. This had been a particular objective since the important conference at Jerusalem; that he and Barnabas should bear the poor in mind was the only injunction which the conference had laid upon Paul. He had been accustomed to do this; now, he says, he "took pains" to do it. He had written to the Corinthians about it before;[10] he had given directions also to the Galatians. The people in Macedonia had done their part.[11] Now Paul proposes to come to Corinth and get their contributions; if the collection is large enough, he will take it to Jerusalem himself (with proper safeguards to insure that no one will suspect him of embezzlement[12]).

Presumably Paul made his way to Corinth. It was from there, apparently, that he wrote his last two letters. One of these is a brief letter of introduction of a woman, Phoebe, of the church of Cenchreae (a suburb of Corinth) to the people of another church. The place to which Phoebe was traveling was presumably Ephesus, since some of the names cited are of persons located there. This letter is now attached to the Letter to the Romans, of which it forms chapter 16.

It would appear, on the basis of internal evidence contained in Paul's letters, that the Letter to the Romans is his last. Its content well suits this view. It is a survey and a prospective view. Its first part (Romans, chaps. 1–8), after an introduction, surveys the world's religious need. First the bad case of the non-Jews is sketched, then the almost equally bad case of the Jews. Paul declares that, as the non-Jews had sought God through

8 II Cor. 2:6 ff.

9 II Cor. 7:11–13.   11 II Cor. 8:1 ff.

10 I Cor. 16:1–4.   12 II Cor. 8:20.

wisdom and failed to find him, so the Jews had sought him in the Law and had failed to find him. But Paul does not stop with the negative. He shows that the only way to find God is through faith. That "the man who is pronounced acquitted lives by his faith" is the theme. Thus Paul shows, to his satisfaction (doubtless other Jews would not have accepted his demonstration), that the Jewish Torah was a perversion of what God had intended in revealing himself to his people. Thus God sent Jesus, his Son, to accomplish what had been missed through wisdom and Law. Anyone, non-Jew or Jew, who believes the good news about Jesus is pronounced acquitted. Paul recounts a case, as though it were his own, of the unhappy result which follows the endeavor to live by the Law; and similarly he sketches, in a paean of noble words, the cosmic result of the acceptance of faith in Christ.

In Romans, chapters 9–11, Paul adverts to a perplexing contemporary fact. It was God's promise that his people should be saved. For them to be saved they must believe, must exercise faith in Jesus. But the Jews had not done so. Did this mean that God's promises were invalid? This, of course, Paul cannot admit. He has recourse to two means of explaining away the obvious fact. On the one hand, he makes the point that anyone who believes is a descendant of Abraham and thus one of God's people. On the other hand, he accounts for Israel's failure to believe by an ingenious explanation. God, he says, has hardened Israel's heart. This he did so that the good news might first be taken to the non-Jews. But this obduracy was to be only temporary; now that the good news has been taken to the non-Jews, soon God will soften Israel's heart, and Israel, too, will believe.

Romans, chapters 12–14, is occupied with teachings of a generally applicable nature, i.e., not limited to the Romans but intended for believers everywhere. Here are discussed some of the old problems: spiritual gifts, basic ethical practices, the question of the state, keeping special days, practicing dietary distinctions, and others.

In Romans, chapter 15, Paul gives some indications of his plans. He is going to Jerusalem with the money collected; presumably the amount is satisfactory to him.[13] He had more than once wished to visit Rome, but other needs had prevented.[14] But when he has discharged this obligation in Jerusalem, he expects to go next to Spain; and at that time he hopes to stop for a while in Rome.

Paul expects grave difficulties in Jerusalem. This is plainly shown in his request that the Romans "agonize" with him in prayer for "those who are disobedient" in Judea.[15] Apparently his experiences up to this point warned him what he might expect.

What was the outcome? Since there is no further letter from Paul, the historian must depend upon secondary sources and tradition. The closing chapters of Luke-Acts relate that Paul did, indeed, encounter the trouble which he had feared. It was instigated by Asian Jews.[16] This is significant. The great crisis had been largely Asian; and it, too, was instigated by Jews. This datum appears to be a correlating element between Paul's letters and tradition. Paul was arrested; and after long detention and various vicissitudes, he claimed, so the tradition states, his right to appeal his case to the emperor and was transported to Rome.

Here secondary written tradition ends. Other tradition agrees that Paul died in Rome, a martyr. His death removed from the scene one of the most creative leaders ever produced in Christianity. In his letters and in the churches which his energy had brought into being, he continued to live.

The particular usefulness of Paul's letters for the historian of religion is that they document his religion. They show that he articulated principles which were latent in Christianity from the days of its beginning. Indeed, it may be said—and the point is not merely academic—that Paul particularized and brought to focal development processes which were indispensable for Christianity's progress as a world religion. That this is not merely academic appears from the fact that there were other leaders, also, who helped to effect the transition of Christianity from its place

---

[13] Vss. 25 ff.

[14] Vss. 22 ff.

[15] Rom. 15:30-33.

[16] Acts 21:27, 24:18.

within Judaism to its position of power in competition with all contemporary cults.

The point was, of course, that Judaism was a quasi-national religion. Although the Jewish people were not a nation, they were and they continued to be a folk, so that to practice the Jewish religion required a person to be or to become a Jew. Christianity, when it could be called such, was a thoroughly individualistic religion, even though many of its aspects were social.

As Hellenistic Judaism was a bridge from Palestinian Judaism to gentile Christianity, Paul was one of those who constructed the bridge. In understanding his religion, the starting-point is the perception of the basic fact that his religion was Judaism—but, further, that it was Hellenistic Judaism. Paul was never conscious of being aught but a loyal Jew. But his unhappy experience of legalism had led him to shift the focus from the Torah to faith and spirit, and this led to an articulation of religion which Jews then and ever since have felt to be incompatible with traditional Judaism.

Modern scholars have devoted much attention to the various factors which led Paul to this adaptation. Some of them have come to the conclusion that the explanation is simple: Paul responded to his gentile environment by "taking over" aspects and values of the contemporary gentile cults, particularly the mystery religions. As these scholars see it, it was simply a case of adaptation to environment. But, as usual, when it is said that a development is "simply" something or other, the statement is an oversimplification. When, for example, it is said that the "parallels" to the mystery religions reflected in Paul's letters indicate that he must have joined one[17]—e.g., the Orphic cult—this is to overlook the fact that no one could have done that and have remained a Jew. The horror of idolatry which characterized Jews generally would have been sufficient to have precluded this.

Other scholars, on the contrary, look to Judaism to discover the "source" of everything in Paul's religion. Certainly much of

[17] See V. D. Macchioro, *From Orpheus to Paul* (New York: Henry Holt & Co., 1930).

its content is thus accounted for: the use of Jewish Scripture, some of the "theological" content (e.g., the conception of God, ideas of the Messiah, the apocalyptic expectation, much of the ethical teaching), characteristic ways of thought and expression, religious vocabulary, and the like. It is said that, in spite of his antipathy to law, Paul's discussions reflect the rabbi's manner of teaching. The statement of Acts, "I sat at Gamaliel's feet," is enough to convince many that Paul had studied for the rabbinate. The question is a technical one; it must suffice to say here that the data of Paul's letters do not bear this allegation out. While (as in I Cor. 10:1–5) Paul uses what is known as the "haggadic" method of interpreting Scripture, there is not a single example in his writings of the type of interpretation which the professional interpreters customarily used (such as is incorporated in the Talmuds). What can safely be said is that Paul reflects the method of using Scripture which any Jewish "layman" would have imbibed in the synagogue.

Further, there are certain elements in Paul's religion, appearing in the way of life which he inculcated in his churches, that cannot have been derived from Judaism. For example, the Lord's Supper certainly, and baptism probably, were sacramental in nature in Paul's understanding of them. Judaism had no sacraments. The nearest approach to sacrament in Judaism was the Temple cultus, and for the common Jewish life the Temple was quite secondary to the synagogue and the school.

How, then, are the objective facts to be understood? The key to the whole matter is Paul's own experience of religion. As a Hellenistic Jew he did his best to live in his traditional pattern. He was precocious; and, as history subsequently witnessed, he was a religious genius. His Hellenistic environment subjected him to the influence of values from gentile culture, including religious values. In his experience of Judaism, including that of a persecutor of followers of Jesus, he saw that non-Jews were capable of a worthy and a valid religious experience, and often exhibited this in their lives. He therefore drew the conclusion that the rigid limits of Judaism as the religion of a people were untenable. The pattern of individualistic religious experience was before him in his gentile environment. He therefore responded to its influence and adapted his conception of the religious life accordingly.

There can be no doubt that "Pauline Christianity" was a salvation cult—a religion of the salvation of the individual. It is inescapable that its pattern was the result of adaptation to the values which he saw in his environment. His attitude toward these values had changed. Without being conscious that he was any less the Jew, certainly without "joining" a gentile religion, he affirmed strongly the value which he had violently rejected before.

It is another inescapable fact that neither the "life" nor the teaching of Jesus was of primary importance in Paul's religion. He says that he got his good news by revelation from God: God revealed his Son "in" him. This means that in his own experience of religion he had some kind of vision of Jesus in which he made another reversal of values: whereas before he had persecuted people who called Jesus "Messiah," he now made that identification himself. In his subsequent reflections upon the all-important experience he seems to have interpreted it in terms of Jewish apocalyptic messianism. But by the same token he also applied terms which had their natural source in Greek religion: Jesus is "Lord" as well as Christ. Thus in his *formulation* of his religion he used terms, frames of reference, and vehicles of expression which were gentile in origin—just as he used content, concepts, and vocabulary derived from Judaism.

The important point for the reader to bear in mind is that Paul's experience and achievements had the result of freeing the nascent religion from certain limitations. Paul was not alone in this, as he himself readily points out. It happens that because of his energy his achievement was conspicuously great; it happens, also, that because Paul wrote letters which were preserved we know much more of what he accomplished. Christianity had to adapt to its environment or not survive; it is not likely that as a trend within Judaism it would have survived, unless perhaps as a Jewish sect.

But the fact was that Christianity had an infinite capacity for adaptation. At all events, it did change. It is of the utmost significance that its adaptation took the form of a religion of individual salvation. This was what was needed. There were many such religions current, as chapter iv of this book has shown. The history of Christianity is the story of its successful competition with all contemporary religions—Judaism and gentile cults. Christianity succeeded in this struggle because it had something to offer to the people of its time. The values which owed their origin to Judaism were of the first importance; it should not be forgotten that from almost any standard of measurement Judaism was certainly the "best" religion in its world. But Judaism was and remained the religion of a people. If Christianity had, so to speak, remained "within" Judaism—if Paul's opponents in the great crisis had prevailed—there would not have been any "Christianity." In other words, the emerging religion would have had so little distinctiveness that it would have been absorbed in the competing religions which were older and established.

On the contrary, Christianity survived along with Judaism. Christianity endured because it satisfied all the needs which the various religions satisfied only in part—and satisfied more needs. Christianity survived because it assimilated all sorts of people, many of whom made their contributions. Continuing Christianity was inclusive of many elements, some of which were extremely diverse. Christianity triumphed because it had the capacity to adapt, to assimilate, and to create. Being new and unbound, it could become what it needed to be in order to compete successfully. Because its leaders had remarkable energy and because its people had boundless enthusiasm, Christianity's rise and expansion were phenomenally rapid. Within a short time it became inclusive of non-Jews and began the evangelization of Gentiles in their own lands. Probably within a generation the non-Jews outnumbered the Jews within it, and in influence the Gentiles were far the more important to Christianity's further expansion.

Within Paul's generation Christian institutions began to take shape. Churches were founded, and there was developed a consciousness of the relation of the churches of one section to those of another. Paul's letters show a lively consciousness of "all the churches,"[18] and there is a glimmer[19] of the conception of "the church." In Christianity generally, and in Paul's churches particularly, ways of life became patterned; Christians developed their ethical codes from experience. Obviously, the people in Palestine had their characteristic ways of life; gentile Christians differed from these patterns markedly. There was no one "Christian" way of life; there were several, but ways of life developed and became "Christian" in each case. There were distinctive cult practices. There were certain teachings. Christians met for common worship, and this inevitably became patterned. Obviously, there were liturgical elements in the common worship. Christians took over Jewish Scripture—in Greek translation—and made it their own. It was not long after Paul's death that the beginnings of a Christian Scripture were made. Interestingly enough, Paul's own letters, although they were not written with any such idea in mind, became the first nucleus of Christian Scripture. Church workers presently found their duties patterned, so that "ministries" emerged—again not the same in different localities, but with wide divergence in detail.

It is fortunate, indeed, that we have Paul's letters, for they inform us not of Paul's work alone but also of other leaders. Much of Paul's greatness lay in the fact that he had the capacity to create and to adapt. His own experience led him to broaden the horizons of his own religion; this had the unexpected result that it broadened the horizons of growing Christianity.

[18] II Cor. 11:28, 8:24.   [19] Col. 1:18, 24 f.

XIV

THE SYNOPTIC GOSPELS AS LITERATURE (A)

THE gospels were the books of the early church. They represent collections of materials which the early evangelists found useful for religious edification. Gospels were produced in response to felt religious needs within the developing communities; they reflect at the same time the traditions about the earthly Jesus and the interpretations which the early preachers made concerning him. After Paul they represent the earliest records of the developing theology of the Christian evangelists. It was the activity of the church which caused them to be written; they were the church's books.

Literary and historical study of the Synoptic Gospels has attempted to understand the relationships which exist among them, the conditions under which they were composed, the traditions which stretched behind them, the purposes and aims which motivated the editors, the identity of the editors or compilers, and the religious values within them. It has not been the aim of the so-called "higher critics" to destroy but rather to analyze and to reconstruct.

A cursory examination of the literary character of the gospels brings the conclusion that the materials spring from several strata of folk activity. A first reading of any one of the Synoptic Gospels informs the analytical mind that the sermons, the old stories, the parables, the sayings, the miracle tales, and the legends represent collections from the life of a people; they did not originate in the imagination of one creative author. A second conclusion is also inescapable: the primary concern of all this literature is religious motivation and indoctrination.

Study of the gospels early led to the conclusion that the first three (or Synoptic) books were intricately interrelated. Almost unquestioned now is the conclusion that Matthew and Luke had the Gospel of Mark before them as they wrote. Some scholars maintained that this was an earlier "edition" of Mark than that which we now have,[1] but the great majority insisted that the evidence demanded no "rough" edition of the earliest gospel. That the Matthean and Lucan compilers used Mark is attested by their adherence to his order. Usually both Matthew and Luke follow Mark slavishly; where one differs from his order, the other follows; in no case do the two agree against their model. Again, Matthew and Luke tend to agree in the wording of materials contained also in Mark, but in materials common to them but not in Mark the differences are more noticeable. Further, changes in the wording or order from Mark to either of the other Synoptics show a movement toward refinement of meaning, or from simple to complex—a tendency which indicates the results of additional years of tradition-making and editing. Finally, Matthew and Luke, together, reproduce in fairly exact form all of Mark with the exception of twenty-seven verses, a fact which indicates a heavy degree of dependency.

In addition to the Gospel of Mark, the editors of Matthew and Luke-Acts had before them several sources which can be more or less accurately identified. A collection made up largely of teaching materials must have been in circulation at the time Mark was composed. Either it was unavailable to Mark, or he knew of its use and preferred to have it read separately, or inclusion of materials from it did not suit his dramatic purpose—which of these is the correct explanation we cannot be certain. The agreement of Matthew and Luke is very noticeable on many non-Marcan materials; these have been reconstructed (in various forms) by many scholars into a source called "Q," from the German *Quelle*, or source.

The Lucan and Matthean compilers further availed themselves

---

[1] The Ur-Marcus theory; see especially the critical treatment and references in James Moffatt, *An Introduction to the Literature of the New Testament* (3d ed.; New York: Charles Scribner's Sons, 1929), pp. 191–94.

of special sources, now most difficult to identify. Luke seems to have used a collection which has been called "L," which may have involved a special passion narrative. His infancy narrative has usually been attributed to still another source. The Matthean compiler evidently had access to special materials which have been identified as Palestinian-Syrian, including a birth story. The special Matthean materials were grouped by Canon Streeter[2] in a minor source which he denominated as "M." These attempts to identify large sources within the Synoptic Gospels culminated in the multiple-source theories, to which many scholars contributed.[3]

Where the multiple-source theories ended, the work of form criticism (*Formgeschichte*) began. Its interest was to separate the editorial, introductory, and transitional materials from the stories as they circulated in the early communities. Its proponents began with the sources as the scholars had delineated them and sought to push back to the individual pericopes, to discover on the basis of form and of environmental tests what stories, sayings, parables, miracle tales, sermons, and legends were used in early gatherings of believers. The aim of form criticism is thus simply to see the first step in gospel production, the naïve and unadorned pericopes as they appeared to the individuals who first thought of welding them into a "source."[4] Some of the results of the form critics' work have already been seen in chapter vii.

We have thus traced the labors of the New Testament scholars back from the finished gospels to the sources and thence to the individual units which circulated in the early communities. Let us now attempt a reconstruction of the process in chronological

---

[2] *The Four Gospels.*

[3] See the summary discussions in F. C. Grant, *The Growth of the Gospels* (New York: Abingdon, 1933), and Riddle, *Early Christian Life.* For the multiple-source theory in application, consult H. B. Sharman, *Records of the Life of Jesus* (Chicago, 1917), which adheres to the Burton-Goodspeed reconstruction. The earliest statement of this theory may be seen in E. D. Burton, "Some Principles of Literary Criticism as Applied to the Synoptic Gospels," in *The Decennial Publications* (Chicago, 1904). For the four-source theory, see Streeter, *The Four Gospels.*

[4] See particularly the works of Dibelius and Bultmann.

order, noting the probable effects upon the tradition in each stage of the movement "toward a gospel."

The traditions indicate that Jesus was a nonprofessional teacher whose following was largely from the "common people." The extent of his popularity during his lifetime cannot be accurately gauged, but the fact of his death and the ensuing "resurrection appearances" stimulated the beginning of a movement which rapidly became "Christianity." It is often a source of wonder that gospels were not written earlier. In brief, the delay was brought about by several causes: (1) The intellectual and economic status of the group with which Jesus was most intimately associated was sufficiently low to deter writing. (2) By the time the movement reached important proportions, the collection of data presented an extreme difficulty. (3) The early believers lived in imminent expectation of the "return of the Lord." Collection of data and the writing of books paled in significance before preparation for the *Parousia*. (4) The habit of teachers of religion in Palestine was to memorize, and not to write down, the tradition.

Jesus lived and taught, finally meeting death upon a Roman cross. The resurrection experiences gave rise to beliefs and practices which marked the new movement as separate from Judaism. The first and most important story to be told was the history of redemption, the passion narrative of Jesus. So important was this story, and so oft-repeated, that its form and substance became crystallized, apparently while still in oral form. The narrative was woven about a framework of biblical quotations which Jesus was believed to have fulfilled. Other needs of the Christian evangelists brought other interests. Conflicts with the Jewish teachers and authorities brought recollections of incidents in which Jesus seemed to oppose the current Jewish practices and beliefs. Problems of illness and mental difficulties surrounding them aroused citations of Jesus' attitudes toward the sick and the wonderful cures which he performed. Questions as to conduct called for the teachings of their leader.

So it was that the oral traditions grew up and began to circulate. Changes and variations were inevitable. The important concern was to transmit faithfully the pronouncement or the actual words of Jesus. The circumstances of the story varied with the fancy of the storyteller: a glance at the gospels shows the effects of this variation. Chronology was so unimportant that it was omitted almost completely; local color was added to suit the community. Sometimes the intense needs of a changing community forced conscious and unconscious changes in the actual quotation from Jesus; his words were normative, therefore they must relate to each situation as it arose. Ample illustrations of the effects of oral transmission may be seen in a cursory examination of a critical harmony of the Synoptic Gospels.[5] The reader will notice that the same teaching of Jesus is clothed with different details of time, place, and circumstance from gospel to gospel. Less often, but still noticeable, is the variation in the actual pronouncement attributed to Jesus.

The second stage in gospel production was reached when early Christian evangelists, operating largely in Hellenistic communities under Greek literary influence, began to write down some of the materials of preaching. These at first were very minor collections of pericopes on similar subject matter. A collection of "proof-texts" had formed one of the structural bases for the oral passion narrative; this principle was now extended to other areas of Jesus' activity, and many of the old stories were associated with quotations of Scripture. Written genealogies were also in circulation: two of the variant forms appear in Matthew and Luke. Healing stories had a tendency to cohere; occasionally they were so closely associated that they grew together, forming one continuous narrative.[6] Controversy stories proved so useful to the early communities that collections of these were made. An examination of the gospels indicates at once that this close association has left its traces in the finished product. In addition, teachings attributed to Jesus were collected for ready reference.

[5] See, e.g., E. D. Burton and E. J. Goodspeed, *A Harmony of the Synoptic Gospels for Historical and Critical Study* (New York: Charles Scribner's Sons, 1917), or *A Harmony of the Synoptic Gospels in Greek* (Chicago, 1920); also Albert Huck, *A Synopsis of the First Three Gospels*, ed. Hans Lietzmann, trans. Frank L. Cross (9th ed.; Tübingen: Mohr, 1936).

[6] Mark 5:22–43.

Some of these circulated separately and drew conclusions which were applicable to the small collection but not to the gospel as a whole when later they were incorporated.[7]

A second phase of this stage in the production of gospels saw the collection of written fragments into longer ''sources.'' The character of several of these longer written collections has already been described. These were woven by the gospel editors into the individual patterns which mark the finished product, being adjusted to the aims of the complete work.

The final stage in gospel production was the process of compiling and editing the actual Gospel of Mark, or Matthew, or Luke and its companion volume of Acts. It is most difficult to determine just how correct one may be to apply the term ''author'' to the gospel editors. By the strict logic of form criticism the ''authors'' of the Synoptic Gospels would be merely compilers of traditions bequeathed them by the Christian communities. The responsibility of these compilers would be simply one of arrangement; their own composition would end with the transitional and editorial sentences, together with some minor pointing of the traditions. This position is hardly adequate. The very processes of selection of material, arrangement, conscious and unconscious modification and adaptation of materials to a well-defined set of aims, and ability correctly to anticipate the needs of a community would demand the application of the title of ''editor,'' at least. Whether more ''authorship'' is to be identified will depend upon our analysis of each gospel.

A problem which has called forth excessive heat in proportion to the light generated is that concerning the language in which the gospels were first written. Our oldest manuscripts of the gospels are in Greek, the universal language of the Hellenistic era. It has generally been accepted that, since Jesus and his disciples spoke Aramaic (a contemporary language derived from the Hebrew), the first oral circulation of his teachings and the message about him was in Aramaic. As the ''gospel'' moved into extra-Palestinian circles, Greek came to be the natural vehicle for the preaching; and when the literature of the movement arose,

[7] Mark 4:1-34.

Greek was the single logical choice. In fact, so strong was the Jewish tradition against written religious commentary on Scripture that no literature of this type is extant in Aramaic; still more telling is the paucity of Aramaic literature of any kind from the period in which the gospels were written. On the other hand, voluminous literature in the *koine* (common Greek) of the first century has been proved by the discovery of the papyri. This is the language of the Greek New Testament, as has been demonstrated by scholarly studies which showed the falsity of the old position that the New Testament was composed in "biblical Greek," as contrasted with classical Greek.

This accepted point of view has been challenged in recent years by a group of Semitists who feel that the oldest Greek manuscripts of the gospels are documents translated from the Aramaic, in which they were supposedly written. The most active exponents of this position are C. F. Burney[8] and C. C. Torrey,[9] who contend that the "Aramaisms" or "Semitisms" in the gospel Greek indicate that it has been translated from Aramaic. While there is value in the continued emphasis of this group upon the Aramaic form in which many of the traditions once circulated, there is little reason to believe that the tradition at this time was other than spoken. The absence of Aramaic literature (written) of this period and the late date at which the gospels were produced are telling arguments against this position. Add to this the fact that no two Semitic scholars agree on lists of the so-called "Aramaisms" and that the overwhelming majority of the expressions appear in the nonbiblical Greek of the papyri and Epictetus, and the evidence in favor of Greek as the original written form seems unshaken.[10] Coupled with these factors is the consideration that the movement so early reached out into Hellenistic circles—indeed, it acquired its distinctive characteristics

[8] *The Aramaic Origin of the Fourth Gospel* (Oxford: Clarendon Press, 1922).

[9] *The Four Gospels* (New York: Harper & Bros., 1933) and *Documents of the Primitive Church* (New York: Harper & Bros., 1941).

[10] See, e.g., the evaluations in F. C. Grant, *The Earliest Gospel* (Nashville: Abingdon-Cokesbury Press, 1943); E. J. Goodspeed, *An Introduction to the New Testament* (Chicago: University of Chicago Press, 1937); E. C. Colwell, *The Greek of the Fourth Gospel: A Study of Its Aramaisms in the Light of Hellenistic Greek* (Chicago: University of Chicago Press, 1931).

there—that Greek would have been the only acceptable language. The reader is invited to evaluate the evidence for himself.

The earliest gospel was produced in Rome about A.D. 70. The name of Mark was, by the early patristic writings and by tradition, associated with the disciple Peter and with Rome; and the internal evidence of the gospel supports the theory of an extra-Palestinian origin. The gospel form itself represents a new type of literature. Greek biography offers no exact parallels. Much closer to the form and purpose of the Gospel of Mark are the cycles of stories about Elijah and Elisha in the books of Kings.[11] But the primary purpose of Mark stands apart from these: it is to picture the dramatic religious work of the divine Son of God.

The earliest patristic reference to Mark's work occurs in a fragment from the writings of Papias, bishop of Hierapolis, who was prominent about A.D. 140. Papias indicated that Mark, the interpreter of Peter, wrote down accurately everything that he remembered, but not in order. Peter, so Papias states, had no design of giving a connected account of the Lord's oracles but rather adapted his instructions to the needs of his hearers.[12] Irenaeus of Lyons, writing about A.D. 185, indicates that Mark wrote down those things which he remembered that Peter had said.[13] Clement of Alexandria, who flourished about A.D. 200, believed that Mark had composed his gospel after showing his work to the apostle Peter, who was then preaching in Rome.[14]

The careful reader will perceive that many statements within the Gospel of Mark show that the work was not intended for a Palestinian reading public. Palestinian coinage must be explained to the reader in the parable of the widow's lepta.[15] The season at which the Jewish Passover is celebrated is unknown to those who will read the gospel.[16] The customs of the Pharisees are not understood: some of the ceremonial observations are cited.[17] Ara-

---

[11] I Kings 17:1—II Kings 13:21; see Goodspeed, *An Introduction to the New Testament*, pp. 125–26.

[12] Eusebius *Church History* iii. 39. 15.

[13] *Ibid.*, v. 8. 2–3.

[14] *Ibid.*, vi. 14. 5–7.

[15] Mark 12:42.

[16] Mark 11:13.

[17] Mark 7:3–4.

maic expressions are not understood by the intended readers; *Taleitha koum* and *Ephphatha* must be translated.[18] These explanations of customs and language familiar to inhabitants of Palestine indicate that the gospel was intended for a gentile reading public.

Thus we have the fairly well-established traditions of the connection of this earliest gospel with the name of Peter and with the city of Rome. In addition, internal factors point to a non-Palestinian group for which the work was intended. The connection with the name of Peter seems to have been magnified by the traditions. The distinctively Marcan materials bear the stamp of eyewitness accounts no more than do the other non-Marcan sources. The tone of the Marcan materials was determined by their traditional history, as was the case with the teaching pericopes of "Q" or the distinctive materials of Matthew or Luke-Acts. The important part which Peter is pictured as playing in the gospel drama, together with his traditional importance in the work of the church at Rome, probably determined his identification with this Roman gospel. The argument for the Petrine character of the Marcan materials cannot, without difficulty, be supported by an analysis of the gospel.

The Gospel of Mark is correctly pictured as dramatic. The character of the language and the arrangement of the materials support this conclusion. The gospel opens with rapid action and drives to its conclusion with dramatic speed and effect. The Greek of the gospel is filled with verbs of dramatic character. The adverb *euthus*, meaning "straightway" or "immediately," is used in Mark more than the other three gospels combined. Important from the dramatic point of view also is the plan of the gospel: Jesus is pictured as a tragic hero along the familiar Greek lines. One notes the three phases of the Greek tragic drama: the rising action, in which the true nature of Jesus is revealed to the reader and in which the hero enjoys a measure of popularity; the recognition scene, in which Jesus is revealed to the inner group; and the falling action, in which the hero is enmeshed in the net of his enemies and is killed, but through which he wins a mighty

[18] Mark 5:41, 7:34.

victory. The entire effect of the gospel is to make clear the mighty drama of salvation and to give meaning to the tragic in the life of Jesus and of those Christians who were being called upon to suffer in the name of the movement.[19]

The dramatic character of the gospel is heightened by the choice and arrangement of pericopes. Action proceeds rapidly through the use of stories in which Jesus is constantly pictured as healing, worsting his enemies in controversies, or controlling the forces of nature. There are few pericopes of teaching materials included in Mark in comparison with either Matthew or Luke. Thus the tragic hero of the gospel story is pictured as a man of action. He is introduced abruptly, as he accepts the baptism of repentance at the hands of John the Baptist. His power and true character are revealed by the wondrous deeds which he performs and by the authoritative words which he speaks. He is not a teacher in the tradition of the scribes and the Pharisees, but one who speaks with authority, for he does not appeal to the tradition of the elders to support his religious deliverances. Demons, admittedly supernatural beings, attest to his peculiar relationship to God. He reveals himself gradually to his disciples; finally they are able to recognize his messianic character in the experience at Caesarea Philippi. Here, halfway through the gospel, the story begins to point to the redemptive action of the passion narrative. He sets his face toward Jerusalem, constantly warning and counseling his disciples. The days at Jerusalem are filled with conflict and triumph over his enemies, even though they finally succeed in crucifying him. The ancient gospel ended with the very dramatic picture of the fear of the women as they fled from the empty tomb, trembling and bewildered. The tragic hero had triumphed, even over death.

The first readers of the Gospel of Mark saw in the sufferings and death of Jesus an example of the treatment which many of them must receive. The martyr motif runs throughout the entire

[19] See further E. W. Burch, "Tragic Action in the Second Gospel," *Journal of Religion*, XI (1931), 346–48; and Riddle, *The Martyrs*, pp. 180–97.

work: it can, in fact, be called a "primitive martyrology."[20] It set the pattern for later stories of martyrdom meant to inspire Christians who lived in constant danger of persecution at the hands of the state.

The tradition which connects the writing of Mark with the last days of the disciple Peter in the city of Rome would give us a clue as to the date at which the earliest gospel was composed. Peter was believed by the early church to have perished in the persecution of Nero about A.D. 63. But internal evidence adds a further word. The "Small Apocalypse" of chapter 13 definitely shows the influence of the events of the Jewish rebellion of A.D. 66–70. It was in the light of the horrible suffering and destruction of those years that the "predictions" of Jesus concerning the end of the Temple were expanded and made specific. The very end of the Jewish world had come, or so it seemed to those who witnessed its sufferings at the hands of Vespasian and Titus. The Gospel of Mark may thus be dated at A.D. 70 or soon thereafter.

Thus in the first written gospel we have the results of a long process, covering forty years, in which the oral gospel and written fragments played their part. Much of the credit for the effectiveness of this first of the gospel type goes to the compiler and editor, traditionally thought to be John Mark. His work was, first of all, one of compilation and selection with a view to the aims he hoped to reach in his production. Careful attention to the general framework of the narrative and to the transitional sections will demonstrate the skill of the editor in initiating the gospel type. Although the title of "author" perhaps cannot be applied to him, still the excellence of plan and arrangement, coupled with deft handling of sources and tradition still in the oral form, merits for him the title of "editor par excellence." This first gospel writer was to have many imitators, even though some as late as the time of Papias still preferred the oral gospel.

[20] Cf. D. W. Riddle, "The Martyr Motif in the Gospel of Mark," *Journal of Religion*, IV (1924), 379–410, and *The Martyrs*, chap. viii.

XV

THE SYNOPTIC GOSPELS AS LITERATURE (B)

THE appearance of the Gospel of Mark served as a stimulus for the writing of other gospels. Approximately fifteen years after the earliest gospel pictured Jesus to Christian readers as the tragic hero, the Gospel of Matthew hailed him as the great teacher and the second lawgiver. Not that the editor of Matthew thought of his work as supplemental to that of Mark; instead, he reproduced most of the pericopes in that earliest gospel and added many of his own choosing. The Gospel of Matthew presented a complete rearrangement of many of the early stories and teaching materials, taking liberties not only with the details of a story but often also with the sayings attributed to Jesus himself. Thus the editor of Matthew pictured Jesus as the mighty teacher, arranging his deliverances carefully according to the Jewish pattern.

The date of the Gospel of Matthew is indicated by the detailed use made of the earliest gospel, by the heightened apocalyptic effect, by the revision of earlier and more naïve attitudes, and by the ecclesiastical rules and regulations set forth. A careful study of a harmony of the Synoptic Gospels will at once show how dependent upon Mark the Matthean compiler was. Particularly in matters of order is this noticeable, where the Matthean policy is to interpolate organized groups of additional material rather than alter the Marcan plan. This is the key to the organization of the gospel.

Several additions to the Marcan scheme form the opening chapters of the Gospel of Matthew. A genealogy, beginning with Abraham and ending with Jesus, introduces the work. How many of these traditional genealogies of Jesus were circulating in the early Christian communities cannot be known: Matthew uses one, and Luke-Acts employs another. Their purpose was to show that Jesus' lineage was in the best Jewish tradition—indeed, that he was descended from David, even though the total effect of the genealogy is greatly lessened by the inclusion of Joseph rather than Mary. There follows the Matthean version of the miraculous birth of Jesus, which relies heavily upon references to Scripture. The flight into Egypt, the "slaughter of the innocents," and the settlement at Nazareth likewise take their form largely from scriptural citations. It is at this point that the order of Mark becomes dominant.

The plan of Matthew is to insert six great sermons at intervals in the general outline of Mark. The first of these, the familiar Sermon on the Mount, embraces chapters 5–7. Jesus has already been introduced as a person of miraculous birth, of the best lineage, and as a doer of mighty deeds. Now, in the tradition of the great Jewish teachers, he goes up onto a mountain, seats himself, and begins to teach. The collection of teachings which Matthew has grouped into the Sermon on the Mount is today received by many as the ethical standard of Christianity. It is here that the Matthean writer groups such familiar teachings as the beatitudes, the new law, the Lord's Prayer, and the sayings on judging others. The end of the sermon can be readily identified by the statement: "When Jesus had finished this discourse, the crowds were astounded at his teaching. . . . ."[1] There is little variation in the formal introductions and conclusions from sermon to sermon. The second sermon, contained in chapter 10, gives directions for the preaching of the Kingdom of Heaven. The third sermon consists of a series of parables on the value of the Kingdom and the way in which it grows (13:1–52). The fourth of the Matthean sermons is found in chapter 18; it treats of the type of life which must be found in the Kingdom of Heaven. The fifth discourse pictures Jesus as turning with savage indictment upon the leaders of the Jewish people, excoriating the scribes and the Pharisees (chap. 23). The final sermon (chaps.

[1] Matt. 7:28–29.

24–25) depicts the fall of Jerusalem and the apocalyptic end of the age.

The closing chapters of Matthew show a few additions to the Marcan narrative of the passion. Of interest is the curious tradition on the remorse and death of Judas and the naming of the Field of Blood.[2] Added to the Marcan narrative, also, is the story of the guard at the tomb of Jesus[3] and the reputed Jewish explanation that his disciples stole his body while the guards were asleep.[4] The resurrection appearances are expanded to include an experience with the eleven disciples on a mountain in Galilee and the consequent giving of the commission to evangelize the whole world.[5]

Of tremendous importance for an understanding of the aims of the Gospel of Matthew is the series of sayings in which Jesus reputedly gives the new law for the guidance of his followers.[6] The section is prefaced by the injunction that he who would enter the Kingdom of Heaven must exceed in righteousness the scribes and the Pharisees. The new law involves the keeping of the old law and improvements thereupon. A succession of contrasting teachings then shows the pre-eminence of Jesus' law to the things which "the men of old" were taught. Plainly, the purpose of this group of teachings is to show the infinite superiority of Jesus to Moses and to utilize the Jewish method of teaching, namely, to set an extremely high standard of attainment. Christian law not only springs from but improves upon Jewish standards.

Further utilization of Jewish values is seen in the constant appeal to Hebrew Scripture. Profuse references to the prophets and the Psalms call attention to Jesus as the Promised One of Israel. The editor of Matthew believes that most of the acts in Jesus' career were "predicted" by Scripture, and he proceeds to document his work liberally.

Because Matthew utilized Jewish values so carefully, many scholars have been led to term it "the Jewish Gospel," feeling

[2] 27:3–10.

[3] Matt. 27:62–66.

[5] Matt. 28:16–20.

[4] Matt. 28:11–15.

[6] 5:17–48.

that it appealed primarily to Jews who might consider the Christian claims. This title is woefully misleading, in that it fails to consider the anti-Jewish elements in the gospel. Typical of the anti-Jewish invective is the long succession of indictments of the recognized leaders of Judaism—the scribes and the Pharisees.[7] This section, read back into the life of Jesus from the later rivalries of the growing church and the synagogue, excoriates all the Jewish leaders without exception. They are cited as people who "talk but do not act," who manipulate the Law entirely to their own advantage, who "do everything they do to have men see it." They are, without exception, hypocrites who will not enter the Kingdom themselves; nor will they let others enter, leaders who "pay tithes on mint, dill, and cummin, and . . . . let the weightier matters of the Law go—justice, mercy, and integrity." Thus Jesus is pictured as attacking the very foundational principles of Judaism—the Torah and its careful interpretation by recognized scholars and leaders. It can in no wise be called "Jewish" in this respect.

A further indictment of Judaism occurs in the so-called "displacement parables," of which there are more in Matthew than in either of the other gospels. Of significance, also, is the explicit didactic which is drawn from each of these parables, making unmistakable the conclusion that God has found the Jews incapable of receiving the good news of Jesus Christ. The earlier sections of Matthew had indicated that the message was not to be given to the heathen or to the Samaritans, but first to "the lost sheep of Israel's house."[8] But during the passion week, Matthew shows the reversal of his decision, for to the high priests and the elders he gives the parable of the two sons who were asked to work in the vineyard.[9] The didactic is stated: "I tell you, the tax-collectors and prostitutes are going into the Kingdom of God ahead of you." The parable of the wicked tenants[10] likewise means for the Matthean editor one thing: "The Kingdom of God will be taken away from you, and given to a people that will produce its proper fruit. Whoever falls on that stone

---

[7] Matt. 23:1–39.

[8] 10:6.

[9] 21:28–32.

[10] 21:33–44.

will be shattered, but whoever it falls upon will be pulverized."
The editorial interpretation of Matthew will be seen immediately upon comparison with the Marcan parallel,[11] where the didactic is inferred rather than sharply stated. Equally clear is the
displacement inference of the Matthean parable of the king who
gave a wedding banquet.[12] These displacement parables indicate
the widening breach between developing Christianity and Judaism and very specifically represent the rationalization on the part
of Christian leaders for the failure of Jews to accept their point
of view.

Thus the Gospel of Matthew must be described as both Jewish
and anti-Jewish in its attitudes. Its picture of Christianity in
terms of law, its description of Jesus as the great teacher and lawgiver, and its utilization of Hebrew Scripture as background and
justification for the developing Christian movement represent
dominantly Jewish values. On the other hand, its invective
against the recognized leaders of Judaism and its picture of Gentiles as replacing Jews in the favor of God mark it definitely
as anti-Jewish in its appeal.

Matthew has been described as "the Ecclesiastical Gospel"[13]
and as a "handbook of the early church "[14] These descriptive
titles recognize the churchly character of the gospel; certainly,
it formed an ideal handbook for the guidance of the early evangelists. Literary and historical development can be traced from
Mark to Matthew, particularly in attempts to refine the meaning
of certain bald statements in the earliest gospel or to clarify
Jesus' meaning in the light of later events. This may be seen in
the Matthean attempt to explain Jesus' acceptance of John's
baptism of repentance,[15] the distinct elevation of Jesus above the
Temple and the Sabbath,[16] and the detailed explanation of the
figure of the weeds in the field.[17]

---

[11] Mark 12:1–11.   [12] Matt. 22:2–10.

[13] Grant, *Growth of the Gospels*, chap. vii.

[14] D. W. Riddle, *The Gospels: Their Origin and Growth* (Chicago: University of Chicago
Press, 1939), chap. x.

[15] Matt. 3:13–15; cf. Mark 1:9.

[16] Matt. 12:5–7; cf. Mark 2:25–26.   [17] Matt. 13:36–43; cf. Mark 4:30 ff.

The churchly nature of the Gospel of Matthew may be seen in its approach to a Christian code of ethics, illustrated particularly in the Sermon on the Mount. This gospel shows many characteristics of an institutional manual for the guidance of church leaders. Prophets and upright men were to be welcomed to the churches.[18] Erring brothers were to be corrected first in private, second in the presence of one or two others, last before the congregation; if then they proved incorrigible, they were to be cast out.[19] The elect (the church) are to act for Jesus on earth, and even small gatherings may secure the presence of Jesus.[20] These directions indicate tremendous progress in church organization when compared with Mark.

The editor of the Gospel of Matthew worked in a period when the Christian apocalyptic expectation was heightened. Apocalypticism shows a distinct advance from Mark to Matthew, as evidenced by the additions to the Marcan apocalypse made in the Matthean version[21] and by the apocalyptic-eschatological materials peculiar to Matthew.[22] His viewpoint, especially if he wrote close to the Judean scene, fits into the tempo of the period between the war of A.D. 66–70 and the final crushing rebellion in A.D. 132. The date usually assigned to the gospel from an investigation of all angles is A.D. 85–90.

The editor of the Gospel of Matthew probably lived in northern Palestine or Syria—so his apocalyptic outlook and his bias in favor of Galilee would indicate. Noteworthy, also, in this connection are the citations from the gospel made in other early Christian literature emanating from this region.[23] That the gospel in its present form was edited by the disciple called Matthew or Levi is highly improbable. His subservience to Mark is too constant to allow the contention that it is the work of an eye-witness of the events. The gospel bears all the characteristics of

[18] Matt. 10:41.

[19] Matt. 18:15–17.   [20] Matt. 18:18–20.

[21] See esp. Matt. 24:5, 30.

[22] 13:24–30, 20:1–16, 22:1–14, 25:1–13, 31–46.

[23] See, further, on the place at which Matthew was written, Streeter, *The Four Gospels*, pp. 500–523; also Grant, *Growth of the Gospels*, pp. 184–85.

traditional literature. It is possible that the connection of this gospel with the name of the disciple originated in the tradition which Papias records, that "Matthew composed the sayings in the Aramaic language and each one translated them as he was able."[24] Since it is highly improbable that this Aramaic composition was our present Gospel of Matthew, Papias' evident meaning was that Matthew composed an oral gospel.[25] If this oral gospel was an inspiration for the present Greek gospel, the name of the disciple might well have been transferred to the new work to give it prestige.

Thus the Gospel of Matthew represented in many ways a new and improved edition of Mark, and yet there were innovations in arrangement and materials. Sections from Matthew's sermonic collections still serve many people as the ethical basis of Christianity. The Matthean concept of Christianity as the new law and of Jesus as teacher serves as the pattern of belief for many devout readers. In scope, plan, and purpose the Gospel of Matthew merits for its composer the description of skilful editor.

The two-volume work of Luke-Acts was conceived and executed on a far grander scale than the gospels of Mark and Matthew. For this author the story did not end with the resurrection appearances and the promise of world evangelization; rather, it could cease only after relating how the Christian movement spread from Jerusalem to the Gentiles and finally to the very capital of the world itself. This literary labor showed the purpose of the historian: to inform the reader reliably concerning the things which he had previously been taught. But the aim of the Lucan writer was not to present factual information alone; here was history with a purpose—namely, to influence the reader to regard the Christian movement most favorably.

The purposes of Luke-Acts can be understood only when one critically examines the continuous threads running through both volumes. Misunderstanding of each volume has been fairly consistent among scholars of the New Testament because they have

---

24 Eusebius *Church History* iii. 39. 16.

25 On this convincing suggestion, see Goodspeed, *An Introduction to the New Testament*, pp. 173–74.

disregarded this fundamental principle of methodology. Luke-Acts was conceived and written according to a single plan by one individual, utilizing materials common to other writers, of course.[26] Style, arrangement, language, and point of view—all indicate the work of one editor. That the two were early divided through the exigencies of textual history was most unfortunate, for the gospel section circulated with the Fourfold Gospels, while the Acts section was grouped with the Epistles.

The primary purpose of Luke-Acts was to present the case of the growing Christian movement favorably to the eyes of the Roman world. Possibly the two-volume work is addressed to a Roman official named Theophilus, or this may simply be the polite general title for any fair-minded religious reader.[27] Christianity in A.D. 90 did not enjoy the respect of the Roman Empire—indeed, it had not been "licensed," as were the accepted faiths of the day. Its illegal character did not add to its reputation or allow full possibilities for correctly judging it. Luke-Acts was the corrective which the church produced.

Two main avenues of approach were utilized by the editor-author. First, he demonstrated that the new movement was firmly rooted in Judaism, a quasi-licensed religion. The Christian faith now represented the true Judaism, but most of the Jews themselves had failed to understand or accept it; therefore, they were now causing trouble for Christian propagandists. Second, Luke-Acts sought to present a favorable picture of Christianity by indicating that Romans themselves had everywhere been impressed by it, had found it to be thoroughly patriotic, and had witnessed the fact that the Jews in every case were the true troublemakers.

Careful reading of the two volumes will show the skill with which Luke worked to make this an effective apology for the growing and yet unlicensed movement. Although the writer himself was a Gentile, his knowledge of Judaism shines through the pages of his work. Jesus' family is, of course, declared to be of the best Jewish tradition; but Luke also pictures John the Baptist as

[26] The unified point of view has been clearly and consistently set forth by Cadbury, *The Making of Luke-Acts*, and by Riddle, *The Gospels: Their Origin and Growth*, pp. 179–209.

[27] Luke 1:1–4.

a member of a prominent family. Jesus, from his childhood, behaves in the best of Jewish tradition; his acts are substantiated by the witness of Hebrew Scripture; and his teachings are in accordance with the highest interpretation of Judaism. It is the Jews who in their blindness will not recognize him as the true Messiah; not even his resurrection from the dead convinces them. Throughout the second volume, also, the implication is plain: the followers of Jesus behave as the best in Judaism indicates that they should behave, but the God-imposed blindness of the Jews prevents their understanding this logical outgrowth from their own religion. The implicit conclusion which the intelligent reader should draw is that the new movement deserves recognition as the legitimate successor of a "licensed" religion.

Throughout the pages of these two volumes the Romans who have contacts with the believers express favorable judgments concerning them. The story of the Roman centurion whose faith in Jesus brings about the healing of his servant is expanded in the Lucan version to make him a most estimable person even in the eyes of the Jewish elders.[28] This respected Roman official shows an extremely favorable attitude toward the revered leader of the Christian movement. The Lucan account of the trial of Jesus before Pilate is much more explicit than either of the other gospels in absolving the Roman governor of blame for the crucifixion of Jesus and fixing it upon the Jews.[29] Pilate expressly states: "I cannot find anything criminal about this man." It is the Jews who suggest that he is "stirring up the people." A peculiar Lucan tradition, also, is the story concerning the trial before Herod: the ruler of Galilee ridicules Jesus but finds him not guilty, remanding him to Pilate.[30] Three times Pilate is pictured as protesting against the punishment of an innocent person, but the Jews by their clamor override him.[31]

Equally explicit are the favorable judgments of Roman authorities in situations of conflict pictured in the Acts volume. Cornelius the centurion reacts most favorably to the message as preached by Peter, for he and his entire household become con-

[28] Luke 7:1–10; cf. Matt. 8:5–13.
[29] Luke 23:2–5; cf. Mark 15:2–5 and Matt. 27:11–14.
[30] Luke 23:6–16.
[31] Luke 23:22–23.

verts.[32] Herod mistreats members of the church chiefly because it gratifies the Jews.[33] A Roman governor, Sergius Paulus, "believes" when he hears the message and sees the deeds of Barnabas and Paul.[34] Gallio, the Roman proconsul in Corinth, censures the Jews for raising a disturbance over "words and titles" and their "own law," indicating that no charge of rascality or lawbreaking is to be brought against the Christian missionaries.[35] The Roman governors, Felix and Festus, are able to find no unpatriotic activity on Paul's part;[36] while Agrippa, a great favorite of the emperor, states that Paul might have been set free had he not appealed to Rome.[37] The volume ends with a picture of Paul's good treatment in Rome and the obstinacy of those Jews who will not believe the obvious truth.[38] In sharp contrast to the fair attitude of the Romans toward the Christian movement is pictured the base attitude of the Jews. It is they who consistently cause all the trouble, who, by their rioting, bring Christian missionaries before the Roman officials.

In addition to his main interest and purpose, Luke shows many subsidiary ones. He pictures non-Jews in a most favorable light, choosing Samaritans as heroes for several of Jesus' stories and sayings[39] and describing the Gentiles throughout both volumes as more open to truth than their Jewish contemporaries.[40] Women assume an especially prominent part in Luke-Acts.[41] The poor are singled out for particular praise and the rich for condemnation, as seen in the Lucan version of the beatitude on "the poor" and the corresponding woe to the rich[42] and in the parables of the rich man and Lazarus[43] and of the rich fool.[44]

Luke-Acts demonstrates the editor's infancy interest, for he includes not only a birth story of Jesus but one of John the Bap-

---

[32] Acts 10:1–48.

[33] Acts 12:1 ff.

[34] Acts 13:7–12.

[35] Acts 18:12–17.

[36] Acts 23:26—25:21.

[37] Acts 26:1–32.

[38] Acts 28:16–31.

[39] Luke 10:29–37, 17:11–19.

[40] See, e.g., Luke 7:9; Acts 10:45–46, 13:44–50, 14:2, 18–19, and *passim*.

[41] I.e., Luke 7:11–15, 10:38–42, 11:27–28; Acts 9:36–43, 16:14–15, 17:34, 18:1–3.

[42] Luke 6:20, 24; cf. Matt. 5:3.

[43] Luke 16:19–31.

[44] Luke 12:13–21.

tist also. This interest is expanded to include brief items on Jesus' appearance at the Temple at forty days of age and again at twelve years, together with a few sentences on the nature of his growth.[45] An interest in Christian hymnody is manifest in Luke's inclusion of several poems which were later placed in the formal ritual of the church.[46] The resurrection interest in Luke stretches the narrative of Jesus' appearance to forty days of activity. A fairly well-developed concept of the Holy Spirit causes the editor to include numerous references to its activity; this is often related to ecstatic activity and to baptism. The development of church organization is reflected in the Acts section, where the disciples are set up as a directing group operating from Jerusalem as a center. Elders are associated with them,[47] and there are indications that the group called "deaconesses" or "widows" had also been set up by the time that Luke wrote.[48]

The literary interest of the Lucan writer is evidenced by his use of two "prefaces"—one a general introduction to his entire work[49] and the other a brief summary of the first volume and an introduction to the second.[50] Both of these represented common literary devices of the Hellenistic world. Luke employed many sources in the construction of each volume, and his use of materials followed the same method from volume to volume. The gospel sources are more readily identifiable than those used in the Acts volume: Mark is reproduced liberally, about three-fifths of the earliest gospel appearing in Luke; "Q" appears frequently, a special source called "L" is in evidence, and smaller strands of special material are visible.[51] Luke may, with propriety, be called a superb organizer of many diverse materials. In every section which Luke has taken from Mark, except two, the materials stand in exactly the Marcan order, as reference to a harmony of the gospels will show. Luke's method was plainly to interpolate blocks of non-Marcan material in the Marcan scheme; one of these insertions stretches from 9:51 to 18:14.

---

[45] Luke 2:21–52.

[46] Luke 1:42–45, 46–55, 68–79, 2:14, 29–32.

[47] Acts 15:2, 6, 22, 16:4, 14:23.

[48] Acts 9:36, 39.

[49] Luke 1:1–4.

[50] Acts 1:1–4.

[51] For a clear discussion, see Grant, *Growth of the Gospels*, pp. 66–95, 158–75.

Doubtless, numerous sources lie beneath the Acts volume also, for in places the interweaving of materials is evident. One fairly long source was the writing now called the "we-sections" of Acts, the exact origin of which scholarship has been unable to determine. In all probability, the writer of the we-sections and the editor of Luke-Acts are not the same.[52] It purports to be the travel diary of a companion of Paul and adds considerable interest and a tone of authority to the narrative. This, again, was a common literary device of first-century historians.

Luke-Acts is not a complete history of the Christian movement from the birth of Jesus to the arrival of Paul in Rome. Many are the omissions in the gospel and the Acts sections. A comparison of the gospel with the total gospel materials available will show the incomplete character of the first volume. An analysis of the letters of Paul will demonstrate the telescopic character of the second volume, for the so-called "journeys" pictured in Acts can never be reconciled with the complete activity pictured in the brief and occasional letters. By the time that Luke-Acts was written, Paul had risen to hero-proportions: controversies were softened, deeds were magnified, and a schematized biography in miniature was presented by this editor.

The editor of Luke-Acts, whether Luke or a person not now identifiable, demonstrates for us the work of a collector of *logoi*, of traditions. He was affected by both Greek and Jewish methods of history-writing. Certainly he fitted his collected materials to a planned scheme, and in the Greek tradition he composed speeches from the materials at hand wherever those statements were lacking.[53] His work represents a powerful apology for the Christian movement which appeared most probably during the last decade of the first century—a literary production written to stem the rising tide of hatred under Domitian.[54]

[52] Cadbury, *op. cit.*, pp. 355 ff.

[53] See H. J. Cadbury *et al.*, "The Greek and Jewish Traditions of Writing History," *The Beginnings of Christianity*, Part I: "The Acts of the Apostles," eds. F. J. Foakes-Jackson and K. Lake (London: Macmillan, 1922), II, 7–29.

[54] D. W. Riddle, "The Occasion of Luke-Acts," *Journal of Religion*, X (1930), 545–62; Riddle, *The Gospels: Their Origin and Growth*, pp. 193–207.

XVI

THE COLLECTION OF PAUL'S LETTERS: THE
BEGINNINGS OF CHRISTIAN
INSTITUTIONS

IT WAS not only in meeting decisive events that the now rapidly expanding Christian movement made progress subsequent
to the career of Paul and the writing of his letters. Nor were the
significant contributions which written gospels made to early
Christian literature the sole means by which Christianity added
to its strength as well as to its numbers.

The gospels exhibit the ways in which Christianity continued
to succeed in its competition with rival religious groups and the
ways in which it successfully met the problems of its own consolidation. They also show how early Christian leaders met the
problems of relation to the state and survived grave crises. They
offer much information on the development of ways of life which
crystallized into codes and patterns of teaching properly called
"Christian." The development toward self-consciousness can be
seen; the inchoate new movement was becoming self-contained.
Much more clearly than in Paul's letters can there be seen the
emergence of the church.

Toward the close of the first century these trends brought
about another significant development. In the time of the troubled reign of Domitian (81–96), and specifically in the latter
years of that period, a certain Christian leader made a momentous discovery. Apparently he was a native of the province of
Asia. Probably some period of his life had been spent in the city
of Colossae. At all events, he was an Asian, and he knew much
about Paul's work in Ephesus and the entire province of Asia.
He knew Paul's letter to the Colossians thoroughly. He also
knew that small letter directed to an unnamed church (perhaps

the church was in Laodicea) which came into the New Testament as Paul's Letter to Philemon. The knowledge and the sense of value of these letters led him to desire to know more of Paul's correspondence.

Luke-Acts had just been written; it would seem that its first place of circulation was the general region of the Aegean Basin. This Christian leader became acquainted with what Renan called "the most beautiful book ever written." One thing in the content of Luke-Acts made a deep impression upon this man, as it has upon everyone since: the heroic epic of Paul. In still closer detail Luke-Acts gave him—as it has given people ever since—some knowledge of Paul's travels. References to places Paul had evangelized gave this early Christian leader suggestions as to the possible location of Pauline letters. Perhaps stories still repeated by word of mouth sufficed to make him conscious that Paul had written letters to the Corinthians, the Philippians, and the Galatians. At all events, he made some effort to collect other letters of Paul's than the two which he knew so thoroughly. He collected as many as he could locate.

He found and assembled two letters to the Thessalonians, fragments of three or more to the Philippians, a whole and parts of three or four letters to the Corinthians, a letter to the Romans, and a little note of introduction of the woman, Phoebe, to the Ephesians. These were in addition to the two letters which he had known to begin with, the letters to the Colossians and to the Laodiceans.

It may seem strange to the modern student that the note of introduction was all that Paul had written to the Ephesians. It should not seem strange. Paul reached Ephesus only after his major work was done in Greece. Then he spent the most protracted period of work in his career in Ephesus and its environs. Paul knew the Ephesians well, and he had been able to meet their particular problems while he was with them. Thus no letter to the Ephesians had been needed.

The collector of Paul's letters made a momentous discovery: when they are read together as a book of letters, they have a message which is lacking when only one is read or when each is read of itself. In other words, this leader discovered that it is true in more realms than in mathematics that the whole is greater than the sum of its parts. He discovered that when Paul's letters are read together, as a book, they have a message for the church—not merely a number of messages for several churches.

This momentous discovery led the collector of Paul's letters to do a very significant thing. He "published" them. This word is used with entire propriety. Today "publication" necessarily means to print; but only a little reflection is necessary to perceive that the ancients published, even though they did not print. Printing was invented in the fifteenth century, but books were published long before that—in classical times certainly. Many of the books written in classical times were written to be published. To cite only one example, Pliny the younger had publication in mind at the very time that he wrote the letters which he later collected and published. There was a well-organized book trade in classical times. To be sure, all books published had to be written: there were many professional copyists, whose work was paid for at a standard rate, their earnings calculated on the basis of the number of "lines" (*stichoi*, roughly the equivalent of the hexameter line) which they wrote. The price of the various grades of papyrus was standard.

It was the objective of the collector and publisher of Paul's letters thus to make their message to the church available to any and all churches that could be reached—in other words, to give to the church the message which Paul's letters had for its members. It is perhaps well to reiterate that, in doing this, the collector and publisher was doing something which Paul did not have in mind when he wrote them. Let it be repeated that Paul wrote his letters to the individual churches addressed, and wrote them always with reference to a specific, immediate, and pressing problem. Nonetheless, the collector and publisher of the letters was right: Paul's letters do have a message for the church in general, as well as for the churches to which they were written. Christianity has found this to be true throughout its history.

The collector and publisher of Paul's letters was acute enough to see that, although the value of Paul's collected letters was apparent to him, the same conclusion might not be drawn by everyone else. To make this plain and inescapable, the acute leader furnished the collection with a letter of introduction which subtly set forth the ideas and values which he hoped the readers of the book would find in it. This act is another which seems strange to modern readers but which was not at all unusual in those days. He prefaced the letters of Paul with another letter, which he wrote and circulated under Paul's own name; this was the so-called "Letter of Paul to the Ephesians."

Consider two things with reference to this. It is the view set forth here that the so-called "Letter to the Ephesians" was not written by Paul but by the collector and publisher of Paul's letters. That means that the letter was, to use the technical word, pseudonymous: written by one person under the name of another. This would be a reprehensible practice today, but it was not at all reprehensible then. Indeed, such writings were common in the ancient world. A number of the writings of Jewish Scripture were pseudonymous: the Pentateuch is the collection of several writings brought together and ascribed by tradition to Moses; "Isaiah" contains several parts which were written by others than the prophet of that name, some of them much later than his time. Books widely circulated, but not contained in our Old Testament, particularly followed this practice: there are books ascribed to Baruch, Ezra, and even Enoch! In writing Ephesians and ascribing it to Paul this leader was doing nothing improper; he thought he was doing something proper and useful.

Second, this letter does not in its own text claim to have been the Letter to the Ephesians. The manuscripts which are used to determine the closest approximation to the original text of the New Testament, and are therefore commonly regarded as the best, do not have the words "in Ephesus." In fact, the recently discovered and edited Chester Beatty Papyrus, the earliest of all the manuscripts of Paul's letters, does not have these words. That is to say, on the basis of the text of the letter itself there is not adequate reason to regard it as having been in its original form a letter to the Ephesians.

Further, when the letter is analyzed, its contents show plainly that it is—and here it differs from Paul's letters—a letter not to any particular church but to the church in general. This was perceived long ago by the poet Coleridge, who pointed out that the letter is in its nature an encyclical. However, more should be said than this—for the letter is more than an encyclical to several churches: it is a letter to the church.

Its ideas and teachings show this unmistakably. It is written to "consecrated people who are steadfast in Christ Jesus."[1] It uses throughout an inclusive "us" and "we." It refers to "the church"[2]; as compared with the occurrence of the word in Paul's letters, the more frequent use here is striking and significant. Still more significant than this incidence of the term, however, are the evidences of the clear concept of the church as an institution. The church appears in figures of speech and in details; e.g., in the building of the church the apostles and prophets are the foundation and Jesus is the cornerstone.[3] The church appears in the repeated pleas for unity,[4] particularly in the insistence that there is only one legitimate body, Spirit, hope, Lord, faith, baptism, God. Obviously, this insistence reveals the fact that there was considerable disunity. The writer is pleading that unity ought to exist and must exist—because he sees that it does not exist. The problems of the heterogeneity of Christianity soon became pressing and important; this source gives us an early picture of their appearance. In any case, in the ideal of unity there is the strongest evidence of the consciousness of the church as such.

The ideas and teachings of this introductory letter are Paul's, but it is easy to see that they place Paul's thought in a much later setting than his own day. For example, Eph. 2:11–22 discusses the relations between non-Jews and Jews. The ideal is that there should be no distinction between them, that God had sent Christ, whose atoning sacrifice broke down all the barriers. Anyone can recognize this as an idea of Paul's; but by the same token anyone can see that the situation in Paul's days showed Jews reluctant to admit the non-Jews, while in the time of the circulation of Paul's letters as a book the situation was reversed: Christianity was now gentile, and there was an unwillingness to admit Jews.

[1] Eph. 1:1.　　　　[2] Eph. 1:22, 3:10, 5:23, 29, 32.

[3] Eph. 2:20–22. Cf. I Cor. 3:10 ff., in which Paul says clearly that Jesus is the foundation, not the cornerstone.

[4] Eph. 1:10, 4:4–6, 16.

The words of the introductory letter are thoroughly Pauline. Time after time, the letter has whole phrases and clauses that closely resemble passages in Paul's letters. This suggests, of course, that the writer of the letter was thoroughly steeped in the knowledge of Paul's letters.[5] Just as the literary relation between Colossians and this letter is especially close, so, too, it is to be explained that the collector and publisher had known Colossians longest. But when he had collected all other available letters, he must have mastered them, too, for their words, ideas, and teachings recur in the introductory letter which he wrote.

But even though they recur, they are different in their total effect, for there is a difference in their total relationship and in their application. While Paul's own letters are written in the light of specific church situations, this is a letter to the church as a whole.

There is every reason to conclude that the momentous discovery, followed by the notable act of the collection and publication of Paul's letters, was of great and permanent result. The first result was to be seen in the wide circulation of Paul's letters, which later stimulated other Christian collections. The corpus of Paul's letters was thus so firmly established that it remained a fixed unit within the later "canon" of Christian Scripture. It is certain that there was no dearth of copies of Paul's letters. It is inescapable that they were widely circulated as a book and that they became prized possessions of many Christian churches. Consequently, Paul's teachings came to have a much wider and deeper effect than would have been possible had the letters remained within individual churches.

Thus there came about a strange thing. Not only did Paul write with no thought that his letters would become Scripture, but he was so convinced that the end was at hand that the very idea of book-writing would have seemed preposterous. In this,

[5] Not all scholars agree that Ephesians was a letter of introduction to the Pauline corpus. The evidence for this conclusion is presented in E. J. Goodspeed, *The Meaning of Ephesians* (Chicago: University of Chicago Press, 1933) and *An Introduction to the New Testament*, pp. 210–21. The position that Paul was the author of Ephesians is strongly argued in E. F. Scott, *The Epistles of Paul to the Colossians, to Philemon, and to the Ephesians* (New York: Richard R. Smith, 1930).

of course, he was mistaken. Therefore, his successors were faced with the problems of an institution which seemed destined for quasi-permanence. It was still some time before people gave up the idea that the world was to end soon; but, even as they held this idea, the sensible acted as though the world was going to last for some time. Thus, the people of the churches developed their teachings, codes, and patterns—in a word, their morals and ethics. They developed church organization. Church workers presently found their duties patterned, and officials came to be charged with definite responsibilities. All this meant the growth of institutional Christianity. This introduction to the book of Paul's letters carried further the instruction concerning the public worship of the church[6] and quoted a well-known Christian hymn.[7]

And, as has been intimated, the publication of Paul's letters as a book secured for them something of the status of Scripture. For, instead of each being read solely in the church to which it was addressed, all of Paul's letters were widely read wherever the collection was circulated. This circulation and this reading were the first of the many long steps which were taken to give Paul's letters the status of Scripture. Let it be repeated: this status was never intended by Paul, and it was not envisaged by the collector. But it was one of the outcomes of his momentous discovery and his decisive act.

Much of the strength of the Christian movement is to be seen in this development. To be sure, as Christianity moved away from its primitive status, many of its aspects of charm were lost: it was much less creative (although the Fourth Gospel, I Peter, and James, among other writings, were yet to be produced), and it no longer had the same virility as in the days when its youth permitted it to meet problems with utter abandon. But, just as Christianity found the way to survive, it discovered that it had the dynamic strength to meet the terribly difficult problems of survival. If in becoming institutionalized it lost some of its earlier charm, it gained the eclectic beauty of a mighty, assimilative religious movement.

[6] Eph. 5:19–21.   [7] Eph. 5:14.

XVII

CHRISTIANITY CONFRONTS THE STATE

HEBREWS, REVELATION, AND I PETER

IN THE years during which the gospels were written, the major problems of Christianity were of two related types: (1) those incident to the expansion of the new movement and (2) those accompanying consolidation. The movement was becoming conscious of itself as a self-contained religion. It developed its own characteristic ways of life. These led to the articulation of distinctive patterns of behavior and to distinctive teachings. The gospels were responses to these needs.

There was, as the preceding chapter has shown, development of Christianity on the institutional side. Christianity was a highly inclusive movement, and in its expansion it embraced all sorts and conditions of people. These people had to be sufficiently affected by their new religion that their feelings, behavior, and thoughts were controlled by it. As the church grew institutionally, as well as in numbers and in geographical expanse, its teachings, its public worship, and its charitable endeavors were affected and influenced by the people whom it embraced. They, in turn, were molded by this new loyalty.

There was one factor which had appeared intermittently but which became especially important in the latter years of the reign of Domitian. It was a factor which has never been absent in the history of Christianity: the relation between the church and the state. That the force of this problem was recognized by Christian leaders is shown unmistakably by the gospels. It was the heavy hand of Rome which had nailed Jesus to the cross. No more regrettable or unfortunate perversion of truth has ever come into history than the aspersion that it was the Jews who had killed Jesus. It was the state which killed Jesus. Paul had many times felt the same heavy hand—finally it encompassed his death, too. Persecution in one form or another is reflected in many of the gospel stories and sayings.

All this occurred in spite of the fact that Jesus and the Christians were people of peace. It was the Roman law which precipitated persecution; the fear of revolution which caused Roman administrators to act ruthlessly and find out the truth afterward.

When Octavius (Augustus) shaped the Roman Empire, he made effective use of law and religion to perpetuate the regime. Religion, he well knew, was an effective conserving force, and he used it to his own ends. Roman religion and law were always conservative, and in the empire religion was carefully watched. One feature which caused endless difficulty to early Christianity was the Roman law which declared new religions illegal—no such religion had a right to exist. Therefore, when Christianity came to the attention of the state, it was in a position of peril. In its earliest days, when the movement had within it a large proportion of Jews, it might be mistaken for Judaism or regarded as a branch of that faith. When this was no longer possible, trouble was averted so long as nothing occurred to bring the rising movement to the attention of state administrators. When it did come to their attention, grave difficulty ensued—witness the tradition that Nero used the Christian groups as a scapegoat to divert suspicion from himself in connection with the burning of Rome.

In these latter years of Domitian a single factor precipitated the gravest crisis which had yet arisen in the relation of Christians to the state. This was his particular demand to be worshiped as a god.

Emperor-worship was no new thing. Alexander had been deified, as had many another person. It was common for members of Roman imperial families to be deified after their death. Indeed, it was exceptional when they were not; an emperor had to be unusually evil, like Caligula, or unusually unpopular, like Tiberius, not to be deified after death.

In the provinces, indeed, the emperor was worshiped during

his lifetime. Some people of the province of Asia had petitioned Augustus for permission to institute a cult in his honor. It was only after some hesitation that he permitted it, though stipulating that the abstraction, Rome, be worshiped with him. The practice of worshiping Rome and the emperor had continued; there were provincial cults and also municipal cults of emperor-worship.

But Domitian not only accepted this in the provinces; he demanded it in Rome. This was something new, and it was resisted. The Roman religion was inherently conservative. Proud patricians who looked at the letter of the law declared that the emperor was only *primus inter pares*, the designated chief among his equals; and they were no more willing to worship him than to demand worship for themselves. Some Roman families suffered for this resistance.

The Christians were in a particularly untenable position. Unlike other religions, Christianity was monotheistic. Many a person came into Christianity after belonging to other cults in which there was no such exclusiveness, but they were expected to worship only the one God as Christians. Obviously, they should not worship the emperor.

Even though nominally Jews were in the same position, practically their case was better. They were a large and formidable minority group. More than once they demanded their civil rights and obtained them. Further, they made a concession: a daily prayer was offered for the emperor in the Temple cultus. This was accepted as sufficient, and did indeed suffice except when some local situation broke out into the equivalent of a pogrom.

Domitian's demand was felt throughout the empire. It is reflected in a large cluster of Jewish and Christian writings. The Jewish apocalypse known as "IV Ezra" reflects it almost as plainly as does the Apocalypse of the New Testament, and the difference between Josephus' *War* and his *Antiquities* is the mark of the threat of Domitian's persecution as it was felt by Jews. Of Christian writings, Luke-Acts, the so-called "Epistle to the Hebrews," a noncanonical writing known as "I Clement," and the Revelation of John exhibit various stages of its imminence and its course. These writings show Christianity confronting the state.

That Luke-Acts was written as the persecution of Domitian loomed large upon the horizon is shown by its obvious political interest. It labors to show that Christianity is not, as might seem, a new religion, but that it is as old as Judaism. Luke-Acts may be fairly interpreted as a plea for the legal permission of Christianity to exist. Its hostility to Judaism is an aspect of this.

The so-called "Epistle to the Hebrews" indicates that the persecution was under way but had not yet become severe in the community to which the writing is addressed. This work is an address, not a letter. Its form as an address is clearly shown by its rhetorical quality. The quality of its Greek is good, as compared to other examples of Greek in early Christian writings. It reads with rhythmic sonorousness; it is an eloquent speech in written form. Its thought is so similar to other examples of Alexandrian allegory that it is an inescapable conclusion that in Hebrews we have the earliest specimen of a document of Alexandrian Christianity. The language, thought, and method of the writing are very much like documents of Alexandrian Judaism, which had seen a long history. There the Jewish Scriptures had been translated into Greek, and there Judaism had made an adaptation to Hellenistic ways, which may be taken as an example of Judaism's adaptation throughout the Dispersion. Philo, though a loyal nationalistic Jew, had put Judaism in terms of Platonic philosophy. Taking over allegorical method from the Greeks, he used it to state mystically for the benefit of Gentiles the "inner," "hidden" meaning of Judaism. Thus it is not remarkable to find in the Epistle to the Hebrews a Christian example of essentially the same thing.

Certainly that is what Hebrews is. It is a speech written to encourage people who were facing a grave danger. Using the allegorical method, and with abundant quotation of the Greek translation of Jewish Scripture, it labors to prevent apostasy.[1] The former status of the people addressed is contrasted with their present position; once they were heroic, now they are faltering.[2]

[1] Heb. 2:1, 4:1, 11, 14.   [2] Heb. 5:11—6:8, 10:32–39.

They are exhorted to stand fast.[3] The data suggest the conclusion that Hebrews was addressed to the Roman community; the former experience of persecution, which they had met nobly, was the traditional Neronic episode; the present one, in which they were not behaving with the same fortitude, was the Domitianic persecution. If this is true, the persecution had not yet been applied in the community with severity (Heb. 12:4: "You have not resisted to the point of death").

This fits the total picture of the lighter pressure applied by Domitian in Rome, as compared with the greater severity of persecution in Asia. It also suits the facts revealed by another early Christian writing, which was not included in the New Testament. This letter, known as "I Clement," is a communication from the church at Rome to the church of Corinth. Early sections of the letter reflect the Domitianic persecution; at the same time, it is the earliest witness of the currency of the Epistle to the Hebrews. The best explanation of the data is that Hebrews was addressed to the Roman church to exhort them to greater resistance; I Clement shows that the exhortation was acted upon; therefore, in some sense I Clement was called forth by Hebrews and was a reply to it.

The messages of Hebrews, couched in eloquent language, are simple enough. The background of Alexandrian culture contributes to its lofty language, to figures of speech which are often obscure (understood only when one is accustomed to the allegorical interpretation of Jewish Scripture), and to supposedly philosophical terms. Its argument that Christianity is a "better" covenant suggests that it is worth struggling to maintain. It reiterates the point of the sin of apostasy. It constantly exhorts the people to hold fast. The message of persecution sometimes becomes explicit, as has been pointed out. In the effective passage of 11:1—12:13 the point is unmistakable: the heroes of faith suffered and many died as martyrs. Now, surrounded by this cloud of martyrs ("witness" and "martyr" are the same word in Greek), those faced with persecution must follow Jesus through death, if need be.

[3] Heb. 10:19-31.

The address is fashioned into a letter by appending a general exhortation[4] and an epistolary conclusion.[5] It is this last which led some of the ancients to believe that Hebrews was a letter of Paul's. Doubtless this belief secured its inclusion in the New Testament. While there have been many guesses as to its authorship, the only certainty is that it was not written by Paul.

In the method of Alexandrian allegorism, Hebrews is a document reflecting early intellectualism in the Christian movement. It is easy to see that in its circle there is definite dogma (faith in Hebrews means not an act of belief, as in Paul's letters, but the belief in a definite body of doctrine). But still more indicative is its abundant use of Scripture, its seeking for the "higher" meaning, and its use of allegory to obtain that meaning.

The Revelation of John is a very different type of writing. In literary form it is an example of the apocalypse, of which there are many examples known. Indeed, from about 250 B.C. Judaism frequently used the apocalypse as a kind of "tract for hard times." The Book of Isaiah contains an apocalyptic section (chaps. 24–27); the books of Joel and Zechariah are apocalypses; while Daniel is a typical example of the form. Besides these, there were several other Jewish apocalypses: the composite book known as "I Enoch" contains several, Baruch has been analyzed into six apocalyptic parts, another is II Enoch, and the latest of the Jewish apocalypses is IV Ezra. These are only a few of the total number which once flourished.

An apocalypse attempts to show the reason for the exceptional difficulties and to picture the final outcome. It customarily uses fantastic imagery and curious figures. It expects that the meaning of these will be apparent to the readers, for basic to the written apocalypses was the world view which makes them readily understood.

As was pointed out in discussing Paul's expectation of the end of the world, the apocalyptic view was that God, although ultimately supreme, has abandoned the world to the devil. For the devil's purposes the world's rulers oppress and persecute God's people—an explanation of their present situation. The message

---

[4] Heb. 12:14—13:17.   [5] Heb. 13:18–25.

of the apocalypse is that, if the people hold fast, God will soon intervene, smash the present world to bits; and, in the new world which he will create, the suffering people will be the people of the Kingdom of God.

The Revelation of John is made up of an introduction,[6] a general letter of "John" to the churches of the province of Asia,[7] seven letters to seven churches in the province,[8] and a series of apocalyptic sections.[9] The apocalyptic sections seem to have been derived from a number of sources; some of their literary relationships have been determined by scholars who specialize in this field.

The book as a whole, however, does what any apocalypse undertakes. The people addressed are undergoing severe persecution. One person has already died a martyr,[10] and it is expected that there will be a multitude of others.[11] Clearly the people addressed are the Christians of Asia—that is the point of the letters to the seven Asian churches—and equally clearly the persecutor is Rome, particularly the emperor. This is unmistakable, although the figures of speech are intentionally obscure (as safety to the reader necessitated): the prostitute who is a city on seven hills is obviously Rome; the imperial house is identified by the "beast" with the varying number of heads and horns.

The readily satisfactory interpretation of the curious figures is that the emperor was Domitian, and the persecution the troubled time which broke when (A.D. 96) Domitian attempted to force his claim to worship. It is significant, for example, that the one martyr who is named, Antipas, was a member of the church at Pergamum. Pergamum was then the seat of the provincial cult of the emperor, and the frieze of the altar of its great temple—referred to in Revelation as "Satan's throne"—is now in a museum in Berlin.

Some of the details are obscure enough. For example, the "number of the beast," 666, is obviously intended to identify a

[6] 1:1–3.

[7] 1:4–20.   [9] 4:1—22:21.

[8] 2:1—3:22.   [10] 2:13.

[11] 7:4–10, where the typical number twelve times twelve thousand is used as a figure.

man. The Greek language did not have numerals; it used letters of the alphabet in place of numbers. Thus the 666 is intended to suggest a name the numerical equivalent of whose letters totals 6 hundreds, 6 tens, and 6 digits. The generally accepted interpretation is that the word is Nero, written in Aramaic characters. How does this, then, suit an apocalypse of the persecution of Domitian? The point is simple: this part of Revelation may have been a Neronic source. Further, there was a common expectation in antiquity that Nero would "return"—the "Nero redivivus" myth. Thus the reigning emperor (identified by one of the heads and horns of the beast) is the revived Nero.[12] "Nero," in fact, was one of the names applied to Domitian by contemporary writers.[13]

Revelation is a book of blood, with nothing of the commonly ascribed Christian virtues in it except steadfastness. The picture of the Messiah is that of a bloodthirsty warrior;[14] certainly a river of blood two hundred miles wide and so deep as to come to horses' bridles is blood enough.[15]

This bloodthirstiness was necessary, in the writer's conviction. For the situation of God's people was desperate. They were in danger because they were compelled to worship the emperor,[16] and the point of the whole book was to encourage resistance. Steadfastness is the great virtue, and the promise of reward (balanced by the threat of punishment) to those who resist emperor-worship is the simple technique. The immediate situation is related to the cosmic outcome: the persecuted are fighting God's battle, are fighting on the side of Jesus; if only they are steadfast and do not give way, soon God will smash the power of Rome and of the devil, for whom the emperor is only a tool.

Revelation is a seditious book. This explains the strange apocalyptic figures of its messages; the initiates will understand, while outsiders will not get the book's point. This explains, too, the curious quality of the Greek in this book. It is very ungram-

[12] Rev. 13:1–10, esp. 13:3; cf. 17:3–14, esp. 17:11.

[13] Juvenal *Satires* iv. 37, 38; Martial *Epigrams* xi. 33.

[14] 19:11–21.

[15] 14:9–20.   [16] 13:15, 14:9, 11, 16:2, 19:20, 20:4.

matical, and the language in general is qualitatively poor. This may not indicate inferior intellect on the part of the writer; rather, it could result from hasty copying by people without literate skill.

It is unfortunate that throughout the succeeding centuries the Book of Revelation has been interpreted not with reference to the situation at the time of its writing but as though its messages were intended for the time of any given interpreter. Thus the most fantastically mistaken interpretations have been made. For example, the beast numbered 666 has been understood as the Pope, Mohammed, Kaiser Wilhelm II, Hitler, and numerous other people. The figure of the thousand years[17] has been tortured by various millenarian groups. All such misuse is regrettable, for it takes attention away from the intended purpose of the book.

The Revelation of John was written as early Christianity confronted a hostile state. It was absolutely essential, if the movement were to survive, that this critical danger be met courageously and with effective leadership. This was not the first time that the heavy hand of the state had been felt, nor was it to be the last. The significant thing is that, when Christianity and the state came into conflict, religious force proved to be stronger than political.

A further stage of the conflict between Christianity and the Roman state is reflected in I Peter. The data of persecution are obvious;[18] it is a question, however, as to what the exact situation was that brought forth the document. The traditional persecution of Nero is the only one which could suit the authorship of the letter by Peter, but there are convincing reasons why the letter is later than this date. These and other reasons are sufficient to prove that I Peter, like Revelation and other books of the New Testament, is pseudonymous.

The literary form of I Peter is itself puzzling. Its epistolary salutation and conclusion do not disguise the fact that the main part of the document is not a letter. The passage 1:3—3:22 is an address; the best judgment is that it is a bishop's address to a class of those who had been instructed in preparation for bap-

---

[17] Rev. 20:4–6.   [18] I Pet. 1:6 f., 4:12–19, 5:9 f.

tism.[19] Chapters 4 and 5 are chiefly, as the former part is incidentally,[20] concerned with behavior of the people in persecution. I Peter, therefore, seems to be a combination of a bishop's address to a baptismal class and several epistolary parts.[21]

The data of the religious life show, at the same time, that the writer of the "letter" was not Peter and that it was written from a date later than Peter's time. In general, the type of the religious experience reflected agrees with that observed in the Pauline churches. The people are Gentiles; they were pagans[22] before they were "born again."[23] They came into their present religious life through believing, i.e., faith;[24] and the process of salvation was the same as in the Pauline communities. As in Paul's way of life, spiritual gifts are important.[25] Indeed, the literary relations between I Peter and Paul's letters are plain. The relationships are particularly observable in Romans and Ephesians; therefore, it must be concluded that the author of I Peter wrote after the publication of Paul's letters as a book.

Since these considerations preclude a Neronic date, the data of persecution must be interrogated to determine which persecution they reflect. The majority of scholars agree that I Peter reflects the Domitianic persecution. There is excellent reason, however, for concluding that it came from the still later Trajanic persecution, regarding which information is given by one of the letters of the younger Pliny. This correspondence originated when Pliny was governor of Bithynia, and it consists of several letters to the emperor Trajan.

The decisive point is that, whereas there is no evidence that any Christian suffered in the Neronic or the Domitianic persecution for the crime of being a Christian, this was the basis of the Trajanic persecution, and this is reflected in I Peter. Such "persecution" as there was in the days of Nero was meted out because those who suffered were suspected of having set fire to the city of Rome and because they were people who, to the Romans, were

---

[19] See, further, Streeter, *The Primitive Church*, pp. 121–41.

[20] E.g., I Pet. 1:6 f., 2:12, 13–17, 3:14–17.   [23] I Pet. 1:3, 23.

[21] 1:1–2, 4:1—5:14.   [24] I Pet. 1:5, 9.

[22] I Pet. 1:18, 2:10, 12, 4:3 f.   [25] I Pet. 4:10, 11.

odiously stubborn. In the Domitianic persecution Christians were liable to punishment if they refused to worship the emperor (i.e., if they refused to participate in the cult of the emperor). There was a distinct difference in the persecution of Trajan. Pliny's letter shows clearly that, now that the old Roman law prohibiting any new religion was being invoked, Christians were liable to arrest and punishment on the ground that they were Christians. The fact alone was sufficient to convict them.

I Peter shows that people were being persecuted simply because they were Christians. In 4:14 it appears that people are liable to abuse "for the sake of Christ." In 4:16 the fact is explicit: people suffer for being Christians. In other words, the legal basis for persecution differs as between I Peter and earlier documents. The same difference can be observed in Pliny's letter to Trajan. Hence it should be concluded that I Peter is Trajanic.

The general data suit this view. In its reflection of a way of life I Peter is highly developed; its vocabulary includes several terms which were used by the mystery cults, and its theological basis is a development from Paul. Jesus has been dead a long time —these people love him whom they have not seen[26] (this resembles John 20:29, also late); officers of the church have specific duties (this resembles the situation of the Pastoral Epistles); and the counsels concerning the daily life indicate an advanced growth of the Christian movement (e.g., wealth is a problem, as is shown by the advice to ladies not to wear jewels).

Thus, both in its reflection of the general religious life and in its particular reference to the behavior of the people with reference to the state, I Peter is an advanced work. The quality of its Greek is high, so far as the New Testament Greek is evaluated. It is the work not of a Galilean fisherman (this epithet, needless to say, is not derogatory but indicative) but of a leader in an advanced development of gentile Christianity. The document is thus of great value as a source of information of Christianity in the period when it was expanding rapidly in many regions of the Mediterranean world.

[26] I Pet. 1:8.

XVIII

THE MIND AND THE SPIRIT: THE FOURTH GOSPEL AND THE LETTER OF JAMES

IT WOULD be difficult to find two more dissimilar documents than the Fourth Gospel and the so-called "Epistle of James." They seem to have been written not far from each other in time, and each expresses a distinctive feature of developing Christianity. Thus they illustrate the different types of religious life in early Christianity.

Why was the Fourth Gospel written? Its differences from the earlier gospels give the lead to the answer. Like the others, it is a particular writing of the good news of Jesus. Like its predecessors, it was written to voice the messages of a certain trend within the Christian movement in order to gain disciples for its view and thus to further the movement. But its differences indicate the particular viewpoint and trend.

The reader can learn much by noting the differences between the Fourth and the other canonical gospels. It has no genealogy or birth story of Jesus. It has no Sermon on the Mount, no Lord's Prayer, no list of the Twelve, no story of Peter's confession or of the transfiguration. In it Jesus teaches differently; there are no parables. In the other gospels the scene of the early action is Galilee (save for the birth stories); in the Fourth Gospel, Jesus is often in Jerusalem. Indeed, there is little realistic setting in the Fourth Gospel—background and history count for little. Here, although the Pharisees are sometimes mentioned, Sadducees, Samaritans, demoniacs, Zealots, do not appear; the "other people" of the Fourth Gospel are lumped together and called "the Jews."

In its own distinctive content, too, the Fourth Gospel differs from the Synoptic Gospels. It begins with a stately prologue; and in it Jesus discourses in a sort of philosophical way on recurrent themes, with a particular vocabulary of light, darkness, life, and belief. While it has some of the same stories as are told in the other gospels (e.g., the feeding of five thousand people), even its miracles are different. There are seven of them in the body of the gospel, and each is a sort of symbol. The vehicle of the teaching of Jesus is characteristically dialogue. In chapters 14–17 there is a sustained discourse which, in form and content, is unique.

In the passion story the narrative approaches that of the other gospels more closely; but this, too, has its differences. As Jesus is first introduced as "the lamb of God who takes away the world's sin," so in his death the figure is carried out; Jesus does not eat the Passover meal with his associates but is put to death at the time the Passover lamb was slain.

These differences indicate that the latest of the New Testament gospels was written not to supplement the earlier gospels but to supplant them. And in its particular content the gospel shows that its purpose was to present an interpretation of Jesus which, for want of a better word, can be called "mystical."

The work tells its purpose: "Jesus did many other omens; these are written that you may believe that Jesus is the Anointed, God's Son, and that in believing you may have life in his name."[1] The particular force of "belief" in the Fourth Gospel shows that the work was built upon a foundation similar to the function of faith in Paul's gospel and way of life. But it is a further development of this. An intellectual element is involved.

The development of Christianity on the intellectual level was, of course, relatively late. This is the necessary and inevitable sequence in any rising religious movement. Evangelism and expansion naturally come first, followed by consolidation and the achievement of self-consciousness. Only after these foundational results have been reached can there be development of the intellectual element. This element did, indeed, appear late. To some extent it is seen in early Christianity in the so-called "Epistle to the Hebrews." Elsewhere it first appears as a reflex of the prob-

[1] John 20:31.

lem of unity; unity involves some agreement of belief, which becomes a doctrinal matter—and in religion doctrine is an intellectual matter. But this does not account for the Fourth Gospel. To discover its intellectualism a different area must be observed. This is found in Hellenistic mysticism.

There were certain trends in Hellenistic culture in which ordinary "rational" processes were disavowed in favor of mysticism. In philosophy this was exemplified variously: by the Neo-Pythagoreans (who lived in semireligious, quasi-monastic groups and cultivated the higher thought by mathematics and other studies), by the movement which became Neo-Platonism, and by the philosophical trends (like the thought of Philo) which were both religious and philosophical. In religion this mysticism is to be observed in the mystery cults and, in a curious form, in Gnosticism. Still more widely to be found was the use of allegory as an intellectual method. For example, going back to what was also in Plato, Plutarch reinterpreted the myth and the practices of the Isis cult by allegory. As was true of Philo also, Plutarch attempted to show that the "physical" aspects of the myth and the crude practices were not the real and essential ones but that their reality was to be grasped only in their mystical meaning.

This is the key to the understanding of the Fourth Gospel. It tells the story of Jesus differently, with "higher" meaning. Its preference for this higher meaning is to be observed in all its content. It has a deliberate disregard for the "historical" (of course, it does not use this word) in favor of the mystical. It is entirely deliberate about this.

For example, the story of Nicodemus brings this out clearly. Nicodemus is said to have sought out Jesus to learn from him; but whenever Jesus speaks, Nicodemus misunderstands and takes the wrong meaning. He always takes the lower, physical meaning. But when the purpose of the Fourth Gospel is perceived, it is discovered that Nicodemus is expected to do this. In each case Jesus is pictured as using a word which is ambiguous—capable of a higher and a lower, a physical and a spiritual, meaning. When Jesus says, "You must be born *anothen*" (the word means both "again" and "from above"), Nicodemus takes it to mean that a man must re-enter his mother's body and be born in the physical way a second time. What he should understand, of course, is that everyone must be reborn spiritually. When Jesus says, "The *pneuma* ["wind," "breath," or "spirit"] *pnei* ["blows" or "breathes"] where it chooses, and you hear the *phone* ["voice" or "sound"] of it," poor Nicodemus is hardly to be blamed if he fails to understand precisely what the ambiguous words mean—translators have failed to agree ever since.

The point is that it was intended that Nicodemus should misunderstand, for he typifies the physically minded person. He illustrates the whole intention of the Fourth Gospel. The work is written on the basis of the perception that, while many, perhaps most, people think and behave on the physical level, or near it, there are some who are capable of understanding the "higher," "spiritual" meaning; and this Gospel was written for them.

This means that, when the Fourth Gospel was written, there were those in Christianity who could form a public for a mystical gospel. In other words, in Christianity's development it came to include some of these intellectual mystics, and in the writer of the Fourth Gospel they found their leader.

This requires the reader to see that the Fourth Gospel represents a considerable development of gentile Christianity. The fact is plain in its contents. For example, the anti-Jewishness of the work is manifest. The story reads back into the story of Jesus the situation which was true when the work was written. The breach between Christianity and Judaism is not only wide; that it is not to be bridged is taken as an assumed fact. The hostility to Judaism which the work reflects is uniform throughout. It reaches a height in John 8:30 ff., at which point Jesus embarks upon a dialogue with Jews who believe in him; when the story reaches 8:44 they are called "sons of the devil." The speeches of 8:34–38, 42–47, are public pronouncements of the fate of the Jews. There is no sympathy with Judaism in the Fourth Gospel; the work represents gentile Christianity at a period well after it had become apparent that there was to be no *rapprochement* between Judaism and Christianity.

Indeed, the Fourth Gospel pictures Jesus as hardly a Jew himself. This is to be seen not only in the quasi-philosophical way in which Jesus speaks (which is quite un-Jewish) and in the un-Jewish themes and vocabulary but in certain items highly suggestive of attitude. For example, Pilate speaks to the Jews (18:31) of "your law"; obviously, it was not his law. But Jesus in 8:17 uses the same expression "your law," as though it were not his.

The correct way to view this feature is to regard it as the writer's reading back into his story of Jesus the attitudes current at the time the gospel was written. This appears plainly in the epilogue to the Nicodemus story. To be sure, it is plain only in the Greek (or in the archaic English of the King James or the American Standard versions). The point may be made plain in contemporary English, however. In 3:10 Jesus says: "Are you [i.e., Nicodemus] the teacher of Israel . . . . ? We know what we say, and you [here the word is plural and obviously does not refer to Nicodemus] reject our [*sic*] testimony." The point is that Nicodemus in the whole story is a type for Judaism, and the point of the story and the dialogue which follows is that Jews generally reject the Christian messages.

The same facts appear in the thought relationships throughout the Fourth Gospel. Some of its concepts are very similar to Paul's teaching: the thoroughgoing individualism[2] and the emphasis upon belief (faith) in Jesus. This element in the Fourth Gospel is not the teaching of Paul, but, like the teaching of Paul, it is the outcome of the impact of the gentile world upon Christianity.

The viewpoint in the Fourth Gospel is a further development of gentile Christianity. For example, in the underlying concept of the end of the age and of life after death the viewpoint is that of an intellectualized development. The former expectation of the soon-to-come end of the age has been given up; the view appears only in vestigial language. The concept of life after death is not the Jewish thought of a resurrection of the body, but a form of the Greek idea of the immortality of the soul—one who believes in Jesus never dies.[3]

The development has reached the point that an advanced conception of the church is evident. While the church is not men-

[2] Cf. John 1:12 f.   [3] John 11:25 f.

tioned in the Fourth Gospel, it is obviously assumed. Chapters 14–17 are a discourse for the guidance of the "New Community." The allegory of the good shepherd and of the sheepfold shows that the inclusion of Gentiles is an assumed fact.[4] The church is envisaged long after Jesus' death; in the prayer of chapter 17 Jesus prays for those who believe through the messages of his followers.[5] The point is implicit throughout the work, and it becomes explicit in 12:20 ff., when the Greeks come to Jesus. This is recognized as the climax. "My hour has not come yet" has been said before; but now Jesus says, "Now the time has come"[6] and "If I am lifted up from the ground I shall draw all men to myself."

The plea for unity and the obvious polemic against sectaries bring out the same point of the highly advanced concept of the church. Unity was a great value in the so-called "Epistle to the Ephesians"; it is so here also. It appears in an allegory at 10:16 and is a theme of the discourse on the New Community, especially in the prayer "that they may all be one."[7] The hostility to the John the Baptist sect is almost as plain; this is the reason for the studied depreciation of John the Baptizer.[8]

But it is not merely the advanced development of Christianity which is apparent in the Fourth Gospel. It is the particular development toward the intellectual, mystical features which indicates its quality and character. This is what accounts for the obvious differences between the Fourth Gospel and the Synoptics. The point is not simply that they are historical while this gospel is interpretative; all gospels are interpretative. But the Fourth Gospel has a deliberate disregard of "history" in favor of that understanding of Jesus which is "above history." Far more than in Paul's thought, Jesus is a cosmic figure. And the view is expressed in terms of Greek thought—e.g., the idea that Jesus was the Logos, the creative Word of God.

The symbolism is to the same effect. It is doubtless important that in the body of this gospel there are seven miracles. Usually

[4] John 10:16.
[5] John 17:20.
[6] John 12:23.
[7] John 17:20–23.
[8] John 1:20 ff., 3:27–30.

each is symbolic. The plainest examples are the feeding of the five thousand, which assumes (without explaining it) the sacramental Lord's Supper, and the healing of the man born blind, which is the basis for the dialogue about the Light of the World. Very probably these seven miracles make individual sections of the gospel and were so shaped in the gospel because of ceremonies in the church. At all events, they illustrate how the gospel always points to a "hidden," "higher" meaning. It is a development of Hellenistic mysticism, as the public of Christianity came to include such people.

It is impossible to date the Fourth Gospel with certainty, and it is impossible to identify its author. No claim of authorship is made in it, and tradition is so confused that no assured answer can be obtained. What can be said with assurance is that the Fourth Gospel is the work of one who thought in Greek terms, and specifically in terms of Hellenistic mysticism. This stage of development would date the work no earlier than the first decade of the second century.

Of a very different type is the so-called "Epistle of James." Indeed, its literary form has long been a puzzle. Included in the New Testament as an epistle, its only epistolary characteristic is a salutation. It has long been recognized as an address, similar to Hebrews. Of late, its coincidence in form with the Cynic-Stoic diatribe has been observed. Still more recently, its similarity to a certain type of Hellenistic moral literature has been shown; formerly the nearest parallel in literary form was thought to be the Jewish Wisdom Literature. It is obviously the work of a teacher; its messages are those of a moral code which was intended to be applied generally.

Thus, while the Fourth Gospel takes its reader into the realm of intellectualized mysticism, James represents a different kind of didactic. Both these later documents of the New Testament represent the work of Hellenistic teachers.

The particular aspects of James are to be noted in the observation of its contents. If the student undertakes to write an outline of it, he soon discovers that the work is not "about" any one thing, nor is there a logical development in related sections of any several themes.

The generality of its messages is an integral feature of its nature. The work differs from Paul's letters in this respect. With few exceptions, as was noted, Paul's letters always related to a specific situation in a particular church, and his messages were intended to apply to that single situation. The Epistle of James was intended for general application. For example, when it offers teaching about rich and poor, it does not follow that in only the one group addressed were there these problems of rich and poor. Nor does it follow that when James was written wealth had become a problem in the church, as it had not been before. What follows is that rich and poor are discussed as classes, and the moral problems involved exist because the rich are rich and the poor are poor. The moralizing is general; it is intended to be such.

This general moral exhortation is called "paraenesis." Romans 12:9–14 illustrates it. The gospels contain it; interestingly enough, much the same attitude toward wealth and poverty is expressed in Luke-Acts as is contained in James. The point is that, as Christianity flourished and grew, it developed its moral codes, and its leaders articulated them in general patterns. Functionally, this is what the Sermon on the Mount was. Jewish literature has much of this paraenetic type of didactic. There is, as noted above, a category of Hellenistic literature which contains it, with one document furnishing close parallels in content to James. This literature has been miscalled "Jewish Greek"; actually, it is genuinely Greek, with its form given it by the emphasis upon ethics in the Stoic philosophy. A document known as "Pseudo-Phocylides," written in hexameter lines, resembles James in content much more closely than the parallels adduced from the Jewish Wisdom Literature.

Although the writer of James was not a philosopher and not a Stoic, the coincidence of its form with the Cynic-Stoic diatribe must be discussed. In its beginning and its early development Stoicism laid primary emphasis upon metaphysics—the problem of the nature of being. But in its later development it laid much greater emphasis upon ethics; this is seen in such a Stoic as Epictetus. Stoicism also became increasingly practical, as, indeed, all Greek philosophy did. Its representatives were no longer cloistered in an academy or a lyceum; they were to be found on the street corners, haranguing the people who passed, attempting to attract them to stop and listen. Stoicism in the days of Jesus and Paul had a missionary zeal. Wearing the philosopher's garb, the speaker in the market place learned how to present his moral messages to the general public and discovered a way to make them interesting.

This vehicle of instruction was the diatribe (from the word *diatribo*, "I rub together"). Typical examples are furnished by the diatribes of Epictetus. These addresses consisted of very short units of simple structure. In part it was in dialogue, and it often secured the effect of dialogue by using the rhetorical question— a question which always answered itself. Imperatives were of frequent occurrence. Although a sentence might be long, it was, nevertheless, structurally simple, usually consisting of short, crisp phrases. The nature of the Greek language being what it was, the effect of rhyme was approximated, and rhythm was obvious.

A careful study of the Epistle of James brings to light many of the features of the diatribe. The apparently discursive nature of its contents coincides with the diatribe form. James is full of imperatives, and rhetorical questions are common. The intended generality of application of its messages suits the diatribe form. Its Greek is of high quality; if the student reads James in Greek after reading Epictetus, he does not have to look up nearly as many words in the lexicon as the reverse study requires. Then, if he compares James with Pseudo-Phocylides, he has the basis for understanding how it came into being.

One of the paradoxical features of James is its apparently Jewish quality. There is almost complete coincidence of its vocabulary with the vocabulary of the Greek translation of the Old Testament. Yet James quotes Jewish Scripture very seldom. Its writer is steeped in it, but he does not quote it. If this can be explained at all, it is by the reason that his knowledge of Jewish Scripture was acquired through the Greek translation, not from experience of Judaism.

Considering this factor with those which have been mentioned, and looking to the development of Christianity in the second century, the reader may see in James the work of a teacher whose approach is the teaching of a moral code which has general reference. In other words, in contrast to the Fourth Gospel, in which the reader finds a flowing-together of mind and spirit, in James he observes the application of mind to the problem of ethical codes and teachings in the new religion.

It is very difficult to suggest a probable date for James, and still more difficult to identify its author. By some scholars it is regarded as the earliest book in the New Testament; by others, one of the latest. That it is relatively late appears from an objective fact. Its place in the rising canon of Christian literature was insecure. Some of the forms of the New Testament do not contain it. Origen, an Alexandrian scholar of the third century, was the first to affirm that its author was James, the brother of Jesus. The bearing of these facts is plain. James was a common name in antiquity. It is possible that the book was written pseudonymously and ascribed to the brother of Jesus. However this may have been, it is probable that the document was written during the second century. The apparent parallels to the teaching of Jesus and in particular to the Sermon on the Mount[9] are best explained by reference to the paraenetic type of writing and teaching.

For, as was mentioned, the task of the teacher in early Christianity was subsequent to the task of the evangelist. The intellectual aspects of religion are not primary but secondary. Some of the processes of the development which was involved have been pointed out. It is simple fact that the features exemplified in the Fourth Gospel and in James are to be observed in Christianity's second century.

The particular time is not of great importance. What is important is to observe the actual sequence of the growth and development of Christianity. Since the developments on the intellectual level are to be found in the second century, to this period the Epistle of James is to be assigned. It is one of the documents which points to a maturing Christianity.

[9] E.g., Jas. 5:12.

XIX

MATURING CHRISTIANITY: I, II, III JOHN;
THE PASTORALS; JUDE; AND II PETER

THERE is considerable contrast between the free, unformed, unfixed, creative Christianity of the first decades and the organized, controlled, conventionalized, and much less creative Christianity of the second quarter of the second century. It requires only a reading of, say, I Corinthians and the Pastoral Epistles to see the difference.

Yet this was wholly natural, inevitable, and necessary. The abandon with which the earliest Christians lived was in part due to their expectation of the early end of the age. When Christians discovered that the world had not been destroyed and that they were to live in it for an indefinite time, they shaped their understanding and their way of the religious life accordingly. Thus Christianity survived and became a permanent institution in the ancient world. It had to pay the price of survival, and part of the price was the loss of freedom and creativity. The religious life had to become patterned; the church took on organization; and the way of life became conventionalized. All this is reflected in the documents of the New Testament which come from this period.

One set of forces and problems operative at this time was the rise of sects. The question of Christianity's unity had appeared as early as the writing of Ephesians, and it is reflected in the Fourth Gospel. It appears in these sources as the problem of general acceptance of teaching, of general uniformity of belief, and of the correctness or the error of doctrine. This, in turn, was an aspect of the intellectual development in Christianity; this fact largely accounts for the late rise of problems of sectaries and heretics.

At all events, an ardent plea for unity always reveals the lack of unity. For Christianity was never homogeneous in its way of life. The religious life of the churches in Palestine differed from that of gentile churches. Within gentile churches further differences are observable, for Pauline communities varied from other areas of gentile Christianity. There was healthy variety and diversity. Thus, when the consolidation of Christianity came and the movement became conscious of itself as a new and independent religion, general acceptance of a given teaching was difficult to achieve. Unity was an ideal but not a reality.

To take the perspective of a longer view, by the time of the Council of Nicea in A.D. 326 there had been achieved a broad and general acceptance of doctrine and churchmanship. But, even then, there were sectarian and heretical movements—always there have been such. It is instructive of the history of early Christianity to observe the early phases of this development as they are revealed in the writings of the New Testament.

I, II, and III John are thus informative sources. It is most efficient to consider them in reverse order. III John is a very brief letter of an unnamed "elder" (the title of a church official; probably there was at that time and in that place no distinction between "elder" and "bishop") to a churchman named Gaius. The behavior of Gaius is approved, for he had received some visiting "brothers" into the hospitality of the local church.[1] But a certain Diotrephes had repelled them and had assumed authority to put out of the church all the members who had accorded these visitors hospitality.[2] Diotrephes is also undermining the authority of the elder who writes.

Thus there is a problem of church discipline. The elder meets it by commending those who have done what he thinks is right and by threatening to come and lay his complaint against Diotrephes before the church for appropriate action.

The area is enlarged in II John. This seems to be a letter to a congregation, for "the chosen lady" who is addressed is doubtless a local church described in a figure of speech. But in this document the situation is different from that in III John. Here the

[1] III John, vss. 5–8. [2] III John, vss. 9 f.

visiting Christian brothers have been spreading the wrong teaching. Obviously, this means that it is considered wrong from the viewpoint of the "elder"; i.e., it is wrong in the eyes of the church which he represents. Thus he directs[3] that no one is to accord these people hospitality—indeed, he orders that people must not even say "Good morning" to them. This, too, is a problem of discipline, with the added detail that correctness of teaching is involved.

It is obvious that, as Christianity developed, it must organize its teaching into doctrines which the people generally were expected to maintain. To the church this was correct, orthodox teaching; anything which differed from it was wrong, unorthodox, heretical. It is plain that in II John a considerable growth of doctrine is to be observed, and with it the rise of doctrine which differed from it. The church regarded all those who dissented in doctrine as sectaries and heretics. As is to be seen in these sources (and in later documents), its way of meeting this problem was to exercise its authority, to exert discipline. The effect of this development was far-reaching.

A still broader picture is to be seen in I John. This is another writing which is miscalled an "epistle." It does not purport to be a letter, for it does not have either epistolary salutation or conclusion. It is a written address. From vocabulary and style it is usually thought that I, II, and III John are by the same writer, who was also the author of the Fourth Gospel; but it will be shown that there are significant and essential differences between them and the Fourth Gospel. In any case, II and III John are so brief that evidence of style is inconclusive, and there is little basis for conclusions drawn from the data of vocabulary.

However this may be, it is plain that the problem of the sectaries is important in I John. The people who are castigated used to be within the church[4] (meaning the church of the writer, or the general church of his locality). Some of their "false" teachings are cited. They claim moral perfection.[5] They deny that Jesus is Christ.[6] They have their characteristic teachings, which the

---

[3] II John, vss. 7–11.   [5] I John 1:8, 10.

[4] I John 2:19.   [6] I John 2:22.

writer calls "error."[7] Apparently they reject some of the church's sacraments and ordinances (in the references to water, blood, and spirit it must be that, in the first two, baptism and the Lord's Supper are referred to).[8] Apparently the sectaries are radical spiritists, for the writer insists that the church people test all utterances of spirit.[9]

In some respects the description of these sectaries corresponds with what is known from other sources[10] as "Docetists" ("seemists"). These Docetists made a radical distinction between spirit and flesh and thus became radical dualists. They denied that Jesus had a "real" body, i.e., a body of human flesh, and insisted that his body was spirit and only seemed to be flesh. They said, similarly, that Jesus did not really suffer, since he was spirit, but only seemed to suffer. To Ignatius of Antioch and to other orthodox church leaders the Docetists were dangerous heretics. References to this particular "heresy" serve to connect these documents of the New Testament with the time of Ignatius, about the years 112–17, and throw light on the ways developed to meet these flourishing sectaries.

Ignatius, the bishop of Antioch, undertook to meet it by the strict application of church discipline, by refusing to admit to the Lord's Supper any who would not submit to the control of the bishop and his subordinates. This is not different from conditions in II John. Indeed, all three of these New Testament documents reflect the method of control by authority; they exhibit, respectively, its application to an individual, a church, and a group of churches in a given region (in effect, a bishop's diocese).

The Pastoral Epistles indicate the process by which the work of church officials came to be more clearly defined. Even though they, also, reflect problems of heresy, their distinctive mark is the wealth of information about church workers.

It is this information which indicates the date of the Pastorals. These letters to Timothy and Titus were written in the name of

[7] I John 4:6.

[8] I John 5:8.   [9] I John 4:1–3.

[10] Particularly the Epistles of Ignatius, bishop of Antioch, which date from approximately the same time as I, II, and III John.

Paul, but it requires only a little study to perceive that they do not fit into any situation of Paul's lifetime. They are, therefore, pseudonymous; written by someone else and ascribed to Paul. Their picture of the church's growth in organization is the clue to the time of their composition. There are three separate "orders" of ministers: bishop (or overseer), elder, and deacon. In addition, there are minor church officers and workers; the Pastorals are particularly concerned with the "widows." It is known from other sources that the church came to have, as minor orders of the ministry, readers and exorcists. The widows named by the Pastorals must be classed as an order of the ministry.

Great advance in organization is indicated in the Pastorals. The work of church officials is now standardized, so that the duties of the workers can be stated. What is still more important, the candidates for the offices can be measured for their probable fitness, and the incumbents appraised for their success and ability. The offices were being sought.[11] Workers were paid salaries.[12] Indeed, the development of Christianity on the organizational side was such that money had become a problem; some of the church workers used their offices for their own gain.[13] That this was not the first instance of a similar situation is shown by I Peter,[14] which dates from the early second century. There is further evidence in another writing contemporary to the Pastorals, the Epistle of Polycarp. Evidently the second quarter of the second century witnessed many problems incident to Christianity's institutional growth.

The Pastoral Epistles reflect a particular aspect of heresy and schism. It is seen in several passages in which the evidence is definite enough to point to the rise of the heresy connected with the name of Marcion. Marcion, a native of Pontus, was a radical dualist, and his vigorous thought was most troublesome to the general church. He came to Rome, joined the church there, and made a substantial gift of money. When his independence of thought became apparent, he was expelled, and his money was

11 I Tim. 3:1. 13 I Tim. 3:3, 8.
12 I Tim. 5:17. 14 5:2.

returned to him. But his influence was of such power that a strong sect came into being.

A notable feature or Marcion's dualism was his sharp distinction concerning the "nature" of God. Marcion concluded that the loving Father of Jesus could not be the same as the vengeful creator God of the Old Testament; there must be two Gods or two distinct natures within God. Since the Jewish Scripture was concerned with the creating and vengeful God, it was, therefore, of no value. But Marcion did not stop with the rejection of the Scripture which the church had appropriated; he compiled a collection of Christian writings to replace it, circulating the gospel section of Luke-Acts and the Pauline corpus as rival Scripture. This was accompanied by the publication of his own book—an exposition of the "antitheses," which were his major subject of thought.

Several of the teachings of Marcion seem to be argued in the Pastorals. In affirming that there is only one God,[15] in controverting some of the ascetic practices of the Marcionites,[16] and in affirming that *all* Scripture is inspired and useful,[17] the Pastorals are alluding to the very things that Marcion taught. In I Tim. 6:20 it may be that Marcion's theological book is mentioned by name; if not, the reference applies perfectly to the heretic's teachings, for the reader is warned against "the worldly, empty phrases and antitheses [this is the word in Greek; the same word which was used as the title of Marcion's book] of the falsely so-called knowledge."

If it is true that the Pastorals controvert Marcionism, their date can be fixed. Marcion became influential during the second quarter of the second century, and the date of his expulsion from the Roman church is fixed at A.D. 144. Thus the Pastorals were probably written at about this time. The precise date is not important, but it is of some value to know that they reflect the general period when Christianity was attaining maturity.

The method by which the problems of heresy were met by the writer of the Pastorals is not different from that which has been

[15] I Tim. 2:5.
[16] I Tim. 4:3–5.   [17] II Tim. 3:16.

observed in other sources. It was by the exercise of authority. There was an objective test of correctness of belief, and all who did not meet it were to be expelled from communion.[18]

The highly organized church of the Pastorals was conscious of its place in the world, and social approval or disapproval was important. This factor is prominent in the directions for measuring and testing officers and workers. The candidate for the office of bishop must be a man of good standing with outsiders.[19] Obviously, too, such elemental aspects as sobriety were relevant in this connection.

One of the aspects of organization reflected in the Pastorals is the function of charity. Basically this is the reason for the employment of widows as church workers. In early Christianity the praiseworthy attempt was made to care for all the Christian needy. Hospitality was an aspect of this; II and III John are pictures of its operation. Widowed women presented a particular problem. The church undertook to care for them and did so, enrolling them as workers for specific duties. These widows now constituted a problem by their very number. Consequently, the Pastorals meet this by urging that relatives care for them wherever possible, so that the burden of the church may be lightened.[20]

In Jude and II Peter the problems of heresy are reflected in an acute stage. These documents appear to be the latest of all the early Christian writings included in the New Testament. Evidently Jude is prior to II Peter, since the latter incorporates nearly all of it. Heresy is controverted by the method of warning people against its exponents, and in particular by the use of epithets. There is little attempt to meet thought with thought, idea with idea, teaching with teaching. Presumably, it was more effective to affirm the correctness of the church's teaching and castigate any conflicting teaching, calling it "heresy" and characterizing it by derogatory epithets.

A considerable advance in one feature, however, is to be observed in II Peter. A close reading of it shows that its author was acquainted with several Christian writings. I Peter is referred

---

[18] I Tim. 6:2b–5; Titus 3:10.

[19] I Tim. 3:7.   [20] I Tim. 5:3–16.

to;[21] there is an allusion to one of the gospels;[22] "all" of Paul's letters are referred to;[23] and Jude is certainly a source. What is more, the way Paul's letters are mentioned shows two important facts: they are known in their collected form, and they are now recognized as Scripture.[24] Thus a great development on the institutional side is to be seen in this latest book of the New Testament: early Christian writings were recognized and used as Scripture. It is not affirmed that the gospels were yet in that status, but there is sufficient reason to infer that they were. Marcion had already designated the Gospel of Luke as Scripture, and before these latest books of the New Testament were written the gospels were being circulated and used in the same form which they came to have in the New Testament, the Fourfold Gospel.

II Peter is certainly pseudonymous. Written as late as it was, the apostle could not have been its author. The use of Peter as a figure to whom early Christian writings were ascribed is itself an interesting phenomenon. In addition to the two letters ascribed to him in the New Testament, there was also a Gospel of Peter, an Acts of Peter, an Apocalypse of Peter, and voluminous stories and sayings in other "apocryphal" books.

This epistle is unmistakably Greek and unmistakably late. The Greek quality can be seen in its statements about the end of the world. For the primitive expectation of a catastrophic end soon to come, the writer substitutes the Greek idea of a place of punishment for the spirits of the wicked dead[25] and the teaching that impatience about the end of the world is out of order—it may come much later than was expected.[26]

The evidence of the letter bears out the whole picture of the later development of Christianity. Not only does it reflect a full canon of Christian Scripture; it exhibits one of the characteristic features of official Christianity in this regard. Scripture is not to be privately interpreted; it is to be understood in the light of its interpretation by the church.[27]

[21] II Pet. 3:1.
[22] II Pet. 1:17 f.
[23] II Pet. 3:16.
[24] II Pet. 3:16.
[25] II Pet. 2:4.
[26] II Pet. 3:3–7.
[27] II Pet. 1:20 f.

As was pointed out, all these later sources contrast with the earlier, primitive writings. The earlier writings pictured living with abandon, giving a high place to individual spiritistic behavior, and reflecting the marvelous creativity which characterized primitive Christianity. By contrast, the religious life reflected in these later works is much more prosaic, conventional, and patterned. This does not, of course, mean that these writings are less valuable; it means that they are different. Christianity necessarily lost something in becoming at home in its world; it had to pay the price of survival. To survive, it had to become institutionalized; and its institutionalization was at the expense of its free, spontaneous expression and much of its creativity. But there is no question that survival was a sufficient good. At least, Christianity in these days was sufficiently creative and adaptable to meet the problems of survival. If the movement lost much of its former charm, it gained great power. For Christianity, by embracing all sorts and conditions of men within itself, won in its competition with all rival cults and assimilated to itself most of the values which these had offered. In the process Christianity triumphed.

XX

THE EVOLUTION OF THE NEW TESTAMENT
CANON, TEXT, AND TRANSLATION

ALL the books of the New Testament had been written, and yet there was no New Testament. The New Testament itself, like the books which compose it, was the product of the religious life of the early Christians.

In observing the growth of the New Testament it must be borne in mind that there were several early Christian writings which were produced while books of the New Testament were being written. In part contemporary with the Revelation of John, there was a type of apocalypse called the "Shepherd of Hermas." The letters of Ignatius have been mentioned; there were seven of these to churches and one to Polycarp, bishop of Smyrna. There was an "Epistle of Barnabas." As has been mentioned, there were a Gospel and a Revelation ascribed to Peter. There were several "apocryphal" gospels, a few of which were written within the period of the New Testament. There was a didactic book called "The Teaching of the Lord through the Twelve Apostles" (commonly known as the "Didache"). Before the latest book of the New Testament was written, there were composed a few defenses of Christianity. The earliest are known only in fragment and in occasional quotations in the writings of the Church Fathers; but the apologies of Quadratus and Aristides are thus known, and a so-called "Preaching of Peter" was really a defense of Christianity. Perhaps a little earlier than the latest book of the New Testament—certainly not much later—there appeared a new type of Christian writing, exemplified first in the Martyrdom of Polycarp. The Epistle of Polycarp to the Philippians has been mentioned; criticism indicates that it is composite, consisting of two letters.

Thus it must be realized that leaders in early Christianity expressed themselves voluminously in writing and that the books of the New Testament represent only a part of early Christian literature. Further, it must be realized that in the growth of Christian Scripture there was a process of selection: the twenty-seven books which constitute our New Testament were selected from the total of early Christian writings. This means, of course, that many works considered valuable by Christian communities failed to be included in the New Testament. Some of them came close to inclusion. Indeed, as shall be shown, some were included in the New Testament as it was constituted in various parts of the Christian world. Conversely, some of the books in our New Testament were not listed in the New Testaments of different localities.

The word "canon" means literally "a rod" or "a measuring stick." Hence the term came to be applied to those biblical works which "passed measure" and were accepted into the Bible. The first factor in the canonical status of a New Testament document was its use. The degree to which a "book" was known was the first measure of the probability that it would be included in New Testaments when these came into being. Thus age was a factor; the books written early (other things being equal) were the ones more widely known and used.

It will be noticed that the plural, "New Testaments," was used above. It was used deliberately. There were several New Testaments, and there was variation in their contents. As has been mentioned, the first collection of Christian writings intended to be used as Scripture was made by the heretic, Marcion; it included the Lucan Gospel and ten letters of Paul. The Bishop of Lyons (Gaul), Irenaeus (*ca.* A.D. 185), had a New Testament of twenty-two books. A list of Christian Scripture which represented the Roman church toward the end of the second century numbered twenty-five. It included in detail our Four Gospels, Acts, fourteen letters of Paul (i.e., listing Hebrews and the Pastorals as Paul's), Jude, I and II John, the Wisdom of Solomon, the Revelation of John, the Revelation of Peter (the list mentions that this is rejected by some), and the Shepherd of Hermas (there is a qualification to this, also; it is stated that it may be read privately, but not publicly in church, since it was written recently). The inclusion of one of the Old Testament Apocrypha is curious, and it is a distinctive feature that Rome had three apocalypses, not merely one.

The New Testament of the Syrian churches also had a "short" canon. Even in the fifth century its books numbered but twenty-two. In this New Testament there were the Four Gospels, Acts, fourteen letters of Paul, James, I Peter, and I John. This canon differs strikingly from that of Rome in that it had no apocalypse at all.

The section of Christianity which had the largest New Testament was the Alexandrian. This corresponds to the content of the Alexandrian Old Testament, which was fuller than the Palestinian. The Greek Old Testament of Alexandria contained the Apocrypha. But, of course, these books were integrally part of that Old Testament.

Alexandria was hospitable to scholarship. The first Christian school was located there, and several of the Alexandrian leaders were excellent scholars. One of these, Origen, made certain distinctions which he applied in determining the content of the New Testament. There were, he mentioned, certain books which were commonly accepted as unquestionably canonical. Then there were some the propriety of whose inclusion was disputed. There were some which were patently spurious It is an interesting fact that, when Origen's first two categories are combined, his New Testament had exactly the same content as that of one of the famous New Testament manuscripts, the Codex Sinaiticus: the Four Gospels, Acts, fourteen letters of Paul, the Revelation of John, I and II Peter, James, I, II, and III John, Jude, the Shepherd of Hermas, and the Epistle of Barnabas.

It is thus to be seen that one should speak of "New Testaments," not of the "New Testament," while the content of the canon was in process of evolution. But there were certain factors basic to all this growth and development. It has been pointed out that the collection of Paul's letters to the seven churches and their publication as a book secured for them at least quasi-scriptural status. One effect, of far-reaching importance, was that Paul's letters thus became the first nucleus about which the New Testaments grew. Another effect, also far-reaching, was that this collection had a great influence upon subsequent early Christian writing. The letters of Ignatius were collected. Very probably the Pastoral Epistles were written and circulated together in collected form. I, II, and III John, written separately, were collected. The Four Gospels were brought together, but now they were no longer considered as four separate gospels; they were "the" gospel in four writings —the Fourfold Gospel. They became a second nucleus about which the New Testaments grew.

The differences in the content of the various New Testaments were in part due to the various localities in which they were collected. The widest difference in content was that between the Syrian churches and Alexandria, with Rome in an intermediate position. The point is that people in various centers of Christianity appraised writings differently, for the religious life had its differences.

Problems of schism and heresy were important in determining the content of the New Testament. The New Testament was a product of the church, and in part the church created it to meet the problems of heresy. That is to say, the determination of the canon was an exercise of the church's authoritarian control, and it was used to prevent the further growth of heresy and to checkmate its effect upon church people. Quite a number of the "apocryphal" Christian writings were produced in the interest of heretical movements (e.g., the Apocalypse of Peter was Docetic; some of the gospels were Gnostic); obviously, the church must define what was Scripture and what was not.

Thus the emergence of the New Testament coincides generally with the development of the church to the position which might be called "catholic" (i.e., general, universal). Irenaeus makes the point that there are four gospels, and only four, because there could be no more nor less; these four are the church's four pillars in defense of its doctrine. Similarly, although considerably later, it was a representative of eastern Christianity, Athanasius, bishop of Alexandria, who, in his "Festal Letter" in the year 367, authoritatively defined the canon of the New Testament to consist of exactly those twenty-seven books which now make up its content.

But there were yet certain vicissitudes in the content of the New Testament. When Luther published his translation of it from the Greek, he made a distinction between James, Hebrews, Jude, and Revelation and the remaining books. This was on the ground of his theology; these books did not "drive Christ" as the others did; consequently, he put them in a secondary class. As late as 1729 an edition of the New Testament in Sweden printed these four books as apocrypha, with pagination separate from that of the books which were thus regarded as fully canonical. Difference in use continued. The Eastern Orthodox churches to this day do not read lessons in church from Revelation. John Calvin published commentaries on every book of the New Testament except Revelation.

Thus the story of the canon is an aspect of the varied history of the church. Those works which had the firm backing of large sections of the church were obviously candidates for Christian Scripture. Important, too, was the doctrinal viewpoint of a book in matters which the church came to regard as crucial. The twenty-seven books which we now call our New Testament were the church's selection, over a period of approximately three hundred years, from the mass of literature which early Christianity produced.[1]

The textual history of the books of the New Testament begins with their first appearance, probably upon papyrus. They were written in the roll form, not as leafed books. Most of them, of course, could be written on a single roll, although Luke-Acts in its original form must have occupied two. It has been calculated that Paul's collected letters were contained in two papyrus rolls.

Sections of the New Testament were perhaps written on rolls

[1] For an interesting and brief treatment showing the growth of the canon, see Edgar J. Goodspeed, *The Formation of the New Testament* (Chicago: University of Chicago Press, 1926).

at first; but presently, because of the cumbersome form of lengthy rolls, they came to be written in the form of leafed books of papyrus (in the so-called "codex" form). It was still later that the skins of animals (vellum or parchment) were used as the materials of the books in which New Testaments were written.

Manuscripts of the New Testament had various contents: some embraced the Four Gospels alone, some contained the gospels and other books, while others embraced Acts and the Epistles. There are some two thousand manuscripts of the gospels, and as many or more of "complete" New Testaments; there are some two hundred of the so-called "Praxapostoli" (manuscripts containing Acts and Epistles). "Complete" New Testaments seldom have the Book of Revelation; there are only about forty-five truly complete New Testament manuscripts containing the twenty-seven books which make up our New Testament.

By the use of these manuscript materials scholars determine the text of the New Testament. Some of the manuscripts are very old; the stately codices named "Vaticanus" (in the Vatican Library) and "Sinaiticus" (now the property of the British Museum) date from the fourth century, and a recently discovered papyrus in codex form (the Chester Beatty Papyrus, which is in part in the Library of the University of Michigan) is still earlier. The great proportion of manuscripts are later. Some manuscripts are in other than the Greek language, representing early "versions" in Syriac, Latin, Coptic (i.e., Egyptian dialects), and other languages.

The purpose of textual criticism is to penetrate as far as possible toward the "original" manuscripts which first appeared in the Christian communities. Needless to say, we do not have the original copy of any work in the New Testament. Rather, our earliest papyrus manuscripts come from the very late second or the third century, while vellum or parchment copies have been dated no earlier than the fourth century. This means that New Testament writings had passed through several stages of copying before our oldest manuscripts came into being. Scribes and copyists are human; therefore errors crept in. Later scribes may have reproduced the now erroneous manuscript faithfully; more probably they added errors of their own; possibly they made corrections where grammar and good sense dictated. Some changes in manuscripts were therefore intentional ones, corrections in harmony with grammar or doctrine. The vast majority, however, were unintentional: omissions, particularly where there were word similarities; duplications, especially in sections where words or phrases recur frequently; and errors similar to those made by typists today.

Study of many manuscripts and observation of their characteristics soon led scholars to classify them into "families." Each manuscript could be identified by its "family" characteristics: inclusion or omission of sections or pericopes, similarity of errors, and general peculiarities. Further study led to conclusions concerning the reliability of families and subfamilies.

This detailed and highly technical work lies beneath the scholarly efforts to reconstruct the most perfect text of the Greek New Testament. Painstaking labor is necessary to evaluate evidence from well over four thousand manuscripts. Errors must be eliminated, so far as this is possible; each reading is evaluated in terms of all others and in terms of probabilities. Specific readings, included in some manuscripts and not in others, must be accepted, rejected, or put into notes on variants.

Thus, by comparing the manuscripts and noting the type of the text in each case, a scientific effort has been made to determine the earliest form of the text of the New Testament writings. Successful results have followed the arduous labors of scholars of several nationalities for more than four centuries. Work in this part of the study of the New Testament is still being carried on.[2]

The work of textual scholarship must precede that of translation. This is, of course, the attempt to render into English (German, French, etc.) the correct meaning of the Greek text. Under the influence of Humanism, the Catholic scholar Erasmus once

---

[2] See, further, K. Lake, *The Text of the New Testament*, ed. Silva New (6th ed.; London: Rivington's, 1933).

expressed the hope that the knowledge of the New Testament would become available to artisans as well as to scholars. Martin Luther early produced, as an aspect of his leadership, a translation of the New Testament into the German vernacular (1522). Previous to this, there had been some sporadic translation into the German and French vernacular; but from Luther's time this effort went on apace. Although John Wyclif had produced in 1382 an English translation from the Latin, William Tyndale in 1525 published the first translation of the Greek New Testament into English; he was followed by other individuals and groups of scholars, until in 1611 the King James Version became the standard English translation.

But English translation of the New Testament and the Bible did not stop then. Indeed, the King James Version immediately underwent its own evolution. It was successively revised, with considerable change from the 1611 edition. If the reader were to locate a 1611 edition of the King James, he would have difficulty in reading it; the copy of the so-called "King James Version" to which he is accustomed is a considerably modernized reprint of a much later edition of it.

For, of course, the English language has changed. The 1611 King James more or less represents Elizabethan English (although, to be sure, the fact that it is a translation strongly affects its diction). Contemporary English, and particularly the American language, are characteristically different. Thus, in response to a perfectly normal and sound impulse, the New Testament has been often translated and retranslated to bring to its readers its messages in the language which is their own.

In the proper effort to translate the New Testament into contemporary language, scholars today have certain advantages over their predecessors. For one thing, contemporary scholars have much more of manuscript material. When Erasmus edited the New Testament in Greek, from which edition Luther and Tyndale made their translations, he had only about a half-dozen manuscripts, and none of these was ancient. When the King James Version was made, none of the great ancient manuscripts was fully known to the scholars who produced it. Now some two hundred old manuscripts are available.

Similarly, the knowledge of the Greek language has increased and improved. When Luther and Tyndale did their work, the knowledge of Greek had only recently come to western Europe. Their scholarship is not to be impugned; it was excellent. But they did not have a competent grammar of the Greek language, for one did not exist. In recent times Greek grammar has been studied, with revolutionary result. It was not known, for example, until as recently as fifty years ago that the language in which the New Testament books were written was the "common dialect" of the Hellenistic world. This has been learned by the use of the tens of thousands of nonliterary papyri which have been discovered and patiently studied. The effect of this is that a modern translation of the New Testament into contemporary American English can approximate the very flavor of the original Greek itself. This was impossible in the days of the classic translations.[3]

The interpretation of the New Testament itself has a history. The modern effort begins with the rise of Humanism in Europe. The Revival of Learning led to an appreciation of antiquity, and as one of the by-products the knowledge of the Greek language was revived. The Western church was, of course, Latin; its New Testament was a Latin translation of the Greek. Among other things, Humanism affected the New Testament. One of its effects was to study the New Testament as other books of antiquity were studied—to apply grammatical interpretation to it and to study it in the light of history. A specific factor was the stimulus to study the manuscripts which were rapidly coming to light, so that the study of the text of the New Testament was fruitfully carried on. As has been pointed out, translation followed. By now the Reformation was well under way, and one of its effects was to put the New Testament back into the hands of the people.

As modern scholarship had its development in the European universities, New Testament study was affected. As the Indus-

---

[3] For a picture of the work of the modern translator, consult Edgar J. Goodspeed, *Problems of New Testament Translation* (Chicago: University of Chicago Press, 1945).

trial Revolution made its mark upon thought and as exploration enlarged knowledge of the world, philosophy was influenced; and this, in turn, affected New Testament study.[4] Thus the interpretation of the New Testament passed through successive stages. Under the influence of Humanism the New Testament was studied as literature. Presently it was studied in the light of history. After the middle of the nineteenth century, science strongly affected its study, so that today all disciplines make their contribution to the attempt to understand and interpret the New Testament correctly.

[4] See, further, Harold H. Hutson, "Some Factors in the Rise of Scientific New Testament Criticism," *Journal of Religion*, XXII (January, 1942), 89–95.

Appendix

LEADING IDEAS IN THE NEW TESTAMENT

THE New Testament was the church's book: it therefore reflected accurately the growth of significant ideas among the leadership of the struggling movement. It would be surprising to discover that no changes in thought were discernible from book to book, that the Christian leader in A.D. 50 completely solved every problem to be faced by his successors one hundred years later. Differences among human minds, diversity of religious experience, and variation in circumstances caused a dissimilarity of attitude in any given period. If to this are added the changes necessitated by the passing of time, one sees clearly that only a developmental concept of early Christianity is historically possible. The New Testament itself is a definitive illustration of the growth of Christian concepts from the earliest period to A.D. 150.

Faced by this variety of opinion, it becomes increasingly difficult to speak of *the* New Testament idea of God or of the church. Rather, one discovers that the Christian communities were so alive to the religious problems of their own day that their leaders developed solutions and attitudes directed to a specific situation. There are several ideas of God and of the church discoverable within the church's book. It is true that there is a degree of historical continuity and that often one writer builds upon the concepts of another, but this should not encourage the reader to fall into the "harmonizing" method of study.

As the church faced new situations and encountered powerful opposition, it developed a rationale suited to its growing needs. The New Testament reflects the vitality and adaptability of the early Christian movement. Each book in the New Testament mirrors the needs of the people for which it was written and the ingenuity of the church's leadership. Part of the strength of this handbook lies in its portrayal of the many ideas of God, Jesus

219

Christ, the way of salvation, the church, and ethics. To trace the growth of these concepts is the purpose of this appendix.

Harm has been done to the proper understanding of New Testament teachings about God by the persistence of two fallacious assumptions: (1) that a complete and "full" teaching was expressed by Jesus through the traditions of the Synoptics and (2) that an orderly and predictable growth in the concept of God is visible when one studies the New Testament documents chronologically. The first error has made the remainder of the New Testament simply commentary upon the gospels; the second demands a schematic relationship which is altogether unhistorical. Neither of these approaches correctly appraises conditions in the early Christian communities.

The Synoptic Gospels at once present the problem of separating the attitudes of Jesus from those of the communities which preserved the traditions about him. Application of the tests of environment and form criticism agree in picturing Jesus' thought about God as essentially Jewish. The emphasis was upon God as father and upon the necessity for complete submission to his sovereignty. God was personal in the same sense that man was personal; there is no hint in the Synoptic Gospels of philosophical "immanence." That these views were characteristic of first-century Jewish belief can be demonstrated by a glance at the sources as treated by G. F. Moore,[1] C. G. Montefiore,[2] and I. Abrahams.[3] Jesus' idea of God was drawn chiefly from Deuteronomy, the Psalms, and Isaiah, although the Synoptics omit entirely their emphasis upon the holiness of God. But to these Hebrew writers Jesus added the later Jewish concept of demons and of Satan, retaining with his contemporaries, however, the confidence that God was still supreme and could delegate power over them through faith.[4] Thus monotheism remained unthreatened.

[1] *Judaism*, II, 201–11.

[2] "The Spirit of Judaism," in F. J. Foakes-Jackson and Kirsopp Lake (eds.), *The Beginnings of Christianity*, I (London: Macmillan, 1920), 35–81.

[3] *Studies in Pharisaism and the Gospels*, 1st ser. (Cambridge: University Press, 1917).

[4] See Mark 3:15; Matt. 7:22; Luke 10:18.

It is probable that the disciples early began to preach Jesus as the crucified Messiah who had appeared to them many times and had subsequently ascended to the right hand of God, a person of especial honor in the eyes of God. That he should have been referred to as "Lord" by Palestinian Jews is improbable, even though there are several instances in the gospels which read the later usage into the story.[5] What factors and individuals effected the transition by which Jesus became both Lord and God to the Christian groups? First of all, the rising tide of gentile adherents helped to give the growing movement a theology adapted to non-Jewish religious needs. Second, a Hellenistic Jew named Paul bridged, perhaps unconsciously, the critical rift which threatened to give Christianity two gods. Third, these tendencies found fulfilment in the work of the intellectualizer and mystic, the writer of the Fourth Gospel.

A cursory reading of the New Testament leaves the impression that the first Christian communities among the Gentiles worshiped the Father-God primarily and gradually elevated Jesus to divine status. This, indeed, is the interpretation intended by the editor of Luke-Acts. But the historical situation dictates the reverse of this procedure, as A. C. McGiffert[6] some years ago clearly discerned. Gentile converts to the growing movement brought with them a wealth of background for an understanding of Christ as the dying-and-rising savior-god. This search in every case was for redemption, and their interest was in the figure who could guarantee this boon. It is altogether unnecessary to assume an interest on their part in the monotheistic principle which was held so dear by the Jews.

For the Gentile saw the promise of salvation by and through the Lord Jesus Christ. The Jewish Father-God was of secondary importance, and the Law by which the Jew lived was most "peculiar." Popular gentile religious thinking did not require the monotheistic principle for effective salvation; a plurality of gods served rather to make religious ministrations and guaranties more personal in character. Not steeped in the monotheistic

[5] See esp. Acts 2:36, 11:17.

[6] *The God of the Early Christians* (New York: Charles Scribner's Sons, 1924), pp. 41–88.

heritage of the Jew, nor yet gifted with the reflective power of the philosopher, these converts entered the gateway through Christ and not through God. Put more directly, there is every reason to believe that Jesus was their God. At least, every known example from their background shows that the lord of the cult was always a god.

Possibly we now have a clue to the significance of the tradition that the disciples were first called "Christians" at Antioch.[7] The earliest emphasis upon Jesus as a messianic figure and as a person of importance in the eyes of God would not distinguish the followers of Jesus from typical Jews. When this emphasis is coupled with the gentile interest in Jesus as a dying-and-rising savior-god, the believer can no longer be called a Jew. Thus an old tradition directly attests to the gentile character of the earliest message that was distinctively "Christian." It was only when a Jewish Jesus was seen through gentile eyes and in the light of gentile religious needs that the new movement became distinctive.

Paul, who seems to have shared the cultural background of both Jew and Gentile, drew a distinction between God (*theos*) and Lord (*kurios*) in name, even though he constantly confuses the functions. In his letters Paul repeatedly refers to Jesus as "Lord" (*kurios*), the term by which the Hebrew "Yahweh" was rendered into the Septuagint by the scholars before him. Further, Paul applies to Jesus passages of Scripture which can be understood, by any plain reading, to refer only to Yahweh.[8] Paul seemed, consciously or unconsciously, to be bridging the gap which was evident between Jews who held that God was supreme and Jesus merely a messianic subsidiary and that more numerous gentile group which received Jesus as lord of the cult but cared little for the previous relationship to Yahweh the Father-God.

But Paul's leadership veered still further toward the appreciation of gentile values. He sees Christ exercising divine functions,[9]

---

[7] Acts 11:26*b*.

[8] See, e.g., I Cor. 1:31; II Cor. 3:16, 10:17; II Thess. 1:9.

[9] I Cor. 11:32; II Cor. 5:9-10; Col. 2:6.

standing with God as an object of worship,[10] and embodying all
the fulness of the Godhead.[11] The solution of the relationship lay
for Paul in the title "Son of God." Christ has been sent by his
Father to consummate the coming of the Kingdom and to deliver
it to God. While the phrase "Son of God" constantly recurs in
the letters of Paul, there is good reason to doubt the primitive
Palestinian authenticity of its use, with all these connotations,
in the Synoptic Gospels. Even so famous a saying as "No one understands the Son but the Father, nor does anyone understand
the Father but the Son"[12] fails both the environmental and the
literary tests for primitivity.[13] The same judgment may be passed
upon the oft-quoted formula of the Great Commission.[14]

The crux of the problem lies in the connotations of the phrase
"Son of God" and not in the actual use of the words. While all
Jews believed themselves potential sons of God, and any person
of especial distinction might be termed a "son of God," the messianic connotations of the term certainly arose after the crucifixion of Jesus. To employ the phrase with the suggestion of equality to God would have been abhorrent to any person steeped in
the beliefs of Judaism. It is, therefore, probable that the full
meaning of the term "Son of God" as it is employed in the Synoptics came first to be applied to the revered Jesus by gentile disciples on gentile soil.

Certainly, it was enthusiastically employed by Paul, who thus
declared his belief in the divine being who had come into the
world and through a mighty drama of redemption had effected
the salvation of all those who had faith in him. He distinguished
this being from the supreme God the Father in terminology; but
in function and property he confuses and identifies the two,[15]
often introducing still a third divine agent in the mystic's concept of salvation.[16] If Paul's doctrine of God seems confused, the

[10] Rom. 10:13; I Cor. 1:2; Phil. 2:9–11; II Cor. 12:8.

[11] Col. 2:9.   [12] Matt. 11:27 = Luke 10:22.

[13] See, e.g., Dibelius, *The Message of Jesus Christ*, p. 161.

[14] Matt. 28:19.

[15] II Cor. 5:19; Col. 2:9, 3:3; Rom. 8:9.

[16] II Cor. 1:21–22, 3:17, 5:17, 12:2; Gal. 1:12; Rom. 8:9 f., 15:16; I Cor. 1:2.

explanation lies in his primary concern for salvation rather than philosophical consistency. For him, salvation lay in the escape from evil flesh by union with divine spirit. For Paul, Christ was the only effectual agency for that union.

These ideas find expansion and intellectualization in the Fourth Gospel. As in Paul, God is both personal and a substance which can be apprehended through mystical experience. The word Father occurs with greater frequency in John than in the remainder of the gospels and is understood as the Father of Christ and the Christians. A difference in emphasis is observable in the mysticism of the Fourth Gospel. In Paul the indwelling essence is usually Christ, or the Spirit; in John, God is more often described in mystical terms.

The Fourth Gospel distinguishes the Father from the Son, but both alike are divine. The prologue emphasizes the divinity of the Logos, and many passages show Jesus identifying himself with the Father.[17] After the resurrection Jesus is addressed by Thomas with the words: "My Lord and my God."[18]

Thus the latest of the gospels represented the confluence of a number of streams of thought in early Christianity. Among a small group of the earliest Palestinian disciples of Jesus, God had remained essentially the Yahweh of the Jews, and Jesus was regarded as an altogether subordinate personage. The early gentile Christians, drawn from a background of savior-gods, saw little need for one supreme being; their allegiance was to the hero of the redemptive story, Jesus. Sharing the traditions of both groups, Paul bound together in divinity the Father and the Son, placing supreme emphasis upon mystical union with Christ and the Spirit. To the writer of the Fourth Gospel fell the task not only of furnishing a gospel-like basis for his philosophy but also for restoring the primacy of God while retaining the redemptive function of the Son.

Other New Testament writers show little variation from the patterns set by the gospels and Paul in their reflection on the nature of God. The Revelation of John shows a strong tendency to

[17] John 10:30, 14:7, 20.
[18] John 20:28.

revert to the idea of God shown in some of the imprecatory
Psalms and in the nationalism of the early Hebrews. God becomes a vengeful deity who wrecks devastation upon those who
resist his will. It is, in fact, a far cry from the loving Father-God
described by Jesus in the Synoptics to the wrathful God of the
"saints" in the Apocalypse. The Epistle to Titus speaks of "our
great God and savior Jesus Christ,"[19] indicating that the leadership of the growing church in the early half of the second century ascribed to Jesus full powers of divinity. In the same vein
Jesus is mentioned as "our God and savior Jesus Christ" by the
latest of the New Testament works, II Peter. Throughout these
works, as in the Letter to the Hebrews, Jesus was placed alongside God as a personage worthy of worship.

Early Christian thought about the nature of Jesus was closely
related to the concept of God. Jesus in many ways represented
God acting for the salvation of men. The picture of the individual Jesus and his functions varied from book to book, indicating
the diversity of thought about him in the first communities.

For Paul, Jesus represented all "the fulness of God," a divine
personage with whom mystical contacts could regularly be established. Paul moved in constant obedience to experiences of revelation,[20] and his knowledge of Jesus came through mystical visions.[21] Salvation was to be effected through faith in the justify-
ing acts and death of Christ.[22] The death of Jesus represented the
central support for the entire structure of salvation.[23] Very little
attention was given to the life or to the teachings of Jesus. Instead, Paul's interest was entirely in the central figure of the
great drama of redemption.

The Marcan narrative retains much of the primitive emphasis
upon the sufferings and death of Jesus, but it shows also a lively
interest in his dramatic career. In fact, the entire gospel seems to
be cast in dramatic form, conforming to the canons of Greek
tragedy. Jesus appears as the man of action, the tragic hero whose
true nature is revealed only to the close reader, for even the dis-

[19] 2:13.
[20] Gal. 2:2.
[21] I Cor. 15:8; II Cor. 12:1–4.
[22] Rom. 4:23–25, 5:17, 18.
[23] I Cor. 15:14, 17.

ciples never fully grasp the mission of the main actor. So deft is the arrangement of the oldest gospel that it served as a suggestive model for the later martyrologies which were to inspire death-defying confession of the "illicit" Christian faith.

The Gospel of Matthew pictures Jesus as the great teacher, the successor to Moses, the corrector of the Pharisaic element, and the founder of an embryonic church. The great drama of redemption remains the dominant element in the picture, but this work of salvation is supplemented by emphasis upon the values inherent in the teachings of Jesus. Jesus the teacher serves as his own authority, but his emphases require listeners to surpass the righteousness required by Jewish leaders. Divine attestations to the supernatural character of Jesus begin with his birth and continue through his post-resurrection appearances. Jesus is regarded as the complete fulfilment of all the "predictions" of Hebrew Scripture. The reader of Matthew would conclude that Jesus offered to prospective cult members all the moral and intellectual advantages of Judaism plus salvation supernaturally guaranteed.

The description of Jesus in Luke-Acts relates directly to the total purpose of the work. Great pains are taken to show the intimate relationship of Jesus to his Jewish background; the final rejection of Jesus and his movement by the Jews shows their own inability to perceive the finest in Judaism. Supernatural birth and exceptional wisdom in childhood form but the prelude to a life of such character that even a Roman procurator wonders at the stupid clamor of the Jews demanding his death. This arrangement and pointing of the data tends to support the contention of Luke-Acts that Jesus and the great leaders of the movement were acceptable to Rome, even though unacceptable to the blinded eyes of fellow-Jews. Jesus stands out from the pages of the Lucan gospel as the hero of redemption who utilizes to the full all available Jewish values. Thought about Jesus is expanded in the Acts volume to accord with many of the values claimed by the early Christian preachers. Jesus is not only Lord; he shares the glory of God and sits on his right hand. It is, further, through his direct plan that the church originates; the disciples at his command are to be witnesses "in Jerusalem and all over Judea and Samaria and to the very ends of the earth."[24] Thus the Lucan plan of evangelization, with Jerusalem serving as a radiating center of activities, is read back into the times of Jesus himself.

The Letter to the Ephesians, which serves as an introduction to the collected Pauline letters, universalizes the earlier concept of personal and mystical guidance; in Ephesians it is the church which experiences the mystical leadership of Jesus.[25] Jesus breaks down all barriers which separate men; they are all one through their union with him and the church. The work of Jesus demands that all adherents of his church live according to the laws of the new self. Christ is the justification for a new ethic.

Revelation, I Peter, and Hebrews all reflect the necessity of suffering for one's faith in Jesus Christ. But they differ markedly in the attitudes which they would encourage in the face of this persecution. The Revelation of John leaves no doubt in the mind of the reader that the cause of Jesus is worth immeasurable suffering; Jesus is the "slain lamb," and only those who possess the mark of his Father[26] (in contradistinction to those with the mark of the animal) will be permitted entrance to God's kingdom. The cause of the "Lamb of God" is so righteous that even hatred of earthly persecutors and gloating over their discomfiture is to be encouraged. The way of righteousness (resistance to the demands of the state) stands in sharp contrast to all earthly and satanic forces. A different attitude moves the writer of I Peter. Obedience to "human authority" is counseled "for the Master's sake,"[27] and trouble is to be regarded as a refining fire which enables the loyal Christian to share in a measure the sufferings of Christ.[28] The spirit of Jesus here moves men to regard even those in opposition to them as agents of God; there is no hint that devotion to Christ justifies hatred of one's persecutors. Hebrews encourages the reader to emulate Christ in his sufferings: Jesus was the greatest of all the high priests, both because he was without blemish or imperfection and because he offered himself as the

[24] Acts 1:8.

[25] 1:23, 2:10, 17–22.   [27] I Pet. 2:13–15.

[26] 14:1 ff.   [28] I Pet. 4:12–13.

perfect sacrifice.[29] Jesus fully surpasses any benefit which the Law or sacrifices might bring, for only once was his own sacrifice necessary for complete salvation.[30]

The Letter of James shows little concern for a doctrinal theory on the work of Jesus; faith in the Lord Jesus Christ serves only as a basis for a general system of ethics previously determined. But with the Fourth Gospel it is an entirely different matter. For the character of Jesus is the chief concern of this writer. Throughout the pages of this early second-century work Jesus is seen as the philosopher, the theologian, and the mystic. Historical occurrences are entirely secondary, for they are merely the suggestive circumstances through which the true character of Jesus can be seen. Here is an intellectualistic portrayal of Jesus, but even the mind must be assisted by mystical guidance. Jesus is no common lord; he is the very Word by which the true nature of God is known.[31] More than that, he shared the exact nature of God, even though common men had extreme difficulty apprehending his true character.

What is man's relation to God? How does an individual come into harmony with the will of God? What is the way of "salvation"? There are several answers to these questions in the religious literature which composes our New Testament. For the books of the New Testament show the variety of experiences shared by the early Christian communities as they met the competition of rival cults and sought satisfactory solution for their own problems.

The Synoptic Gospels emphasize salvation as preparation for the coming Kingdom of God and obedience to its laws. Jesus is pictured as demonstrating the perfect law of God and as calling men to its requirements. But more than that is necessary. The person and work of Jesus himself is of cosmic importance; reliance upon him is necessary for redemption. A basic difference from contemporary Judaism is at once evident: Judaism is a religion of attainment, calling men to complete identification with God's will through the keeping of the perfect law, the Torah;

---

[29] Heb. 9:11–14.

[30] Heb. 10:1–14.   [31] John 1:1–5.

Christianity became, from its early days, a religion of redemption. The passion narrative drives to a conclusion that which the traditions about Jesus generally make explicit: mankind is "lost" and needs the "saving" help of Jesus. How early this concept came to control cult thinking is difficult to say; certainly it was dominant by the time gospels came to be written. Judaism could well utilize the idea of a child's returning to his Heavenly Father through obedience to his will, but the emphasis upon "lostness" was gentile. Certainly the formula found in the second volume of Luke-Acts is sufficient to distinguish the movement from contemporary Judaism: "There is no salvation through anyone else, for there is no one else in the world who has been named to men as their only means of being saved."[32] Jesus is undoubtedly Lord of a redemption cult.

In the Pauline communities the experience of Paul himself was regarded as normative. Salvation was effected through immediate dominance of God over the life of an individual. This came about in one way: a person was enveloped in the life of God. A mystical experience made him no longer master of his own motives and activities. He came to be "in Christ" and thus "in God." Redemption had been made possible for men through the work of Jesus. Only through "faith" (union with Christ) could this saving deed be made effective in the individual life. Once a man became Christ-possessed, his bodily desires were metamorphosed; he became a new man in Christ. Thus the moral life for Paul was the inevitable result of one's becoming Christ's. One reached salvation through mystical union with the Redeemer, and thus with God.

There is no effective picture of a man's total relationship to God in the Revelation of John. This apocalypse is too concerned with the impact of the state upon the Christian movement to give counsel in other areas. I Peter and Hebrews infer that Jesus is the author of salvation. Man's proper relationship to God comes through acceptance of the mediating and sacrificial work of Christ. Great faith is needed to see the believer through troubled times—faith such as that which enabled the ancient worthies of

[32] Acts 4:12.

Hebrew history to persevere. The end may come, and one must always be ready.

Simple moral duties fully occupy the attention of the writer of James, but the total relationship of man to God is a serious concern of the Fourth Gospel. Men fail to see truth because it is veiled from them by their own ignorance, their concern with inferior traditions, or their inability to appreciate inner meanings. The way to God is not simply through confession of Jesus as Christ; it involves inner perception of Jesus as the incarnate Word. Hope is not to be fastened upon a mere physical resurrection, but eternal life is promised those who understand the Father through the Son. There is no confidence in an "end of the age" to bring in the Kingdom; rather, the eternity already exists of which the present time is only a fragment. Thus Jesus is an indispensable link for the understanding of God and his purposes.

What does the New Testament show about the development of ideas concerning the church? The early followers of Jesus must, indeed, have been astonished when their Jewish contemporaries regarded them as peculiar. Their bewilderment increased when their beliefs and practices became increasingly unacceptable to Jewish leadership. Like all religious "reforms," the suggested changes seem to be perfectly logical developments to the reformers; but to the majority of the faithful they appear to be dangerous innovations. Before the time of Paul the believers had been forced into their own groups, through which they carried on the work of spreading the good news.

Paul's lifetime witnessed the close organization of groups of individual believers into churches. Christians became the *ekklesia* (literally, "a calling-out"). A reading of Paul's letters shows that he still regarded the Christian groups as representative of the highest in Judaism and that he hoped for the ultimate enlightenment of his "kindred." Members of the churches were "the chosen," in the same sense that Israel had originally been chosen by God. Out of the refining fire of the Exile had come the Righteous Remnant; now further refinement was taking place, for "the chosen" were being called apart from the remainder of the Righteous Remnant. The Christian churches were a selection from a selection. But to Paul the church meant the individual communities of believers. Discipline was still a matter of individual problems.

The Synoptic Gospels reflect still further growth in the concept of a church. This is seen most strikingly in Matthew, where the rudiments of church discipline are found and hints as to the importance of the church are given.[33] Luke-Acts presents an idealized account of the church and its spread. Beginning in Jerusalem, it will move out into Judea, then throughout Samaria, and from there to the uttermost parts of the world.[34] The reader would infer that the church realized its unity from the days of the resurrection experiences; this, however, represents a re-writing of the story on the part of the editor. By the last decade of the first century, when the editor of Luke-Acts reviewed the spread of churches all over the Mediterranean world, it did seem that some unified plan had been in operation from the beginning.

There can be little doubt that the "church universal" is an actuality in the mind of the author of Ephesians. The church is the body of Jesus,[35] has been cleansed by him through baptism,[36] and serves as the agent of his will on earth.[37] I Peter shows a general feeling of brotherhood among all churches suffering persecution.[38] The duties of "elders," together with their responsibilities, are stressed.[39]

Practical churchmanship reaches its height in the Pastoral Epistles. A full list of church officers is given, and the duties of each are detailed. A fair degree of organization has taken place, for not only are there offices open to men only, but "widows" render official service. The meaning of the church services and of the sacraments is assumed.

The Fourth Gospel stands apart in its concept of the church. There is a clear line drawn between the believers and "the Jews." There is an awareness of the church in the author's mind when he speaks of the Beloved Community and of the relation of the

---

[33] 16:18–19, 18:15–20.
[34] Acts 1:8.
[35] Eph. 1:22–23.
[36] Eph. 5:26.
[37] Eph. 1:23, 3:21.
[38] 5:9.
[39] I Pet. 5:1 ff.

vine and the branches. But the intellectualized mysticism of this author tends to make any relationship of a man to God or to Jesus immediate and direct—the church is never the mediating force it becomes under other theological presuppositions.

Almost every church group has endeavored to trace its polity back to the New Testament, and many have claimed that their government is the "New Testament polity." The point is most difficult to substantiate historically, for a survey of the New Testament writings shows a great variety of attitudes toward the church and its officers. The historical probability is that each church developed its own means of control; and not until a late stage of development, such as that seen in the Pastoral Epistles, could any unified approach to the problem be made.

The ethical teachings of the New Testament constitute a lengthy study in themselves. The Synoptic Gospels present a picture of Jesus which places him in the direct line of Jewish moral thought. But Jesus is shown to have deepened the moral conscience and to have directed the attention of his listeners away from the externals of conduct toward the motives of men.[40] It has also been urged by scholars, both Christian and Jewish, that the traditions picture Jesus as emphasizing God's mercy and love to the partial exclusion of his justice.[41] But in the main the moral message of Jesus was built directly upon Jewish foundations.

The writings of Paul show morality to be a secondary but not an unimportant part of the good news. Paul was primarily concerned with the redemptive work of Jesus on the cross. According to his thought, a proper spirit experience would guarantee proper behavior of the body. Not that the body was to be forgotten; rather, its desires would be metamorphosed under the dominance of the spirit. Paul's Jewish background caused him to condemn bitterly those who pretended to believe that life in the spirit released them from all moral laws. But essentially, it is to be remembered, an experience of Jesus was always primary; ethical concepts were but concomitant.

[40] Matt. 5:21-48.

[41] See, further, John Baillie, *The Place of Jesus Christ in Modern Christianity* (New York: Charles Scribner's Sons, 1929), pp. 76 ff.

The ethical concepts of the Revelation of John are far from lofty. Certainly the reader of that book would not be inspired to love his enemies; instead, a harsh justice which approaches retribution dominates the work. More in the spirit of the gospels are the patient suffering and submission counseled by I Peter and Hebrews. Their readers were encouraged to emulate Jesus, "our leader and example in the faith, who in place of the happiness that belonged to him, submitted to a cross, caring nothing for its shame. . . . ."[42] Both the Epistle of James and the Pastoral Epistles deal almost entirely in the undistinguished morality of common sense.

The procession of New Testament life and literature has passed before us. Complete appreciation of its values comes only by thorough study and repeated readings. The New Testament is of interest because it is literature and because of the light which it throws upon the history of the period. Its chief importance, however, lies in its portrayal of the growth of a movement from relative insignificance within Judaism to world-embracing proportions. Its genius lies in its picture of a quality of life which developed through the fires of experience into a revolutionary interest, which finally changed the face of the West much more than it had touched the spirit of the East.

[42] Heb. 12:2.

Select Bibliography

A. GENERAL WORKS ON THE HISTORY AND LITERATURE
OF THE NEW TESTAMENT

Dictionary of the Bible. Ed. JAMES HASTINGS. 5 vols. New York: Charles Scribner's Sons, 1909.

A Dictionary of Christ and the Gospels. Ed. JAMES HASTINGS. 2 vols. New York: Charles Scribner's Sons, 1906–8.

Dictionary of Religion and Ethics. Eds. S. MATHEWS and G. B. SMITH. New York: Macmillan Co., 1921.

Encyclopedia of Religion and Ethics. Ed. JAMES HASTINGS. 13 vols. Edinburgh: T. and T. Clark, 1910–27.

The Jewish Encyclopedia. Ed. ISIDORE SINGER. 2d ed. 12 vols. New York: Funk & Wagnalls, 1925.

AYER, J. C. *A Source Book for Ancient Church History.* New York: Charles Scribner's Sons, 1913.

BOOTH, E. P. (ed.). *New Testament Studies.* Nashville: Abingdon-Cokesbury Press, 1942.

CADOUX, C. J. *The Early Church and the World: A History of the Christian Attitude to Pagan Society and the State down to the Time of Constantius.* Edinburgh: T. and T. Clark, 1925.

CASE, S. J. *The Evolution of Early Christianity.* Chicago: University of Chicago Press, 1913.

———. *Experience with the Supernatural in Early Christian Times.* New York: Century Co., 1929.

———. *The Social Origins of Christianity.* Chicago: University of Chicago Press, 1923.

——— (ed.). *Studies in Early Christianity.* New York: Century Co., 1928.

CRAIG, C. T. *The Beginning of Christianity.* Nashville: Abingdon-Cokesbury Press, 1943.

DIBELIUS, MARTIN. *A Fresh Approach to the New Testament and Early Christian Literature.* New York: Charles Scribner's Sons, 1936.

ENSLIN, M. S. *Christian Beginnings.* New York: Harper & Bros., 1938.

FOSDICK, H. E. *The Modern Use of the Bible.* New York: Macmillan Co., 1924.

GOODSPEED, EDGAR J. *Christianity Goes to Press*. New York: Macmillan Co., 1940.

———. *A History of Early Christian Literature*. Chicago: University of Chicago Press, 1942.

———. *An Introduction to the New Testament*. Chicago: University of Chicago Press, 1937.

HARNACK, A. *Geschichte der altchristlichen Litteratur bis Eusebius*. 3 vols. Leipzig: Hinrichs, 1893–1904.

JAMES, FLEMING, *et al. The Beginnings of Our Religion*. New York: Macmillan Co., 1934.

JAMES, M. R. *The Apocryphal New Testament*. Oxford: Clarendon Press, 1924.

JÜLICHER, ADOLF. *An Introduction to the New Testament*. Trans. JANET P. WARD. New York: G. P. Putnam & Sons, 1904.

LAKE, KIRSOPP, and LAKE, SILVA. *An Introduction to the New Testament*. New York: Harper & Bros., 1937.

LYMAN, MARY E. *The Christian Epic: A Study of the New Testament Literature*. New York: Charles Scribner's Sons, 1936.

MACKINNON, JAMES. *The Gospel in the Early Church: A Study of the Early Development of Christian Thought*. New York: Longmans, Green & Co., 1933.

MCNEILE, A. H. *An Introduction to the Study of the New Testament*. Oxford: Clarendon Press, 1927.

MANSON, T. W. (ed.). *A Companion to the Bible*. New York: Charles Scribner's Sons, 1939.

MOFFATT, JAMES. *An Introduction to the Literature of the New Testament*. New York: Charles Scribner's Sons, 1911.

An Outline of Christianity: The Story of Our Civilization, Vol. I: *The Birth of Christianity*. E. F. SCOTT and B. S. EASTON (eds.). New York: Dodd, Mead & Co., 1926.

PARSONS, E. W. *The Religion of the New Testament*. New York: Harper & Bros., 1939.

PURINTON, H. R. *Literature of the New Testament*. New York: Charles Scribner's Sons, 1925.

RIDDLE, D. W. *Early Christian Life as Reflected in Its Literature*. Chicago: Willett, Clark & Co., 1936.

———. *The Martyrs: A Study in Social Control*. Chicago: University of Chicago Press, 1931.

SANDS, P. C. *Literary Genius of the New Testament*. Oxford: Clarendon Press, 1932.

SCOTT, E. F. *The Gospel and Its Tributaries*. New York: Charles Scribner's Sons, 1930.

———. *The Literature of the New Testament*. New York: Columbia University Press, 1932.

———. *The New Testament Idea of Revelation*. New York: Charles Scribner's Sons, 1935.

———. *The New Testament Today*. New York: Macmillan Co., 1921.

SMITH, G. A. *Historical Geography of the Holy Land*. New York: A. C. Armstrong & Son, 1902.

STRACK, H. L., and BILLERBECK, PAUL. *Kommentar zum Neuen Testament aus Talmud und Midrasch*. 4 vols. München: C. H. Beck, 1922.

STREETER, B. H. *The Primitive Church Studied with Special Reference to the Origins of the Christian Ministry*. New York: Macmillan Co., 1929.

WEISS, JOHANNES. *The History of Primitive Christianity*. Trans. F. C. GRANT *et al.* 2 vols. New York: Wilson-Erickson, 1937.

WILD, L. H. *A Literary Guide to the Bible*. New York: George H. Doran Co., 1922.

B. THE HELLENISTIC WORLD

ANGUS, S. *The Environment of Early Christianity*. New York: Charles Scribner's Sons, 1915.

BOOTH, H. K. *The World of Jesus: A Survey of the Background of the Gospels*. New York: Charles Scribner's Sons, 1933.

BREASTED, J. H. *Ancient Times: A History of the Early World*. New York: Ginn & Co., 1916.

DILL, SAMUEL. *Roman Society from Nero to Marcus Aurelius*. London: Macmillan & Co., 1905.

GLOVER, T. R. *The Ancient World*. New York: Macmillan Co., 1937.

———. *The World of the New Testament*. New York: Macmillan Co., 1931.

JONES, A. H. M. *The Herods of Judaea*. Oxford: Clarendon Press, 1938.

MACGREGOR, G. H. C., and PURDY, A. C. *Jew and Greek, Tutors unto Christ: The Jewish and Hellenistic Background of the New Testament*. New York: Charles Scribner's Sons, 1936.

POLYBIUS. *The Histories*. With an English translation by W. R. PATON. 6 vols. ("Loeb Classical Library.") New York: G. P. Putnam's Sons, 1923.

PRENTICE, W. K. *The Ancient Greeks: Studies toward a Better Understanding of the Ancient World*. Princeton: Princeton University Press, 1940.

ROSTOVTZEFF, M. *A History of the Ancient World*, Vol. I: *The Orient and Greece*. Trans. J. D. Duff. 2d ed. Oxford: Clarendon Press, 1930.

SANFORD, E. M. *The Mediterranean World in Ancient Times*. New York: Ronald Press, 1938.

TARN, W. W. *Hellenistic Civilization*. 2d ed. London: E. Arnold & Co., 1930.

WENDLAND, PAUL. *Die hellenistisch-römische Kultur in ihren Beziehungen zu Judentum und Christentum*. 2d and 3d eds. ("Handbuch zum Neuen Testament.") Tübingen: J. C. B. Mohr, 1912.

C. JUDAISM

ABRAHAMS, I. *Studies in Pharisaism and the Gospels*. 1st ser. Cambridge: University Press, 1917.

BELKIN, SAMUEL. *Philo and the Oral Law: The Philonic Interpretation of Biblical Law in Relation to the Palestinian Halakah*. Cambridge: Harvard University Press, 1940.

BEVAN, EDWIN R. *Jerusalem under the High Priests*. London: Arnold, 1904.

BINNS, L. ELLIOTT. *The Jewish People and Their Faith*, Part I of *The Rise of the Christian Church*. ("The Christian Religion; Its Origin and Process" [J. F. BETHUNE-BAKER (ed.)]). Cambridge: University Press, 1929.

BOOTH, H. K. *The Bridge between the Testaments*. New York: Charles Scribner's Sons, 1929.

BOUSSET, WILHELM. *Die Religion des Judentums in späthellenistischen Zeitalter*. 3d ed. Ed. HUGO GRESSMANN. ("Handbuch zum Neuen Testament.") Tübingen: J. C. B. Mohr, 1926.

CHARLES, R. H. *Religious Development between the Old and New Testaments*. ("Home University Library.") New York: Henry Holt & Co., 1914.

COHEN, A., *et al*. *Judaism and the Beginnings of Christianity*. London: George Routledge & Sons, 1923.

DANBY, HERBERT (ed. and trans.). *The Mishnah*. London: Oxford University Press (Humphrey Milford), 1933.

FAIRWEATHER, WILLIAM. *The Background of the Gospels: Or Judaism in the Period between the Old and New Testaments*. Edinburgh: T. and T. Clark, 1926.

FINKELSTEIN, LOUIS. *The Pharisees: The Sociological Background of Their Faith*. 2d ed. rev. 2 vols. Philadelphia: Jewish Publication Society of America, 1940.

FOAKES-JACKSON, F. J. *Josephus and the Jews: The Religion and History of the Jews as Explained by Flavius Josephus*. London: Society for Promoting Christian Knowledge, 1930.

FREEDMAN, H., and SIMON, M. (eds.). *Midrash Rabbah, Translated into English with Notes, Glossary, and Indices.* 10 vols. London: Soncino Press, 1939.

GAVIN, F. *Jewish Antecedents of the Christian Sacraments.* London: Society for Promoting Christian Knowledge, 1928.

GOODENOUGH, E. R. *An Introduction to Philo Judaeus.* New Haven: Yale University Press, 1940.

———. *By Light, Light: The Mystic Gospel of Hellenistic Judaism.* New Haven: Yale University Press, 1935.

HERFORD, R. T. *Judaism in the New Testament Period.* London: Lindsay Press, 1928.

———. *The Pharisees.* New York: Macmillan Co., 1924.

———. *Talmud and Apocrypha: A Comparative Study of the Jewish Ethical Teaching in the Rabbinical and Non-rabbinical Sources in the Early Centuries.* London: Soncino Press, 1933.

JOSEPHUS, FLAVIUS. *The Complete Works of Flavius Josephus.* Trans. WILLIAM WHISTON. Hartford: S. S. Scranton Co., 1916.

KOHLER, K. *Jewish Theology Systematically and Historically Considered.* New York: Macmillan Co., 1918.

———. *Origins of the Synagogue and the Church.* Ed. H. G. ENELOW. New York: Macmillan Co., 1929.

LOEWE, H. (ed.). *The Contact of Pharisaism with Other Cultures,* Vol. II of *Judaism and Christianity.* New York: Macmillan Co., 1937.

MATHEWS, SHAILER. *New Testament Times in Palestine.* New York: Macmillan Co., 1933.

MOORE, G. F. *Judaism in the First Centuries of the Christian Era, the Age of the Tannaim.* 3 vols. Cambridge: Harvard University Press, 1927.

OESTERLEY, W. O. E. *Second Esdras (the Ezra Apocalypse).* ("Westminster Commentaries.") London: Methuen Co., 1933.

——— (ed.). *The Age of Transition,* Vol. I of *Judaism and Christianity.* New York: Macmillan Co., 1937.

OESTERLEY, W. O. E., and BOX, G. H. *The Religion and Worship of the Synagogue.* New York: Charles Scribner's Sons, 1907.

RODKINSON, M. L. *The History of the Talmud from the Time of Its Formation, about 200 B.C., up to the Present Time.* 2 vols. in 1. Boston: Talmud Society, 1918.

——— (ed. and trans.). *The Babylonian Talmud.* 2d ed. by ISAAC M. WISE. 9 vols. Boston: Talmud Society, 1918.

ROSENTHAL, ERWIN I. J. (ed.). *Law and Religion,* Vol. III of *Judaism and Christianity.* New York: Macmillan Co., 1938.

SCHAUSS, H. *The Jewish Festivals from Their Beginnings to Our Own Day.* Cincinnati: Union of American Hebrew Congregations, 1938.

SCHECHTER, S. *Some Aspects of Rabbinic Theology.* London: Black, 1909.

SCHÜRER, EMIL. *History of the Jewish People in the Time of Jesus Christ.* Trans. J. MACPHERSON and S. TAYLOR. 2d ed. 5 vols. Edinburgh: T. and T. Clark, 1885–1919.

SILVER, ABBA HILLEL. *A History of Messianic Speculation in Israel from the First through the Seventeenth Centuries.* New York: Macmillan Co., 1927.

STRACK, HERMANN L. *Introduction to the Talmud and Midrash.* Trans. from the 5th German ed. Philadelphia: Jewish Publication Society of America, 1931.

TAYLOR, CHARLES (ed. and trans.). *Sayings of the Jewish Fathers, Comprising Pirqe Aboth in Hebrew and English, with Notes and Excursuses.* 2d ed. Cambridge: University Press, 1897.

WAXMAN, MEYER. *A History of Jewish Literature.* New York: Black, 1938.

YONGE, C. D. (trans.). *The Works of Philo Judaeus, the Contemporary of Josephus.* London: H. G. Bohn, 1854–55.

D. GENTILE RELIGIOUS LIFE

ANGUS, S. *The Mystery Religions and Christianity: A Study in the Religious Background of Early Christianity.* New York: Charles Scribner's Sons, 1928.

———. *The Religious Quests of the Graeco-Roman World: A Study in the Historical Background of Early Christianity.* New York: Charles Scribner's Sons, 1929.

APULEIUS, L. *The Golden Ass, Being the Metamorphoses of Lucius Apuleius.* With an English translation by W. ADLINGTON. ("Loeb Classical Library.") New York: Macmillan Co., 1915.

ARNOLD, E. V. *Roman Stoicism.* Cambridge: University Press, 1911.

BEVAN, E. R. *Later Greek Religion.* New York, 1927.

———. *Stoics and Sceptics.* Oxford: Clarendon Press, 1913.

CATON, R. C. *The Temple and Ritual of Asklepius at Epidauras and Athens.* London, 1900.

CUMONT, F. R. *Astrology and Religion among Greeks and Romans.* New York, 1912.

———. *After Life in Roman Paganism.* New Haven: Yale University Press, 1922.

———. *The Mysteries of Mithra.* Trans. from 2d rev. French ed. by THOMAS J. McCORMACK. Chicago: Open Court Publishing Co., 1910.

CUMONT, F. R. *The Oriental Religions in Roman Paganism.* Trans. GRANT SHOWERMAN. Chicago, 1911.

FARNELL, L. R. *The Cults of the Greek States.* 3 vols. Oxford: Clarendon Press, 1896–1909.

———. *Greek Hero Cults and Ideas of Immortality.* Oxford: Clarendon Press, 1921.

FOWLER, W. W. *The Religious Experience of the Roman People from the Earliest Times to the Age of Augustus.* London: Macmillan & Co., 1933.

GEDEN, A. S. (ed. and trans.). *Select Passages Illustrating Mithraism.* London: Society for Promoting Christian Knowledge, 1925.

GLOVER, T. R. *The Conflict of Religions in the Early Roman Empire.* 11th ed. London: Methuen, 1927.

GRAILLOT, H. *Le Culte de Cybèle, mère des dieux.* Paris, 1912.

HALLIDAY, W. R. *The Pagan Background of Early Christianity.* Liverpool: University Press of Liverpool, 1925.

HEINRICI, C. F. G. *Die Hermes-Mystik und das Neue Testament.* Leipzig, 1918.

HERN, OTTO. *Orphicorum fragmenta.* Berlin, 1922.

HICKS, R. D. *Stoic and Epicurean.* New York: Charles Scribner's Sons, 1910.

HOOKE, S. H. (ed.). *The Labyrinth: Further Studies in the Relation between Myth and Ritual in the Ancient World.* New York: Macmillan Co., 1935.

LEGGE, F. *Forerunners and Rivals of Christianity, Being Studies in Religious History from 330 B.C. to 330 A.D.* Cambridge: University Press, 1915.

MACCHIORO, V. D. *From Orpheus to Paul: A History of Orphism.* New York: Henry Holt & Co., 1930.

MEADE, G. R. S. *Thrice Greatest Hermes.* London, 1906.

NILSSON, M. P. *Greek Popular Religion.* New York: Columbia University Press, 1940.

———. *A History of the Greek Religion.* Trans. F. J. FIELDEN. Oxford: Clarendon Press, 1925.

NOCK, A. D. *Conversion, the Old and the New in Religion from Alexander the Great to Augustine of Hippo.* Oxford: Clarendon Press, 1933.

PHYTHIAN-ADAMS, W. J. *Mithraism.* London, 1915.

REITZENSTEIN, RICHARD. *Die hellenistischen Mysterien-Religionen nach ihren Grundgedanken und Wirkungen.* 3d ed. Leipzig: B. G. Teubner, 1927.

WILLOUGHBY, H. R. *Pagan Regeneration: A Study of Mystery Initiations in the Graeco-Roman World.* Chicago: University of Chicago Press, 1929.

E. THE CAREER OF JESUS

BACON, B. W. *Jesus the Son of God.* New York: Henry Holt & Co., 1930.

BAILLIE, JOHN. *The Place of Jesus Christ in Modern Christianity.* New York: Charles Scribner's Sons, 1929.

BARNETT, A. E. *Understanding the Parables of Our Lord.* Nashville: Cokesbury Press, 1940.

BRANSCOMB, B. H. *Jesus and the Law of Moses.* New York: Richard R. Smith, 1930.

———. *The Teachings of Jesus.* Nashville: Cokesbury Press, 1931.

BULTMANN, RUDOLF. *Jesus and the Word.* Trans. L. P. SMITH and E. HUNTRESS. New York: Charles Scribner's Sons, 1934.

BURKITT, F. C. *Jesus Christ, an Historical Outline.* Glasgow: Blackie, 1932.

BURTON, E. D. *A Source Book for the Study of the Teaching of Jesus in Its Historical Relationships.* Chicago: University of Chicago Press, 1924.

CADBURY, H. J. *The Peril of Modernizing Jesus.* New York: Macmillan Co., 1937.

CASE, S. J. *The Historicity of Jesus.* 2d ed. Chicago: University of Chicago Press, 1928.

———. *Jesus: A New Biography.* Chicago: University of Chicago Press, 1927.

DIBELIUS, MARTIN. *Gospel Criticism and Christology.* London: Ivor Nicholson & Watson, 1935.

———. *The Message of Jesus Christ.* Trans. FREDERICK C. GRANT. New York: Charles Scribner's Sons, 1939.

DODD, C. H. *The Parables of the Kingdom.* New York: Charles Scribner's Sons, 1936.

EASTON, B. S. *Christ in the Gospels.* New York: Charles Scribner's Sons, 1930.

GOGUEL, MAURICE. *Jesus the Nazarene: Myth or History?* Trans. FREDERICK STEPHENS. New York: D. Appleton & Co., 1926.

———. *The Life of Jesus.* Trans. OLIVE WYON. London: George Allen & Unwin, 1933.

GRANT, F. C. *The Gospel of the Kingdom.* New York: Macmillan Co., 1940.

———. *The Life and Times of Jesus.* New York: Abingdon Press, 1921.

——— (ed. and trans.). *Form Criticism.* New York: Willett, Clark & Co., 1934.

HEADLAM, A. C. *The Life and Teachings of Jesus the Christ.* London: Murray, 1923.

HERFORD, R. T. *Christianity in Talmud and Midrash.* London: Williams & Norgate, 1903.

KEPLER, T. S. (ed.). *Contemporary Thinking about Jesus.* Nashville: Abingdon-Cokesbury Press, 1944.

KLAUSNER, J. *Jesus of Nazareth.* Trans. HERBERT DANBY. New York: Macmillan Co., 1925.

LYMAN, MARY E. *Jesus.* ("Hazen Series.") New York: Association Press, 1937.

McCASLAND, S. V. *The Resurrection of Jesus.* New York: T. Nelson & Sons, 1932.

McCOWN, C. C. *The Search for the Real Jesus.* New York: Charles Scribner's Sons, 1940.

MACKINNON, JAMES. *The Historic Jesus.* New York: Longmans, Green & Co., 1931.

MAJOR, H. D. A.; MANSON, T. W.; and WRIGHT, C. J. *The Mission and Message of Jesus.* London: Ivor Nicholson & Watson, 1937.

MANSON, T. W. *The Teaching of Jesus.* Cambridge: University Press, 1931.

MICKLEM, E. R. *Miracles and the New Psychology: A Study of the Healing Miracles of the New Testament.* Oxford: University Press, 1922.

OESTERLEY, W. O. E. *The Gospel Parables in the Light of Their Jewish Background.* New York: Macmillan Co., 1936.

OTTO, RUDOLF. *The Kingdom of God and the Son of Man: A Study in the History of Religion.* Trans. F. V. FILSON and B. L. WOOLF. Grand Rapids: Zondervan Publishing Co., 1938.

RIHBANY, A. M. *The Syrian Christ.* New York: Houghton Mifflin Co., 1916.

SCHWEITZER, ALBERT. *The Quest of the Historical Jesus: A Critical Study of Its Progress from Reimarus to Wrede.* Trans. W. MONTGOMERY. 2d English ed. London: A. and C. Black, 1931.

SCOTT, E. F. *The Ethical Teachings of Jesus.* New York: Macmillan Co., 1924.

———. *The Kingdom of God in the New Testament.* New York: Macmillan Co., 1931.

———. *The Kingdom and the Messiah.* Edinburgh: T. and T. Clark, 1910.

SHARMAN, H. B. *The Son of Man and the Kingdom of God: A Critical Study.* New York: Harper & Bros., 1943.

SIMKHOVITCH, V. G. *Toward the Understanding of Jesus, and Other Historical Studies.* New York: Macmillan Co., 1921.

SMITH, B. T. D. *The Parables of the Synoptic Gospels: A Critical Study.* Cambridge: University Press, 1937.

TAYLOR, VINCENT. *The Historical Evidence for the Virgin Birth.* Oxford: Clarendon Press, 1920.

WARSCHAUER, J. *The Historical Life of Christ.* London: T. Fisher Unwin, 1927.

WEINEL, HEINRICH, and WIDGERY, A. G. *Jesus in the Nineteenth Century and After.* Edinburgh: T. and T. Clark, 1914.

WILDER, A. N. *Eschatology and Ethics in the Teachings of Jesus.* New York: Harper & Bros., 1939.

F. THE CAREER OF PAUL

ANDREWS, MARY E. *The Ethical Teaching of Paul.* Chapel Hill: University of North Carolina Press, 1934.

BULTMANN, RUDOLF. *Der Stil der Paulinischen Predigt und die kynisch-stoische Diatribe.* Göttingen, 1910.

DEISSMANN, G. A. *Paul: A Study in Social and Religious History.* Trans. W. E. WILSON. 2d ed. New York: Doran & Co., 1926.

――――. *The Religion of Jesus and the Faith of Paul.* Trans. W. E. WILSON. New York: Doran & Co., 1923.

DERWACTER, F. M. *Preparing the Way for Paul: The Prosylyte Movement in Later Judaism.* New York: Macmillan Co., 1930.

ENSLIN, M. S. *The Ethics of Paul.* New York: Harper & Bros., 1930.

GLOVER, T. H. *Paul of Tarsus.* New York: Richard R. Smith, 1930.

KENNEDY, H. A. *St. Paul and the Mystery Religions.* London, 1913.

KLAUSNER, JOSEPH. *From Jesus to Paul.* Trans. W. F. STINESPRING. New York: Macmillan Co., 1944.

KNOX, W. L. *St. Paul and the Church of Jerusalem.* Cambridge: University Press, 1925.

MONTEFIORE, C. G. *Judaism and St. Paul.* London, 1914.

NOCK, A. D. *St. Paul.* New York: Harper & Bros., 1938.

RIDDLE, D. W. *Paul, Man of Conflict.* Nashville: Cokesbury Press, 1940.

ROBINSON, B. W. *The Life of Paul.* Chicago: University of Chicago Press, 1928.

SCHWEITZER, ALBERT. *The Mysticism of Paul the Apostle.* Trans. WILLIAM MONTGOMERY. London: A. and C. Black, 1931.

――――. *Paul and His Interpreters: A Critical History.* Trans. WILLIAM MONTGOMERY. London: A. and C. Black, 1912.

SCOTT, C. A. A. *St. Paul, the Man and the Teacher.* Cambridge: University Press, 1936.

WEINEL, H. *St. Paul, the Man and His Work.* Trans. G. A. BIENEMANN; ed. W. D. MORRISON. New York: G. P. Putnam's Sons, 1906.

G. THE LETTERS OF PAUL AND EPHESIANS

ABBOTT, T. K. *A Critical and Exegetical Commentary on the Epistles to the Ephesians and to the Colossians.* ("The International Critical Commentary.") New York: Charles Scribner's Sons, 1905.

BURTON, E. D. *A Critical and Exegetical Commentary on the Epistle to the Galatians.* ("The International Critical Commentary.") New York: Charles Scribner's Sons, 1920.

DIBELIUS, MARTIN. *An die Kolosser, Epheser, an Philemon.* 2d ed. ("Handbuch zum Neuen Testament.") Tübingen: J. C. B. Mohr (P. Siebeck), 1927.

———. *An die Thessalonicher I, II; an die Philipper.* 3d ed. ("Handbuch zum Neuen Testament.") Tübingen: J. C. B. Mohr, 1937.

DODD, C. H. *The Epistle to the Romans.* ("The Moffatt New Testament Commentary.") London: Hodder & Stoughton, 1932.

DUNCAN, G. S. *The Epistle of Paul to the Galatians.* ("The Moffatt New Testament Commentary.") New York: Harper & Bros., 1934.

———. *St. Paul's Ephesian Ministry: A Reconstruction with Special Reference to the Ephesian Origin of the Imprisonment Epistles.* London: Hodder & Stoughton, 1929.

FRAME, J. E. *A Critical and Exegetical Commentary on the Epistles of St. Paul to the Thessalonians.* ("The International Critical Commentary.") New York: Charles Scribner's Sons, 1912.

GOODSPEED, E. J. *The Meaning of Ephesians.* Chicago: University of Chicago Press, 1933.

KNOX, JOHN. *Philemon among the Letters of Paul: A New View of Its Place and Importance.* Chicago: University of Chicago Press, 1935.

LAKE, KIRSOPP. *The Earlier Epistles of St. Paul.* London: Rivington's, 1911.

LIETZMANN, HANS. *An die Galater.* 3d ed. ("Handbuch zum Neuen Testament.") Tübingen: J. C. B. Mohr (P. Siebeck), 1932.

———. *An die Korinther I und II.* 3d ed. ("Handbuch zum Neuen Testament.") Tübingen: J. C. B. Mohr (P. Siebeck), 1931.

———. *An die Römer.* ("Handbuch zum Neuen Testament.") Tübingen: J. C. B. Mohr (P. Siebeck), 1933.

MICHAEL, J. H. *The Epistle of Paul to the Philippians.* ("The Moffatt New Testament Commentary.") New York: Doubleday, Doran & Co., 1929.

MOFFATT, JAMES. *The First Epistle of Paul to the Corinthians.* ("The Moffatt New Testament Commentary.") New York: Harper & Bros., 1938.

ROPES, J. H. *The Singular Problem of the Epistle to the Galatians*. Cambridge: Harvard University Press, 1929.

SANDAY, WILLIAM, and HEADLAM, A. C. *A Critical and Exegetical Commentary on the Epistle to the Romans*. ("The International Critical Commentary.") New York: Charles Scribner's Sons, 1906.

SCOTT, E. F. *The Epistles of Paul to the Colossians, to Philemon, and to the Ephesians*. ("The Moffatt New Testament Commentary.") New York: Richard R. Smith, 1930.

STRACHAN, L. R. N. *The Second Epistle of Paul to the Corinthians*. ("The Moffatt New Testament Commentary.") New York: Harper & Bros., 1935.

H. THE SYNOPTIC GOSPELS AND ACTS

BACON, B. W. *Studies in Matthew*. New York: Henry Holt & Co., 1930.

BRANSCOMB, B. H. *The Gospel of Mark*. ("The Moffatt New Testament Commentary.") New York: Harper & Bros., 1937.

BURTON, E. D., and GOODSPEED, E. J. *A Harmony of the Synoptic Gospels for Historical and Critical Study*. New York: Charles Scribner's Sons, 1929.

CADBURY, H. J. *The Making of Luke-Acts*. New York: Macmillan Co., 1927.

———. *The Style and Literary Method of Luke*. ("Harvard Theological Studies" [MOORE, ROPES, and LAKE (eds.)], Vol. VI.) Cambridge: Harvard University Press, 1920.

DIBELIUS, MARTIN. *From Tradition to Gospel*. Trans. from the 2d German ed. by B. L. WOOLF. New York: Charles Scribner's Sons, 1935.

DODD, C. H. *The Apostolic Preaching and Its Developments*. Chicago: Willett, Clark & Co., 1937.

———. *History and the Gospel*. New York: Charles Scribner's Sons, 1938.

EASTON, B. S. *The Gospel before the Gospels*. New York, 1928.

FILSON, F. V. *Origins of the Gospels*. New York: Abingdon Press, 1938.

FOAKES-JACKSON, F. J. *The Acts of the Apostles*. ("The Moffatt New Testament Commentary.") New York: Richard R. Smith, 1931.

FOAKES-JACKSON, F. J., and LAKE, KIRSOPP (eds.). *The Beginnings of Christianity*. 5 vols. New York: Macmillan Co., 1920–33.

GOODSPEED, E. J. *Strange New Gospels*. Chicago: University of Chicago Press, 1931.

GRANT, F. C. *The Earliest Gospel*. Nashville: Abingdon-Cokesbury Press, 1943.

GRANT, F. C. *The Economic Background of the Gospels*. London: Oxford University Press, 1926.

———. *The Growth of the Gospels*. New York: Abingdon Press, 1933.

HUCK, ALBERT. *A Synopsis of the First Three Gospels*. 9th ed. Revised by HANS LIETZMANN; trans. F. L. CROSS. Tübingen: J. C. B. Mohr, 1936.

LIGHTFOOT, R. H. *History and Interpretation in the Gospels*. New York: Harper & Bros., 1935.

———. *Locality and Doctrine in the Gospels*. New York: Harper & Bros., 1937.

LUCE, H. K. (ed.). *The Gospel According to St. Luke*. ("The Cambridge Bible for Schools and Colleges.") Cambridge: University Press, 1936.

McCOWN, C. C. *The Genesis of the Social Gospel: The Meaning of the Ideals of Jesus in the Light of Their Antecedents*. New York: A. A. Knopf, 1929.

MANSON, WILLIAM. *The Gospel of Luke*. ("The Moffatt New Testament Commentary.") New York: Richard R. Smith, 1930.

MONTEFIORE, C. G. *Rabbinic Literature and Gospel Teachings*. London: Macmillan & Co., 1930.

———. *The Synoptic Gospels*. 3 vols. London: Macmillan & Co., 1909.

OESTERLEY, W. O. E. *The Gospel Parables in the Light of Their Jewish Background*. New York: Macmillan Co., 1936.

RAWLINSON, A. E. J. *St. Mark*. 3d ed. ("Westminster Commentaries.") London: Methuen & Co., 1931.

REDLICH, E. B. *Form Criticism: Its Value and Limitations*. London: Duckworth, 1939.

RIDDLE, D. W. *The Gospels: Their Origin and Growth*. Chicago: University of Chicago Press, 1939.

———. *Jesus and the Pharisees*. Chicago: University of Chicago Press, 1928.

ROBINSON, T. H. *The Gospel of Matthew*. ("The Moffatt New Testament Commentary.") New York: Doubleday, Doran & Co., 1928.

ROPES, J. H. *The Synoptic Gospels*. Cambridge: Harvard University Press, 1934.

SCOTT, E. F. *The Validity of the Gospel Records*. New York: Charles Scribner's Sons, 1938.

SMITH, B. T. D. *The Gospel According to St. Matthew*. ("The Cambridge Bible for Schools and Colleges.") Cambridge: University Press, 1933.

STREETER, B. H. *The Four Gospels*. New York: Macmillan Co., 1935.

TAYLOR, VINCENT. *Behind the Third Gospel: A Study of the Proto-Luke Hypothesis*. Oxford: Clarendon Press, 1926.

———. *The Formation of the Gospel Tradition*. London: Macmillan & Co., 1935.

Torrey, C. C. *Documents of the Primitive Church*. New York: Harper & Bros., 1941.

———. *The Four Gospels*. New York: Harper & Bros., 1933.

I. REVELATION, HEBREWS, AND I PETER

Case, S. J. *The Millenial Hope*. Chicago: University of Chicago Press, 1923.

———. *The Revelation of John*. Chicago: University of Chicago Press, 1919.

Charles, R. H. *A Critical and Exegetical Commentary on the Revelation of St. John*. 2 vols. ("The International Critical Commentary.") New York: Charles Scribner's Sons, 1920.

——— (ed.). *The Apocrypha and Pseudepigrapha of the Old Testament*. 2 vols. Oxford: Clarendon Press, 1913.

Kiddle, Martin. *The Revelation of St. John*. ("The Moffatt New Testament Commentary.") New York: Harper & Bros., 1940.

Lohmeyer, Ernst. *Die Offenbarung des Johannes*. ("Handbuch zum Neuen Testament.") Tübingen: J. C. B. Mohr (P. Siebeck), 1926.

Moffatt, James. *A Critical and Exegetical Commentary on the Epistle to the Hebrews*. ("The International Critical Commentary.") New York: Charles Scribner's Sons, 1924.

———. *The General Epistles, James, Peter, and Judas*. ("The Moffatt New Testament Commentary.") New York: Doubleday, Doran & Co., 1928.

Robinson, T. H. *The Epistle to the Hebrews*. ("The Moffatt New Testament Commentary.") New York: Harper & Bros., 1933.

Scott, E. F. *The Book of Revelation*. New York: Charles Scribner's Sons, 1940.

———. *The Epistle to the Hebrews: Its Doctrine and Significance*. Edinburgh: T. and T. Clark, 1922.

Windisch, Hans. *Der Hebräerbrief*. 2d ed. ("Handbuch zum Neuen Testament.") Tübingen: J. C. B. Mohr (P. Siebeck), 1931.

J. THE LETTER OF JAMES AND THE FOURTH GOSPEL

Bacon, B. W. *The Gospel of the Hellenists*. New York: Henry Holt & Co., 1933.

Bauer, Walter. *Das Johannesevangelium*. 3d ed. ("Handbuch zum Neuen Testament.") Tübingen: J. C. B. Mohr (P. Siebeck), 1933.

Burney, C. F. *The Aramaic Origin of the Fourth Gospel*. Oxford: Clarendon Press, 1922.

COLWELL, E. C. *The Greek of the Fourth Gospel: A Study of Its Aramaisms in the Light of Hellenistic Greek.* Chicago: University of Chicago Press, 1931.

————. *John Defends the Gospel.* Chicago: Willett, Clark & Co., 1936.

HOWARD, W. F. *The Fourth Gospel in Recent Criticism and Interpretation.* London: Epworth Press, 1931.

KUNDSIN, K. *Charakter und Ursprung der Johanneischen Reden.* Riga: Latvijas Universitate, 1939.

MACGREGOR, G. H. C. *The Gospel of John.* ("The Moffatt New Testament Commentary.") New York: Harper & Bros., 1929.

MEYER, A. W. *Das Johannes-Evangelium.* Göttingen: Vandenhoeck & Ruprecht, 1937.

ROPES, J. H. *A Critical and Exegetical Commentary on the Epistle of St. James.* ("The International Critical Commentary.") New York: Charles Scribner's Sons, 1916.

SCOTT, E. F. *The Fourth Gospel: Its Purpose and Theology.* Edinburgh: T. and T. Clark, 1906.

STRACHAN, R. H. *The Fourth Evangelist, Dramatist or Historian?* London: Hodder & Stoughton, 1925.

K. THE EPISTLES OF JOHN, THE PASTORALS, JUDE, AND II PETER

BIGG, CHARLES. *A Critical and Exegetical Commentary on the Epistles of St. Jude and St. Peter.* ("The International Critical Commentary.") New York: Charles Scribner's Sons, 1905.

BROOKE, A. E. *A Critical and Exegetical Commentary on the Johannine Epistles.* ("The International Critical Commentary.") New York: Charles Scribner's Sons, 1912.

DIBELIUS, MARTIN. *Die Pastoralbriefe.* 2d ed. ("Handbuch zum Neuen Testament.") Tübingen: J. C. B. Mohr (P. Siebeck), 1931.

FOAKES-JACKSON, F. J. *Christian Difficulties in the Second and Twentieth Centuries: A Study of Marcion and His Relation to Modern Thought.* Cambridge: University Press, 1903.

HARRISON, P. N. *The Problem of the Pastoral Epistles.* London: Oxford University Press, 1921.

LOCK, WALTER. *A Critical and Exegetical Commentary on the Pastoral Epistles (I and II Timothy and Titus).* ("The International Critical Commentary.") New York: Charles Scribner's Sons, 1924.

SCOTT, E. F. *The Pastoral Epistles.* ("The Moffatt New Testament Commentary.") New York: Harper & Bros., 1936.

WAND, J. W. C. *The General Epistles of St. Peter and St. Jude.* ("Westminster Commentaries.") London: Methuen & Co., 1934.

WINDISCH, HANS. *Die katholischen Briefe.* ("Handbuch zum Neuen Testament.") Tübingen: J. C. B. Mohr (P. Siebeck), 1930.

L. TEXT, CANON, TRANSLATION, AND INTERPRETATION

GOODSPEED, E. J. *The Formation of the New Testament.* Chicago: University of Chicago Press, 1926.

———. *The Making of the English New Testament.* Chicago: University of Chicago Press, 1925.

———. *Problems of New Testament Translation.* Chicago: University of Chicago Press, 1945.

GREGORY, C. R. *Canon and Text of the New Testament.* ("The International Theological Library.") New York, 1907.

HATCH, W. H. P. *The Principal Uncial Manuscripts of the New Testament.* Chicago: University of Chicago Press, 1939.

KENYON, F. G. *Handbook of Textual Criticism of the New Testament.* London: Macmillan & Co., 1926.

———. *Our Bible and the Ancient Manuscripts.* 4th ed. New York: Harper & Bros., 1940.

———. *Recent Developments in the Textual Criticism of the Greek Bible.* London: Oxford University Press, 1933.

———. *The Story of the Bible: A Popular Account of How It Came to Us.* London: Murray, 1936.

———. *The Text of the Greek Bible.* London: Duckworth, 1937.

KNOX, JOHN. *Marcion and the New Testament: An Essay in the Early History of the Canon.* Chicago: University of Chicago Press, 1942.

LAKE, KIRSOPP. *The Text of the New Testament.* 6th ed. Revised by SILVA NEW. London: Rivington's 1933.

MILLIGAN, GEORGE. *The New Testament and Its Transmission.* London: Hodder & Stoughton, 1932.

NASH, H. S. *The History of Higher Criticism of the New Testament.* New York: Macmillan Co., 1900.

NESTLE, EBERHARD. *Novum Testamentum Graece cum apparatu critico.* 16th ed. Revised by ERWIN NESTLE. Stuttgart, 1936.

The New Testament: An American Translation. By EDGAR J. GOODSPEED. Chicago: University of Chicago Press, 1923.

The New Testament in Modern Speech: An Idiomatic Translation into Everyday English from the Text of the Resultant Greek Testament. By R. F. WEYMOUTH. 5th ed. Boston: Pilgrim Press, 1939.

The New Testament: A New Translation. By JAMES MOFFATT. New York: George H. Doran, 1926.

SOUTER, A. *The Text and Canon of the New Testament.* New York: Charles Scribner's Sons, 1910.

THOMPSON, MAUNDE. *Greek and Latin Palaeography.* Oxford, 1912.

WESTCOTT, B. F., and HORT, F. J. A. *The New Testament in the Original Greek.* New York: Macmillan Co., 1881.

M. ARCHEOLOGY AND PAPYRI

BAIKIE, JAMES. *Egyptian Papyri and Papyrus Hunting.* London: Religious Tract Society, 1925.

BELL, H. T., and SKEAT, T. C. (eds.). *Fragments of an Unknown Gospel and Other Early Christian Papyri.* London: British Museum, 1935.

CAIGER, S. L. *Archaeology and the New Testament.* London: Cassell & Co., 1939.

DEISSMANN, ADOLF. *Bible Studies: Contributions Chiefly from Papyri and Inscriptions to the History of the Language, the Literature, and the Religion of Hellenistic Judaism and Primitive Christianity.* Trans. ALEXANDER GRIEVE. Edinburgh: T. and T. Clark, 1901.

————. *Light from the Ancient East.* Trans. L. R. M. STRACHAN. 2d ed. New York: Doran, 1927.

————. *The New Testament in the Light of Modern Research.* New York: Doran, 1929.

KAUFMANN, C. M. *Handbuch der altchristlichen Epigraphik.* Freiburg: Herder, 1917.

————. *Handbuch der christlichen Archäologie.* 3d ed. Paderborn: Schöningh, 1922.

KENYON, FREDERICK G. *The Bible and Archaeology.* London: George G. Harrap & Co., 1940.

McCOWN, C. C. *The Ladder of Progress in Palestine.* New York: Harper & Bros., 1943.

MILLIGAN, G. *Selections from the Greek Papyri.* Cambridge: University Press, 1910.

ROBERTS, C. H. (ed.). *Two Biblical Papyri in the John Rylands Library, Manchester.* Manchester: Manchester University Press, 1936.

————. *An Unpublished Fragment of the Fourth Gospel in the John Rylands Library.* Manchester: Manchester University Press, 1935.

WINTER, JOHN G. *Life and Letters in the Papyri.* Ann Arbor: University of Michigan Press, 1933.

Index of Persons and Subjects